Water Infrastructure

T0361070

Water infrastructure is an essential element in water management. Together with institutions, policies and regulation, it provides basic services to growing populations, especially in developing countries, where much of the growth is taking place. In the Asia-Pacific region, for instance, populations are growing not only in size but also in affluence, straining further the existing infrastructure and demanding urgently the development of a new one. While 79% of total water use in Asia occurs in agriculture, the fastest increases in demand are emanating from industry and urban areas. This trend is a natural consequence of the fastest industrialization and urbanization process in history. By 2030, more than 55% of Asia's population will live in urban areas, an increase of 1.1 billion people. Nevertheless, water infrastructure is of concern not only in the global South but also in the North, where much of the drinking-water infrastructure needs upgrading or replacement, a significant undertaking as infrastructure is more than a hundred years old in many cases. The American Water Works Association estimates that changing all of the water pipes in the United States would cost more than USD 1 trillion. In this book, in-depth case studies on water infrastructure challenges and policy solutions are presented from different parts of the world.

This book was originally published as a special issue of the *International Journal of Water Resources Development*.

Cecilia Tortajada is a Senior Research Fellow at the Institute of Water Policy, National University of Singapore.

Asit K. Biswas is a Distinguished Visiting Professor at the Lee Kuan Yew School of Public Policy in Singapore.

Routledge Special Issues on Water Policy and Governance
Edited by:
Cecilia Tortajada (IJWRD) – *Institute of Water Policy, National University of Singapore*
James Nickum (WI) – *International Water Resources Association, France*

Most of the world's water problems, and their solutions, are directly related to policies and governance, both specific to water and in general. Two of the world's leading journals in this area, the *International Journal of Water Resources Development* and *Water International* (the official journal of the International Water Resources Association), contribute to this special issues series, aimed at disseminating new knowledge on the policy and governance of water resources to a very broad and diverse readership all over the world. The series should be of direct interest to all policy makers, professionals and lay readers concerned with obtaining the latest perspectives on addressing the world's many water issues.

Water Pricing and Public-Private Partnership
Edited by Asit K. Biswas and Cecilia Tortajada

Water and Disasters
Edited by Chennat Gopalakrishnan and Norio Okada

Water as a Human Right for the Middle East and North Africa
Edited by Asit K. Biswas, Eglal Rached and Cecilia Tortajada

Integrated Water Resources Management in Latin America
Edited by Asit K. Biswas, Benedito P. F. Braga, Cecilia Tortajada and Marco Palermo

Water Resources Management in the People's Republic of China
Edited by Xuetao Sun, Robert Speed and Dajun Shen

Improving Water Policy and Governance
Edited by Cecilia Tortajada and Asit K. Biswas

Water Quality Management
Present Situations, Challenges and Future Perspectives
Edited by Asit K. Biswas, Cecilia Tortajada and Rafael Izquerdo

Water, Food and Poverty in River Basins
Defining the Limits
Edited by Myles J. Fisher and Simon E. Cook

Asian Perspectives on Water Policy
Edited by Cecilia Tortajada and Asit K. Biswas

Managing Transboundary Waters of Latin America
Edited by Asit K. Biswas

Water and Security in Central Asia
Solving a Rubik's Cube
Edited by Virpi Stucki, Kai Wegerich, Muhammad Mizanur Rahaman and Olli Varis

Water Policy and Management in Spain
Edited by Francisco González-Gómez, Miguel A. García-Rubio and Jorge Guardiola

Water Infrastructure

Edited by
Cecilia Tortajada and Asit K. Biswas

Routledge
Taylor & Francis Group

LONDON AND NEW YORK

First published 2016 by Routledge

2 Park Square, Milton Park, Abingdon, Oxon OX14 4RN
711 Third Avenue, New York, NY 10017, USA

Routledge is an imprint of the Taylor & Francis Group, an informa business

First issued in paperback 2017

British Library Cataloguing in Publication Data
A catalogue record for this book is available from the British Library

ISBN 13: 978-1-138-91195-6 (hbk)
ISBN 13: 978-1-138-08574-9 (pbk)

Typeset in Times New Roman
by RefineCatch Limited, Bungay, Suffolk

Publisher's Note
The publisher accepts responsibility for any inconsistencies that may have
arisen during the conversion of this book from journal articles to book chapters,
namely the possible inclusion of journal terminology.

Disclaimer
Every effort has been made to contact copyright holders for their permission to
reprint material in this book. The publishers would be grateful to hear from any
copyright holder who is not here acknowledged and will undertake to rectify
any errors or omissions in future editions of this book.

Contents

Policy Brief

Citation Information

The chapters in this book were originally published in the *International Journal of Water Resources Development*, volume 30, issue 1 (March 2014). When citing this material, please use the original page numbering for each article, as follows:

Foreword
Foreword
Kishore Mahbubani
International Journal of Water Resources Development, volume 30, issue 1
(March 2014) pp. 1–2

Chapter 1
Editorial: Infrastructure and development
Cecilia Tortajada and Asit K. Biswas
International Journal of Water Resources Development, volume 30, issue 1
(March 2014) pp. 3–7

Chapter 2
Water infrastructure as an essential element for human development
Cecilia Tortajada
International Journal of Water Resources Development, volume 30, issue 1
(March 2014) pp. 8–19

Chapter 3
The worldwide urban water and wastewater infrastructure challenge
Michael Rouse
International Journal of Water Resources Development, volume 30, issue 1
(March 2014) pp. 20–27

Chapter 4
Is water scarcity a constraint to feeding Asia's growing population?
Colin Chartres
International Journal of Water Resources Development, volume 30, issue 1
(March 2014) pp. 28–36

Chapter 5

Water services industry reforms in Malaysia
Yen Hua Teo
International Journal of Water Resources Development, volume 30, issue 1
(March 2014) pp. 37–46

Chapter 6

Water infrastructure in China: the importance of full project life-cycle cost analysis in addressing water challenges
Shuping Lu
International Journal of Water Resources Development, volume 30, issue 1
(March 2014) pp. 47–59

Chapter 7

Water infrastructure for the Hindu Kush Himalayas
David James Molden, Ramesh Ananda Vaidya, Arun Bhakta Shrestha, Golam Rasul and Mandira Singh Shrestha
International Journal of Water Resources Development, volume 30, issue 1
(March 2014) pp. 60–77

Chapter 8

The Gujarat State-Wide Water Supply Grid: a step towards water security
Andrea Biswas-Tortajada
International Journal of Water Resources Development, volume 30, issue 1
(March 2014) pp. 78–90

Chapter 9

Positive externalities of irrigation from the Sardar Sarovar Project for farm production and domestic water supply
M. Dinesh Kumar, S. Jagadeesan and M.V.K. Sivamohan
International Journal of Water Resources Development, volume 30, issue 1
(March 2014) pp. 91–109

Chapter 10

Opinion: Environmental over enthusiasm
Chetan Pandit
International Journal of Water Resources Development, volume 30, issue 1
(March 2014) pp. 110–120

Chapter 11

The changing role of hydropower: from cheap local energy supply to strategic regional resource
Jacob Snell, Daniel Prowse and Ken Adams
International Journal of Water Resources Development, volume 30, issue 1
(March 2014) pp. 121–134

Chapter 12

Interbasin water transfers at the US–Mexico border city of Nogales, Sonora: implications for aquifers and water security
Andrea Harrop Prichard and Christopher A. Scott
International Journal of Water Resources Development, volume 30, issue 1
(March 2014) pp. 135–151

Chapter 13

Policy Brief: The 2012 Murray-Darling Basin Plan – issues to watch
James Horne
International Journal of Water Resources Development, volume 30, issue 1
(March 2014) pp. 152–163

Chapter 14

Environmental water management in Australia: experience from the Murray-Darling Basin
Benjamin Docker and Ian Robinson
International Journal of Water Resources Development, volume 30, issue 1
(March 2014) pp. 164–177

Please direct any queries you may have about the citations to
clsuk.permissions@cengage.com

FOREWORD

Kishore Mahbubani

Lee Kuan Yew School of Public Policy, National University of Singapore

The management of our water supply and its delivery to the rapidly increasing global population is one of the key challenges of the next century. Today, 2.7 billion people already suffer from some form of water scarcity. The World Economic Forum's *Global Risks 2014* report found that water crises were the third-highest area of concern among survey respondents. At a 2013 Global Water System Project conference in Bonn, 500 of the world's leading water scientists projected that water shortages could affect half of the world's 9 billion people by 2050. Water scarcity has a huge impact on a wide range of policy issues, from food security to industry, from energy to health.

Water infrastructure is an essential element in water management. Together with institutions, policies and regulation, water infrastructure provides basic services to growing populations, especially in developing countries, where much of the growth is taking place. In the Asia-Pacific region, populations are growing not only in size but also in affluence, compounding the strain on existing infrastructure and supply. While 79% of total water use in Asia occurs in agriculture, the fastest increases in demand are emanating from industry and from urban households, a natural consequence of the fastest industrialization and urbanization process in history. By 2030, more than 55% of Asia's population will live in urban areas, an increase of 1.1 billion people.

It is important to emphasize that it is not just in developing countries that water infrastructure is an area of concern. In developed countries, much of the drinking-water infrastructure needs upgrading or replacement, a significant undertaking because in many cases the infrastructure is more than 100 years old. The American Water Works Association estimates that changing all of the water pipes in the United States would cost more than USD 1 trillion.

The increasing magnitude and urgency of our water management needs make this new publication on water infrastructure from Cecilia Tortajada and Asit Biswas truly timely. These in-depth studies on water infrastructure challenges and policy solutions from the Himalayas to Mexico, from Australia to China, are invaluable tools in the fight against water insecurity, a challenge facing vast swathes of the world's population and nearly all governments at all levels in coming years.

Our school is proud that Asit Biswas, a distinguished visiting professor, and Cecilia Tortajada, who has worked closely with our school, have produced another excellent publication that bears the school's imprimatur. Their earlier volume, *The Singapore Water Story*, was widely acclaimed. I am confident that this publication will be equally well received and will help fulfill our school's mission of helping to improve governance in Asia and beyond.

References

Tortajada, C., Joshi, Y., & Biswas, A.K. (2013). *Singapore water story: Sustainable development in an urban city state*. London: Routledge.

World Economic Forum. (2014). *Global risks 2014* (9th ed.). Retrieved from http://www3.weforum.org/docs/WEF_GlobalRisks_Report_2014.pdf

Infrastructure and development

Introduction

Forecasting the future is a difficult task. However, one can predict with complete certainty that the world will change rapidly during the next four decades. Some of these changes may be predictable but others can at best be guessed in general terms. Some will be totally unexpected. For example, it can be predicted that the global population will continue to increase and is likely to be over nine billion by 2050. This increase will occur primarily in developing countries. Urbanization in the African and the Asian countries will increase significantly. Much urbanization has already occurred in Latin America and the developed world. Migration within countries and between countries will increase, bringing with it its own sets of challenges and opportunities. However, it is not possible to predict what new scientific and technological developments may occur in 2020, let alone in 2050.

With increasing population, changing demographic structures, urbanization, and phenomenal growth of the middle class in developing countries, the requirements for all types of resources will increase, unless the current resource-use processes and practices can be improved continuously and significantly. Agricultural productivity may struggle to keep up with the steadily increasing demands of a larger population and changing dietary preferences amongst the rapidly growing middle class. With rapid advances in communication and information technology, people's aspirations and expectations for a better quality of life will steadily advance all over the world. All these developments have to be squarely met amidst the increasing uncertainties imposed by many other complex and unexpected events over which individual nation-states will have at best somewhat limited, or even no control. Among these uncertainties are national and global economic growth rates; social, economic and political upheavals within and between countries; the extent of globalization and free trade, and their implications, positive or negative, on the countries and regions concerned; the magnitude and extent of climate changes; and rapid advances in scientific and technological knowledge. Viewed from any direction, future challenges are likely to be truly formidable, but then so are the likely opportunities if these can be handled properly and in a timely manner.

Infrastructure and development

While the future may be uncertain, one issue can be predicted with complete certainty. In the world as a whole, if the rising aspirations of the people are to be met, it will be essential to have better planned and managed infrastructure of all kinds but also to develop the human capacities and institutions to operate and maintain it properly in a cost-effective and timely manner. For countries to stay even in the same place in terms of socio-economic development and economic competitiveness with the others, they all will have to plan their infrastructure better, develop it faster and maintain it significantly better than

3

any time in human history. Without adequate infrastructure of all kinds, the development progress of countries will be seriously constrained. This is unlikely to sit well with the people who are expecting better standard of living and quality of life.

Numerous studies show the close interrelationships between a country's infrastructure and its economic competitiveness, and thus its long-term economic development. A country's economic development potential depends in a significant way on the extent and the quality of its infrastructure. In spite of this well-known linkage, the fact is that the world's infrastructure deficit has been increasing in recent decades. However, it should be noted that returns on infrastructure investment can only be obtained over the long term.

In 2006, the Organisation for Economic Co-operation and Development (OECD) estimated that the total new spending in infrastructure over 2010–2030 could be as high as USD 71 trillion (OECD, 2006).

Nearly a decade after this study was completed, the methodologies used leave much to be desired. A year later, in 2007, Booz Allen Hamilton estimated that to "modernize obsolescent systems and expanding demand" would require investment of USD 41 trillion between 2005 and 2030. The report also warned, "Much of America's critical infrastructure is failing, threatening our economic growth, national competitiveness and even national security" (Doshi, Schulman & Gabaldon, 2007).

Booz Allen Hamilton's estimates of necessary infrastructure spending by sector were:

- Water and wastewater: USD 22.6 trillion
- Power: USD 9.0 trillion
- Roads and railways: USD 7.8 trillion
- Airports and seaports: USD 1.6 trillion.

It is interesting to note that this report considered that water and wastewater investment spending would be a little over 50% of the required total.

The World Economic Forum estimated in 2010 that over the following 20 years the infrastructure deficit was likely to be USD 2 trillion per year.

The difference between the OECD's USD 71 trillion and Booz Allen Hamilton's USD 41 trillion is very significant. However, global estimates of any kind leave too much range for errors. They depend on the assumptions, quality of data available and analyses, and the experience, knowledge and understanding of the analysts (Ashley & Cashman, 2006). Thus, like all global estimates, these should be considered very approximate. The fact remains that the global infrastructure investment needed in the next 20 years will probably be somewhere between USD 40 trillion and USD 75 trillion. Whatever the exact amount, the fact remains that an enormous amount of investment will be necessary to ensure that the necessary infrastructure is developed and that it is properly maintained.

Water infrastructure

There are three major issues that the world is now confronted with in terms of water infrastructure. First, the population in all developing countries has increased significantly in the recent decades, and the growth in infrastructure has not kept up with the new realities. In all African, Asian and Latin American developing countries, over the recent decades, infrastructural developments have lagged far behind what was needed because of increasing population growth, urbanization, constantly expanding economic activities and higher aspirations of their people. Politicians and bureaucrats have mostly not realized the need and importance of infrastructural development and proper management to cope with new demands and catch up with the previous backlog. Thus, infrastructure development and adequate maintenance often did not receive the priority they deserved from planners and political decision makers.

Second, good and comprehensive planning for water infrastructural development has been rare in most countries. For example, countries have built numerous water and sewage treatment plants without considering where trained and experienced operators may come from. China recently found that over 25% of its newly constructed sewage treatment plants were not working because the pipelines bringing wastewater to the plants could not be completed in time (Lu, 2014). China also mandated suddenly in 2013 that its nationwide water institutions would henceforth be measuring 106 water quality parameters, compared to only 36 before. No serious thought has been given to whether laboratories are available all over the country to sample and measure these parameters or qualified and trained personnel could be recruited to staff them adequately.

While the situation is very similar in other developing countries, the level and extent of the problems vary from one country to another, and then often from one part of the country to another. However, the fact remains that good planning in the area of water infrastructure has mostly been conspicuous by its absence.

In addition, inter-institutional coordination between water and water-related institutions leaves much to be desired. For example, as Pandit (2014) points out in his article in this issue, environmental clearance of major hydropower and irrigation projects in India often takes years – sometimes decades. And, sadly, all the emphasis is on clearance of the projects. No one bothers to check whether the environmental mitigation measures that may have been a condition to have the project cleared have ever been implemented by the public- or private-sector institution constructing the project. In fact, one would be hard pressed to find even a single major water project which the Indian Ministry of the Environment has audited to see to what extent the conditions that were specifically imposed with respect to environmental clearance were ever met. Thus, environmental clearance often becomes a paper exercise whose beneficial impacts become somewhat dubious. Regrettably, the situation is very similar in most developing countries, as well as developed countries.

Third, a major problem with water and sewerage pipes is that they are almost all underground, and thus not visible to the population or to policy makers. Thus, whenever municipalities face a cash crunch, which is frequent, proper maintenance is deferred indefinitely. Consequently, the quality of water service delivery starts to suffer because of the absence of proper timely maintenance.

If the case of the United States, the world's most important economy, is considered, the situation of deferred maintenance and underinvestment can be graphically illustrated. The American Society of Civil Engineers has been carrying out comprehensive assessments of the country's major infrastructure categories since 1998. The report uses a simple A-to-F type of school report card format in considering current infrastructure conditions and requirements. It considers eight criteria for grading: capacity, condition, funding, future needs, operation and maintenance, public safety, resilience and innovation.

Since 1998, the grades have been very poor, in fact near failing, averaging only D's because of delayed maintenance and underinvestment in most categories. In its latest report (2013), the society gave bridges a C^+, ports a C, dams a D, drinking water a D, inland waterways a D^- and wastewater a D. Not surprisingly, water mains burst an average of 250,000 times a year, which increases water losses. Unfortunately, even with the prevailing historically low interest rates, there are no encouraging signs that infrastructure underinvestment and deferred maintenance are likely to change in the foreseeable future.

The situation is worse than the USA in many other countries. If we consider the case of China, in recent decades it has built infrastructure at a break-neck speed, but it has not been enough to meet the national requirements. Chinese infrastructure development has been truly frantic, especially when compared with other Asian countries. For example, in 2009, India had 6000 km of 4-lane highways. In contrast, during only the preceding 10 years, China had built 35,000 km of 4-to-6-lane highways. Each month, China adds nearly the total electricity generating capacity of Bangladesh, a country with 155 million people (around 11% of the population of China).

Even after these developments, China has much to catch up with. For example, its railway network today is shorter than that of the United States in the 1880s. Around 85 cities in China of more than 5 million inhabitants still do not have mass transit systems.

Urbanization will create more and more demand for infrastructure in Asia, especially in countries like China, India and Indonesia whose economies are developing fast. By 2030, an additional 650 million people in Asia are likely to have become urban dwellers. This is estimated to require an additional infrastructure investment requirement of USD 11–12 trillion, equivalent to almost 80% of the region's current GDP (Man, 2013).

Regarding water infrastructure, an important conceptual problem between developed and developing countries is the difference in extreme seasonality of rainfall. For example, if a monsoon country like India is considered, some 80% of its annual rainfall occurs in about a total of 80–120 hours (not continuous) during the rainy season. Hence, the main problem all the monsoon-climate developing countries are facing is how to collect and store this immense amount of rainfall in this short period of time so that enough water of the required quantity and quality is available throughout the year, as well as over varying years, for domestic, industrial and agricultural uses, hydropower generation and other uses. Policy makers, bureaucrats and even water professionals are not aware of this fact or of its implications in terms of water management.

All developing countries which receive such seasonal skewed rainfall have to consider increasing their storage capacities if they wish to achieve water security in the foreseeable future. Sadly, developed countries in temperate climates, and a few others in semi-tropical climates like Australia, which have much more uniform rainfall, have significantly greater storage capacities than any developing country. For example, the United States has a storage capacity of 6155 m^3 per person, and Australia 4733 m^3 per person. In contrast, China has around 2500 m^3 per person, and Brazil 2155 m^3 per person. India has less than 10% of the storage capacity of China, at 225 m^3 per person. Ethiopia and Pakistan have even less.

Lack of storage and the resulting water insecurity can be graphically illustrated by the water situation of one of the rainiest cities of the world, Cherrapunji, India. The average annual rainfall is 12,000 mm per year. In spite of this torrential rain, Cherrapunji has severe water shortages during non-monsoon months because of low storage capacity.

Knowledge and technology have been available for years as to how to store water efficiently and effectively to ensure against intra- and inter-annual water availability. Availability of investment funds is often not the problem. Lack of political will, institutional incompetence, public apathy, absence of serious media scrutiny, and pervasive corruption in the capital-intensive water sector have all contributed to water unsustainability.

Mismanagement and bad planning of infrastructure have also created numerous problems in many different countries. For example, the Supreme Court of India expressed its intense disappointment with water infrastructure expenditures which did not appear to have any impact. It said on 10 October 2012: "It is unfortunate that huge public funds were spent" to clean up the Yamuna River, yet the "the pollution of Yamuna has increased by the day" (Biswas, 2012).

Similarly, China spent USD 112.41 billion on water infrastructure between 2006 and 2011, and yet much of the country's water remains undrinkable. Funds have to be targeted better to produce the desired results.

Concluding remarks

While all over the world there is a deficit of water infrastructure, constructing it without good and comprehensive planning is unlikely to reduce the continuing deficit. Equally, there must be capacity in the country to operate and maintain it properly and in a timely manner. In much of the developing world, proper operation and maintenance seldom receives adequate attention. Thus, often a vicious cycle of build–neglect–rebuild develops which is not only expensive but counterproductive. This process seldom provides long-term sustained benefits.

Acknowledgements

Some of the papers for this infrastructure issue were specially commissioned for a special session on water infrastructure during the 2012 Singapore International Water Week (SIWW). It was sponsored by the Lee Kuan Yew School of Public Policy, SIWW and the Third World Centre for Water Management. The majority of the papers were submitted for possible publication in this journal.

On behalf of the *International Journal of Water Resources Development*, we thank the numerous anonymous peer reviewers who unstintingly helped us to review all the papers received during 2013 within the stipulated period of four weeks. Thanks to their efforts, the quality of all the papers published remains very high. We are most grateful to them for their insightful peer reviews.

Finally, here are our current most-cited articles (2013 Web of Science citations of papers published in 2011 and 2012). As promised, the main authors of these papers will receive free online subscriptions to the *International Journal of Water Resources Development* for 2014:

Robert J. Diaz and Rutger Rosenberg, "Introduction to Environmental and Economic Consequences of Hypoxia", Volume 27, No. 1 http://www.tandfonline.com/doi/full/10.1080/07900627.2010.531379

Kevin Parris, "Impact of Agriculture on Water Pollution in OECD Countries: Recent Trends and Future Prospects", Volume 27, No. 1 http://www.tandfonline.com/doi/full/10.1080/07900627.2010.531898

References

American Society of Civil Engineers. (2013). *Report card for America's infrastructure*. New York, NY: ASCE.

Ashley, R., & Cashman, A. (2006). The impacts of change on the long-term future demand for water sector infrastructure. In Organisation for Economic Co-operation and Development (OECD) (Ed.), *Telecom, land transport, water and electricity* (pp. 241–322). Paris: OECD.

Biswas, A.K. (2012, November 9). *Yamuna, Ganga cleanup: Fact or fiction*. Dainik Jagran.

Doshi, V., Schulman, G., & Gabaldon, D. (2007). Lights! Water! Motion! *Strategy+Business*, 46, 1–7.

Lu, S. (2014). Water infrastructure in China: The importance of full project life-cycle cost analysis in addressing water challenges. *International Journal of Water Resources Development*, 30, 47–59. doi:10.1080/07900627.2013.847760.

Man, R. (2013). *Asia infrastructure shortfall*. Hong Kong: HSBC.

OECD (2006). *Infrastructure to 2030: Telecom, land transport, water and electricity, Vol. 1*. Paris: OECD.

Pandit, C. (2014). Environmental over enthusiasm. *International Journal of Water Resources Development*, 30, 110–120. doi:10.1080/07900627.2013.871480.

World Economic Forum (WEF). (2010). *Positive infrastructure: A framework for revitalizing the global economy*. Cologny: World Economic Forum.

Cecilia Tortajada[a] and Asit K. Biswas[b]
[a]Third World Centre for Water Management, Mexico; [b]Lee Kuan Yew School of Public Policy, Singapore

Water infrastructure as an essential element for human development

Cecilia Tortajada

Third World Centre for Water Management, Atizapán, Mexico

Infrastructure is essential for development, but by itself it will not contribute to improving the quality of life of millions of people unless it is part of an overall framework for development, economic growth, social equity and environmental protection. As mentioned by Nobel laureate Amartya Sen, the absence of infrastructure has a pervasive influence on poverty, but at the same time is not a free-standing factor in lifting people from it. The focus should thus not be on physical infrastructure per se but on infrastructure as a driver for growth and sustainable development. This requires more comprehensive institutional, legal, regulatory, policy and management frameworks than the ones existing at present.

Introduction

As populations have grown, human needs have increased and expectations have changed, the natural environment that supports their growth has deteriorated and the challenges faced by governments and societies have become more complex. In a race to promote the sort of economic growth that is able to sustain human development, inexplicably, people themselves have been pushed from the centre of development debates and dialogues to the periphery (UNDP & RBAS, 2002). People have many times lost the irrefutable priority governments should have awarded them in the search for sustainable development.

In the 1990s, when the concept of 'human development' was first defined, more comprehensive discussions on development and related policy implications were proposed (UNDP, 1990). Development began to be understood as a much broader process than the mere generation of wealth. The focus thus shifted towards the intersection of social, economic and environmental dynamics. It was then logical that 'sustainable development' included the protection of the sources of future economic growth and social progress, because present and future human development depend on it.

Throughout the years, agendas promoting human development have necessarily become multifaceted. Priorities have focused on state and social institutions that advance equitable growth with widespread social, economic and environmental benefits; economic infrastructure and provision of social services; enabling regulatory environments and policy instruments for public and private investments in priority areas for human development; and, more recently, technological mobility (UNDP, 2013).

Significant human development–related progress was achieved during the last three decades. In spite of this, or perhaps because of it, many of the concerns raised in the 1990s, when international movements advocating for sustainable development picked up momentum, continue to be significant at present. These include the appraisal and promotion of human development that is not limited to gross domestic product (GDP) measurements; implementable strategies for planning, managing and financing human development as well as for participatory development; and provision of and universal access to basic public services such as education, health and water (UNDP, 1990, 2013).

Over the years, effective governance has also been recognized as an essential element for human development. It is regarded as a necessary platform through which societal goals can be pursued because it stresses the importance of involving more voices, responsibilities, transparency and accountability of the formal and informal organizations associated with any process and in any development field (Tortajada, 2010). Governance is expected to be part of all decision-making processes and to embrace the relationships between governments and societies, including laws, regulations, institutions, and formal and informal interactions that affect the ways in which governance systems function and decisions are taken (Tortajada, 2007). Governance takes into consideration how governments and social organizations interact, how they relate to societies, and how accountability is rendered (Graham, Amos, & Plumptre, 2003).

In the quest for sustainable development, infrastructure has proved to be an indispensable component of this long-term goal due to its role in reducing poverty and inequality and promoting economic growth. It has a distinct potential to help overcome growth constraints, respond to urbanization pressures, improve social and environmental conditions, encourage competitiveness and productivity, underpin improvements in quality of life and social inclusion, and enlarge and speed up communication and mobility. This should make it a sustained priority for all public and private sectors in society (Bhattacharya, Romani, & Stern, 2012).

As noted by Nobel laureate Amartya Sen, the absence of infrastructure has a pervasive influence on poverty, but at the same time is not a free-standing factor in lifting people out of it:

> It is one thing to understand that lack of infrastructure is often the principal causal influence on the genesis of poverty, it is quite another to see how attempts at deliberate and organized removal of handicaps of underdeveloped infrastructure may actually make a difference. Do public plans and programmes actually work (a natural scepticism given the shrill chorus we hear too often these days that "the best plan is no plan")? Can the differences that are made be seen immediately, or do they take an immensely long time? (2006, p. 4)

Prevailing wisdom suggests that infrastructure development should be based not on political priorities but on social and economic realities. Unfortunately, this is not always the case. It also suggests that growth and equity-promoting strategies should assess what might be necessary for entire populations, mostly the poor, to access basic services, as opposed to deciding, after the infrastructure has been developed, how it could be used by the poor (Agénor & Moreno-Dodson, 2006); the latter may produce disappointing results. Nonetheless, given the size and scale of infrastructure requirements, decisions do not tend to occur without political interference. This seems to have become a fact of life even when many times monopolies based on political relations have resulted in reduced quantities and poor quality of infrastructure services (World Bank, 2012).

Infrastructure and social impacts

Developed and developing countries alike acknowledge that one of the main challenges at present is to develop implementable policies that positively influence the lives of billions of people all over the world. The profound implications for development caused by demographic changes, the severe strains on the environment that result from rapid economic growth, and the limitations that infrastructural deficits place on access to social services in many countries constitute the panorama marking the approach of the end of the Millennium Development Goals (MDGs) (UN, 2013a).

To add to this complexity, the relaxation of the one-child population policy in China (Hongguang, 2013) has the potential to change the global dynamics of growth and development and may increase the already enormous pressure on human and natural environments. According to the 2012 revision of the official United Nations population estimates and projections (UN, 2013b), the world's population, 7.2 billion as of mid-2013, is projected to increase to 9.6 billion in 2050 and 10.9 billion by 2100. These calculations are based on projected fertility declines in countries where large families are still prevalent and slight increases in fertility in countries where, on average, there are less than two children per woman. With the new population policy in the most populous country in the world, the global situation has the potential to change significantly. This decision is likely to have immense implications in terms of environment, water, energy and food securities, not only for China but also for the rest of the world, because it is from the rest of the world that China obtains the resources required to satisfy many of its needs.

As one can appreciate, achievement of the MDGs, ultimately aimed at reducing poverty and inequality (UNDP, 2013), depends on numerous interrelated global issues as well as on many actors that can influence them through multiple pathways. Infrastructure that is properly planned, managed, operated and maintained and which has the potential to deliver universal coverage is one of the critical elements for the achievement of these goals.

There is broad evidence that infrastructure coverage and quality play a vital part in the economic growth of any country as well as in investments in human capital, with both direct and indirect effects in reducing poverty. Even then, the precise extent of public investment in infrastructure is not accurately known; this information is considered to be incomplete and unreliable (Commission on Growth and Development, 2008). So far, its actual impact on society is known qualitatively but not quantitatively.

Estache (2008) presents a comprehensive overview of this situation globally. A survey on infrastructure policy issues in developing and transition economies from the 1990s and early 2000s indicates serious monitoring difficulties due to the lack of data on the performance of infrastructure in terms of access, efficiency, equity and fiscal costs. This applies to the energy, water and sanitation, telecommunication, and transport services subsectors. The survey also indicates that public–private partnerships would be beneficial in achieving sustained efficiency gains and minimizing financing requirements. As the author notes, a serious obstacle for any policy and decision-making process has been the lack of accurate data on the status of existing physical infrastructure; insufficient knowledge of the impacts infrastructure has on human development (whether it works the same way at all stages of development or if it varies, and how); whether it has homogeneous impacts in all regions of a given country (and what are the differences for rural and urban areas). Overall, the work that could be done towards strengthening the infrastructure–poverty alleviation nexus is seriously constrained by the lack of a good baseline that provides reference information on issues such as how much the poor actually spend on and consume infrastructure services. Financial institutions such as the Inter-American Development Bank (IDB) (n.d.) and the Asian Development Bank (ADB), 2013 have also emphasized the policy and decision-making constraints resulting from lack of reliable data and information.

In the context of intensified urbanization, the continuous growth of large and medium-size cities in developing and emerging economies has become a major source of demand for additional services. This has created a sense of urgency in most national and international policy circles. Efficient delivery of services, as well as access to them, depends on much more than infrastructure. It depends on a combination of responsive institutions; regulatory models; well-planned and properly maintained and operated infrastructure; efficient public and private service providers; governance structures associated with infrastructure-project financing; economic and non-economic policies and incentives; auditing and financial accountability; equity, transparency and fiscal considerations; decentralization as a way to increase accountability (although not always efficiency); public participation; and more (Estache, 2008; Rouse, 2013, 2014).

At this point is important to stress that all users, donors and non-governmental organizations (NGOs) should systematically be made accountable for their decisions and actions. Transparency is for all, not only for governments, developers and operators. This is important because donor and NGO transparency has already been questioned on several occasions (Estache, 2008; Pandit, 2014; Rouse, 2013).

The most common means by which different actors can have a say in decision making is through the interest groups to which they belong. However, research on effective participation shows that even projects claiming full participation and empowerment have not necessarily rendered positive results for all members of society. When only such groups (many of them NGOs) are involved, the views that are put forward may not always be sufficiently representative of all the parties involved. Realistically speaking, stakeholder groups do not include all members of the society, nor do they represent all of their needs, views and concerns. In addition, not all stakeholders who are affected by a particular decision or situation are represented in the groups that are prepared to take part in decision making. Many times, members of local institutions, user groups, and normally excluded sections of the population do not see their views expressed (Mallaby, 2004; Söderbaum & Tortajada, 2011). When planning for infrastructure and services, it is important to realize that even the so-called participatory movements are not free of biases (Kumar, Jagadeesan, & Sivamohan, 2014).

Transparency, and also accountability, require accurate and reliable data and information to measure any type of progress. As noted by Estache (2008, p. 71):

> the MDGs are a good start, but accountability should not only be about access, it should also be about affordability, about public and private costs, about risks and about quality. Without more and better data on these dimensions of infrastructure service delivery, there will be no accountability in the sector. So far, when accountability has failed, the poorest users and the taxpayers have tended to bear the bulk of the costs of poor service and of corruption.

In her handbook on evaluating the impact of development projects on poverty, Baker (2000) aims to provide the necessary tools to evaluate project impacts. The author selects case studies from a pool of evaluations carried out by the World Bank and by other donor agencies, research institutions and private groups. Her findings indicate that project impact evaluations are the only means to understand whether infrastructure has produced the intended benefits; whether future projects should be designed differently, and how; whether resources (human, financial and natural) have been used efficiently, and if not, what needs to be improved; and what have been the overall impacts on the population.

Looking towards the future, the main concern governments currently have is the lack of understanding of the possible global impacts of climate change and how they will affect populations all around the world. Further uncertainty arises from the lack of clear knowledge of the type of data that should be collected to attempt to develop mitigation and adaptation strategies that are both efficient and effective. Global investments for possible strategies are in the billions of dollars. World Bank (2010) estimates that the investments required for developing countries to adapt their infrastructure to a changing climate may reach $14–30 billion annually. These figures include the incremental costs of constructing, operating and maintaining the baseline level of infrastructure under new climatic conditions, which are unknown at present.

What should be particularly stressed is that, in most developing countries, climate-related vulnerability is expected to be the result of lack of (or of poorly maintained) infrastructure. It is generally estimated that developing countries need to invest some $1.2–1.5 billion every year to close the existing infrastructure development gap; of this, only about half is actually being invested (Fay, Limi, & Perrissin-Fabert, 2010). In the case of Africa, country-level studies show that most countries are investing only 30–60% of what would be needed to close their development gap (Briceño-Garmendia, Smits, & Foster, 2008).

Clearly, the scale and nature of the challenges to achieving growth and human development are enormous, and increasing. In order to manage, allocate, utilize and protect resources globally for the future to come, multiple complementary improvements are necessary: policies which are implementable and which are developed within a long-term framework; effective and efficient institutions; forward-looking legal and regulatory frameworks; construction, maintenance and efficient use of assets; very large investments; governance matters such as accountability and transparency; and accurate data and information will all have a say in the present and future quality of life and the expectations of millions of people.

Infrastructure investment needs

Even with all the constraints due to lack of detailed information, global investments in infrastructure development, operation and maintenance are estimated to be in the trillions of dollars. For instance, developing countries tend to face a substantial and persistent infrastructure deficit, both economically and in physical assets. In many of them, low public spending on infrastructure construction and maintenance has been a problem for decades. In the early 1990s, for example, technical inefficiencies in the construction and operation of roads, railways, power stations and water services resulted in losses equivalent to a quarter of the annual public investment in infrastructure, affecting also the flow of resources from the private sector (Agénor & Moreno-Dodson, 2006). In the medium term, infrastructure investment and maintenance needs are calculated at more than $1.2 trillion annually, and actual spending is estimated to be about 50% of this (World Bank, 2011b). Figure 1 shows the needs and actual investments of the different regions in the developing world. Even though these are very gross estimates, it shows how far regions are lagging in terms of investments.

To reach the MDGs by 2015, the poorest developing countries would need to spend approximately 9% of their GDP in the operation, maintenance and expansion of their infrastructure to provide the necessary services (Estache, 2008). In the case of Asia, it is estimated that the urban infrastructure deficit is over $60 billion per year (ADB, 2013). It seems, however, that China is an exception. In the 12th Five-Year plan, the country has set a goal of ensuring high-quality economic growth, which includes enhancing water, energy, transport, communications, education and healthcare infrastructure. As a result, numerous provinces and cities have announced major infrastructure developments that

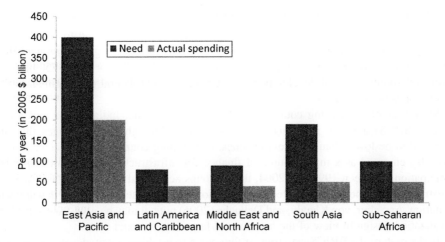

Figure 1. Infrastructure investment in developing countries: needs versus actual spending. Adapted from World Bank (2011b).
Note. Figures include investment and O&M spending. Data are not available for Europe or Central Asia.

reach the billions of dollars (KPMG International Cooperative, 2013) and that are likely to improve the living conditions of the population.

The other emerging country in Asia, India, is in a very different situation. According to the McKinsey Global Institute (2010), India's annual per capital spending for infrastructure is $17 – only 14% of China's $116 per capita. The institute calculates that India will have to invest $1.2 trillion in capital expenditure in its cities over the next 20 years to reach the necessary $134 per capita annually. This figure represents an increase in spending from the present annual average of 0.5% of GDP to 2% of GDP.

In Latin America and the Caribbean, both the Economic Commission for Latin America and the Caribbean (2010) and the IDB (n.d.) estimate that the region needs to invest some 5% of GDP in infrastructure to close the existing gap. The bank, however, notes that this figure does not consider maintenance-related expenses. Equally, it explains that these estimates depend on the goals of the individual countries and whether investments are made to boost GDP or to provide basic needs to the population such as access to safe drinking water, electricity, and good roads.

At the same time, returns from infrastructure investment have the potential to be high in developing countries, where levels of infrastructure are normally low. For example, according to the World Bank (2011b), the estimated annual needs for infrastructure in Sub-Saharan Africa are around $93 billion. If infrastructure in this region were improved to the level of countries like Korea, for example, its growth rate could rise by 2.7 percentage points annually. Similar potential has been identified in Latin America, where the region's growth rate could increase by 2 percentage points per year if it had the same level of infrastructure as East Asia's middle-income countries.

As the IDB (n.d.) notes, infrastructure investment needs should be defined through planning processes that render an implementable long-term vision for the country based on available fiscal resources and the population's ability to pay. This is not necessarily the situation in developing countries, where reforms to improve the efficiency and development effectiveness of investment programmes are not always part of long-term development plans, many times corresponding to presidential terms instead.

Investment initiatives, old and new partners

Current spending on infrastructure in developing countries is estimated to be \$0.8–0.9 trillion per year. Much of this is financed directly through domestic government budgets (\$500–600 billion), private-sector groups (approximately 20–30%, or \$150–250 billion), developed-country official development assistance, and multilateral development banks (5–8%, or \$40–60 billion).

More recently, emerging countries such as Brazil, Russia, India, China and South Africa (BRICS) are also investing in infrastructure, although in percentages that are estimated to be lower than the previous ones. Developing-country private-sector groups have also emerged as a major source of finance for infrastructure projects with private participation. Between 1998 and 2004, these groups accounted for some 52% of private investment in transport, 46% in telecommunications, 27% in energy and 19% in water and sanitation. As Schur, von Klaudy, and Dellacha (2006) note, it may be necessary to modify privatization design in view of the bias toward large international firms.

In the case of the BRICS countries, if they were to establish a new development bank for infrastructure and sustainable development, it could provide an additional borrowing channel for governments in developing countries to finance economically productive infrastructure assets (Bhattacharya et al., 2012). The importance of these emerging-country donors is not so much in the amount of aid they may disburse but in the new assistance roles they may play. This is challenging the traditional architecture of international aid, breaking the North–South aid flow stream and broadening it to South–South cooperation based on mutual national interests. This emerging architecture is modifying the sphere of influence of donor countries and is also challenging the rules under which aid is normally provided (Tortajada, forthcoming-a).

The emerging donor that has acted more proactively all over the world supporting infrastructure development, mostly of large dams, has been China (Kattelus, Rahaman & Varis, 2013; Tortajada, forthcoming-b). Chinese aid to Africa, Latin America and South-East Asia increased from less than \$1 billion in 2002 to an estimated \$25 billion in 2007 (Lum, Fischer, Gomez-Granger, & Leland, 2009). It is argued that China's aid to Africa and Latin America serves the country's long-term economic objectives via infrastructure, public works and natural resource development, whereas those in South-East Asia reflect longer-term diplomatic and strategic objectives.

In 2008, Chinese companies were involved in 97 dam projects in 39 countries. By 2011, the country was supporting the development of 251 dams in 68 countries (Tanaka, 2011). A valid concern at the international level is that economic, social and environmental considerations may not be an important part of dam construction guidelines when the funds come from China. This could be very different from the financial support of development banks with stringent requirements. China claims that its assistance to other developing countries does not come with political strings and only indicates its desire to fulfil its obligations to the international community (Siqian, 2011). As has been the case for aid in the past, perceived economic and political self-interests remain important considerations for all donors. In the case of China, engagement with developing countries at such a massive scale could be considered part of an overall national strategy for acquisition of the much-needed resources to sustain the future economic growth of the country. This is likely to have multidimensional impacts in terms of water, energy, food and environment security if not planned on a long-term horizon by the host countries (Kattelus, et al., 2013; Tortajada, forthcoming-b). Whatever may be China's ultimate objectives, it is a fact that the country is rewriting the terms and conditions of development aid, and the rest of the world is forced to take notice of the plans of this new major actor.

Multilateral development banks and private-sector groups

To support countries in improving infrastructure spending efficiency, the multilateral development banks (MDB)[1] have proposed an infrastructure action plan endorsed by the G20.[2] This set of actions presents a series of initiatives that aim at unlocking infrastructure projects left in the pipeline by (1) allowing increased private-sector participation and financing and (2) improving infrastructure spending efficiency (World Bank, 2011a).

Intensified private-sector participation and financing include actions such as improving the effectiveness of project-preparation funds; developing catalytic regional projects; expanding technical assistance through expanded public–private partnership (PPP) practitioners' networks; increasing incentives for MDB staff to engage in PPP transactions and regional projects; piloting an Africa Infrastructure Marketplace; improving procurement practices to facilitate collaboration with the private sector and amongst MDBs; and helping countries improve spending efficiency. Looking to improve efficiency in infrastructure spending, the main goals are to launch a global Infrastructure Benchmarking Initiative and to scale up the Construction Sector Transparency Initiative.

The objective of the Infrastructure Benchmarking Initiative is to collect data and perform analysis covering trends in infrastructure financing and performance with a globally consistent methodology. It would cover major network infrastructure such as information and communication technologies, power, roads, railways, ports and airports, and urban infrastructure, as well as water and sanitation. It would also enable following regional and national infrastructure trends over time (World Bank, 2011a).

Globally, the domestic private sector is investing mostly in energy and transport, while international private-sector groups are investing mostly in communications and technology (Estache, 2010). Their participation is much less in the transport, water and sewerage subsectors mainly because of the political constraints (or so-called political risk) in achieving the necessary reforms and the long time interval needed for payback. Another reason is that decision making does not always occur at the national level but increasingly at subnational levels, with local governments playing important roles. In infrastructure, private-sector participation has been mostly in terms of management and lease contracts, without assuming investment risks or undertaking major tariff reforms (World Bank, 2013).

In 1990–2001, developing countries transferred the operating risk for almost 2500 infrastructure projects to the private sector, attracting investment commitments of more than $750 billion. Those projects were implemented under schemes that included management contracts, divestitures to greenfield facilities under build-operate-own (BOO) or build-operate-transfer (BOT) contracts, and merchant facilities (World Bank, 2011b; for a detailed explanation of these terms, see the World Bank's PPI Glossary at http://ppi. worldbank.org/resources/ppi_glossary.aspx#management).

Figure 2 shows investment commitments to infrastructure projects with private-sector participation in developing countries, by sector, between 1990 and 2005. Investments were highest in the telecommunications sector, followed by the energy sector and then the water and sanitation subsectors.

Between 1990 and 2012, the private sector invested in water and sewerage projects in some 63 countries. The region with the largest share of this investment was East Asia and

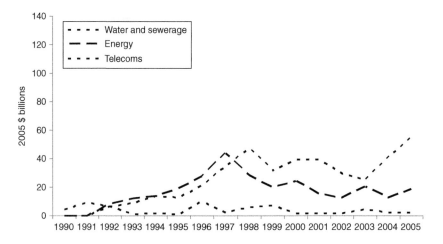

Figure 2. Investment commitments to infrastructure projects with private participation in developing countries, by sector, 1990–2005. Adapted from World Bank Group (2011b).

the Pacific, with 44%. Globally, concessions attracted 62% of private participation in infrastructure, which represents the largest share in investment and covers 41% of projects. Most governments vertically transferred integrated water utilities through concessions, with a few cases of expansion of bulk capacity for water treatment through BOO and BOT contracts (World Bank Private Participation in Infrastructure Database, Sector Data Snapshots, http://ppi.worldbank.org/explore/ppi_exploreSector.aspx?sectorID=4).

The focus on management and lease contracts that do not require private investment suggests private-sector groups are willing to invest, but they are also concerned about taking on risk (Kerf & Izaguirre, 2007). On the other hand, governments may also not be willing to take on risk, especially in a sector such as water that is so sensitive politically.

Policy mechanisms and social expectations: further thoughts

The Organisation for Economic Co-operation and Development has long insisted on the relevance of policy mechanisms that consider economic, social and environmental costs and benefits of water used in all the different sectors (OECD, 2007). Policy frameworks and structural changes as well as efficient institutions and skilled human resources are needed to secure the substantial financing required for countries to build, operate, maintain, extend and/or upgrade the necessary infrastructure for all uses and users of water. This will be the first step towards providing what should ideally be universal coverage of safe drinking water and sanitation, with the resulting improvement in the quality of life of populations in the developing world.

While the financing of water and sanitation services is a major problem mostly for developing countries, it represents only part of the seriousness and complexity of the overall lack of provision of water services. Infrastructure, its management and its operation are often problems that carry more importance. Virtuous cycles, where growth and social policies reinforce each other, are still not in place, in spite of their importance for human development (UNDP, 2013).

The inability of national and subnational governments to meet their populations' basic water needs (many times because of poor infrastructure or lack of it, as well as poor operation and maintenance practices) has resulted in not only economic but also social and environmental costs in developed and developing countries alike. There is an increasingly large and expensive agenda of policy actions and investments in infrastructure that need to be undertaken. The delay in doing so has resulted in growing numbers of people without access to clean water and the resulting deterioration in their quality of life from avoidable illnesses and premature mortality and morbidity; environmental pollution of point and non-point water sources; over-exploited and polluted rivers, lakes and aquifers; depletion of non-renewable resources and higher costs of pumping groundwater; and seawater intrusion and land subsidence. These are just a few of the numerous issues that are affecting populations on a daily basis all over the world and that are, in many cases, already delaying social and economic progress, impacting negatively on livelihoods, degrading the environment and hampering economic development (OECD, 2007).

In his book *Development as Freedom*, Sen (1999) argues the need to go beyond market rules to protect the environment. He points out that the environmental challenge has been recognized as part of a more general problem related to resource allocation involving public goods. There have been proposals for policies and regulations and institutional arrangements, as well as provision of appropriate incentives through taxes and subsidies. However, the efficient provision of public goods requires not only action on the part of the state but also analysis of the role of social values and expectations and a sense of responsibility that may reduce the need for forceful action. Since individuals live and operate in a world of institutions, where opportunities and prospects depend crucially on which institutions exist and how they perform, they should not be considered mechanical devices for development. Given that their use depends on issues like values, expectations, priorities and participation, it would be a mistake to look for some particular 'formula' for an optimum compromise from institutions, policies and society. A better approach would include institutions and policies working to promote the goals and expectations of the societies to which services are offered (Sen, 1999).

The case is the same for the provision of basic infrastructure services, such as water and sanitation, on which quality of livelihoods rely, and the physical means through which water is provided, the infrastructure itself. People's expectations and aspirations have changed significantly in recent years, requiring new policy responses and demanding participation, transparency, accountability and responsibility, which was not the case before. To identify and understand these changes and to propose alternative policies, institutions, regulations and strategies that are more relevant for the twenty-first century, it will be necessary to redirect policy dialogues to the fundamentals: development is about people, a fact that seems to have been forgotten in many places on numerous occasions.

The previous role of policy makers in developing policies and trying to implement them in isolation has only limited value in the present society. The proposed alternatives may not be compatible with reality until and unless societies and their views and expectations are made a mainstream part of development.

Notes

1. The MDB Working Group on Infrastructure includes the African Development Bank, Asian Development Bank, European Investment Bank, Inter-American Development Bank, Islamic Development Bank and World Bank Group.
2. The Group of Twenty Finance Ministers and Central Bank Governors (G20) is composed of 19 countries plus the European Union, and representatives of the International Monetary Fund and the World Bank. The 19 countries are Argentina, Australia, Brazil, Canada, China, France, Germany, India, Indonesia, Italy, Japan, Mexico, Russia, Saudi Arabia, South Africa, Korea, Turkey, the United Kingdom, and the United States.

References

Asian Development Bank (ADB). (2013). *Urban operational plan 2012–2020*. Manila: Asian Development Bank.

Agénor, P. R., & Moreno-Dodson, B. (2006). *Public infrastructure and growth: New channels and policy implications* (Policy Research Working Paper 4064). Washington, DC: The World Bank.

Baker, J. L. (2000). *Evaluating the impact of development projects on poverty: A handbook for practitioners*. Washington, DC: The World Bank.

Bhattacharya, A., Romani, M., & Stern, N. (2012). *Infrastructure for development: Meeting the challenge*. London: Centre for Climate Change Economics and Policy.

Briceño-Garmendia, C., Smits, K., & Foster, V. (2008). *Financing public infrastructure in Sub-Saharan Africa: Patterns and emerging issues* (Background Paper No. 15, Africa Infrastructure Country Diagnostic). Washington, DC: The World Bank.

Commission on Growth and Development. (2008). *The growth report: Strategies for sustained growth and inclusive development*. Washington, DC: The World Bank.

ECLAC (Economic Commission for Latin America and the Caribbean). (2010). *Diagnóstico sobre las restricciones al desarrollo y a una integración económica más profunda* [Diagnosis on the limitations for development and for a deeper economic integration]. Santiago de Chile: Economic Commission for Latin America and the Caribbean.

Estache, A. (2008). Infrastructure and development: A survey of recent and upcoming issues. In F. Bourguignon & B. Pleskovic (Eds.), *Rethinking infrastructure for development* (pp. 47–82). Washington, DC: The World Bank.

Estache, A. (2010). Infrastructure finance in developing countries: An overview. *European Investment Bank Papers*, *15*, 61–88.

Fay, M., Limi, A., & Perrissin-Fabert, B. (2010). Financing greener and climate-resilient infrastructure in developing countries: Challenges and opportunities. *EIB Papers*, *15*, 34–58.

Graham, J., Amos, B., & Plumptre, T. (2003). *Principles for good governance in the 21st century* (Policy brief No. 15). Ottawa: Institute on Governance.

Hongguang, L. (2013, November 15). China to ease one-child policy. Xinhuanet. Retrieved from December 1st 2013 http://news.xinhuanet.com/english/china/2013-11/15/c_132891920.htm

Inter-American Development Bank (IDB). (n.d.). Infrastructure strategy for competitiveness. [Profile]. Retrieved from December 20, 2013 http://www.iadb.org/en/civil-society/public-consultations/public-consultation-infrastructure/public-consultation-idb-infrastructure-strategy,8157.html

Kattelus, M., Rahaman, M. M., & Varis, O. (2013). Myanmar under reform: Emerging pressures on water, energy and food security. *Natural Resources Forum*. doi:10.1111/1477-8947.12032.

Kerf, M., & Izaguirre, A. K. (2007). *Revival of private participation in developing country infrastructure. A look at recent trends and their policy implications*. Washington, DC: The World Bank. Retrieved December 6, 2013, from https://openknowledge.worldbank.org/handle/10986/10720

KPMG International Cooperative. (2013). Infrastructure in China. Sustaining quality growth. Retrieved from January 10, 2014 http://www.kpmg.com/cn/en/issuesandinsights/articlespublications/pages/infrastructure-in-china-201302.aspx

Kumar, D. M., Jagadeesan, S., & Sivamohan, M. V. K. (2014). Positive externalities of irrigation from the Sardar Sarovar project for farm production and domestic water supply. *International Journal of Water Resources Development*, *30*, 91–109. doi:10.1080/07900627.2014.880228.

Lum, T., Fischer, H., Gomez-Granger, J., & Leland, A. (2009). *China's foreign aid activities in Africa, Latin America, and Southeast Asia* (CRS Report for Congress). Washington, DC: Congressional Research Service.

Mallaby, S. (2004). *The world's banker: A story of failed states, financial crises, and the wealth and poverty of nations*. New Haven: Yale University Press.

McKinsey Global Institute. (2010). *India's urban awakening: Building inclusive cities, sustaining economic growth*. Mumbai: McKinsey & Company.

OECD. (2007). *Instruments mixes for environmental policies*. Paris: Organisation for Economic Co-operation and Development.

Pandit, C. (2014). Environmental over enthusiasm. *International Journal of Water Resources Development*, *30*, 110–120. doi:10.1080/07900627.2013.871480.

Rouse, M. (2013). *Institutional governance and regulation of water services: The essential elements* (2nd ed.). London: IWA Publishing.

Rouse, M. (2014). The worldwide urban water and wastewater infrastructure challenge. *International Journal of Water Resources Development, 30*, 20–27. doi:10.1080/07900627.2014.882203.

Schur, M., von Klaudy, S., & Dellacha, G. (2006, April). *The role of developing country firms in infrastructure* Grid Lines, Note no. 3. Washington, DC: The World Bank.

Sen, A. (1999). *Development as freedom*. New Delhi: Oxford University Press.

Sen, A. (2006, March). *Summary of the talk to be given at the launch meeting of Japan-UNDP report making infrastructure work for the poor*. New York, NY. Retrieved from www.un.emb-japan.go.jp

Siqian, M. (2011, April 22). White paper on China's foreign aid. China Daily. Retrieved from 10 December 2013 http://www.chinadaily.com.cn/cndy/2011-04/22/content_12373944.htm

Söderbaum, P., & Tortajada, C. (2011). Perspectives for water management within the context of sustainable development. *Water International, 36*, 812–827.

Tanaka, K. (2011). *China, a new driving force of the world development? Implications of China's engagement in water infrastructure*. Singapore: Lee Kuan Yew School of Public Policy.

Tortajada, C. (2007, June). *Water governance in the MENA region: Critical issues and the way forward. The case of stakeholder participation and public awareness*. Paper presented at the Second Partner' Forum of InWEnt Capacity Building International, Germany, and the Arab Water Council, Cairo.

Tortajada, C. (2010). Water governance: Some critical issues. *International Journal of Water Resources Development, 26*, 297–307.

Tortajada, C. (forthcoming-a). Water resources evolving landscape. In B. Currie-Alder, R. Kanbur, D. Malone, & R. Medhora (Eds.), *International development: Ideas, experience, and prospects*. Oxford: Oxford University Press.

Tortajada, C. (forthcoming-b). Dams: An essential component of development. *Journal of Hydrologic Engineering*, In press.

UN. (2013a). *The millennium development goals report 2013*. New York, NY: United Nations.

UN. (2013b). *World population prospects. The 2012 revision*. New York, NY: United Nations.

UNDP & RBAS. (2002). *The Arab human development report 2002: Creating opportunities for future generations*. New York, NY: United Nations Development Programme and Regional Bureau for Arab States.

UNDP. (1990). *Human development report 1990. Concept and measurement of human development*. New York, NY: United Nations Development Programme.

UNDP. (2006). *Human development report 2006. Beyond scarcity: Power, poverty and the global water crisis*. New York, NY: United Nations Development Programme.

UNDP. (2013). *Human development report 2013. The rise of the south: Human progress in a diverse world*. New York, NY: United Nations Development Programme.

World Bank. (2010). *Beyond the sum of its parts: Blending financial instruments to support low-carbon development*. Washington, DC: The World Bank.

World Bank. (2011a). *Infrastructure action plan (Vol. 1 of multilateral development banks infrastructure action plan: G20 documents)*. Washington, DC: The World Bank. Retrieved from http://documents.worldbank.org/curated/en/2011/10/15470166/multilateral-development-banks-infrastructure-action-plan-g20-documents-vol-1-2-infrastructure-action-plan

World Bank. (2011b). *Framework for strong, sustainable and balanced growth. Rebalancing, growth, and development: An interconnected agenda*. Washington, DC: The World Bank. Retrieved December 2, 2013, from http://econ.worldbank.org/WBSITE/EXTERNAL/EXTDEC/0,contentMDK:23037042~pagePK:64165401~piPK:64165026~theSitePK:469372,00.html

World Bank. (2012). *World development report. Jobs*. Washington, DC: The World Bank.

World Bank. (2013). Private participation in infrastructure: Trends in developing countries in 1990–2001: Energy, telecommunications, transport and water. Retrieved from January 10, 2013 http://ppi.worldbank.org/resources/ppi_book.aspx

The worldwide urban water and wastewater infrastructure challenge

Department of Geography and the Environment, University of Oxford, Oxford, UK

There are two parts to the challenge of providing the infrastructure necessary for universal access to water and sanitation. One challenge is the extension of existing infrastructure and new infrastructure to serve all in today's urban areas and to keep up with the expected rapid growth of cities; the other is the refurbishment of existing infrastructure to maintain access to water and sanitation. Meeting the second challenge is the more costly; it is also essential to meeting the first challenge. Infrastructure is the means, not the end, with a requirement for clear policies on objectives, priorities and service standards. Delivery will require effective planning, regulation, innovation, capacity building and training. Although the infrastructure costs will be high, the benefits will be greater.

Introduction

The overall challenge is to plan for, build and maintain water, wastewater and sanitation infrastructure to facilitate universal access to safe water and dignified sanitation. This might be regarded as making provision for those areas currently unserved, but in practice it is much more complicated. There are two separate but related challenges: developing and extending infrastructure to match the accelerating growth of people who will be born in or migrate to cities (UNDESA, 2011); and refurbishing the existing infrastructure which has been allowed to deteriorate. There will be associated infrastructure needs for increasing energy and food demands, a topic which is beyond the scope of this article. However, it has been estimated that, worldwide, the required investment in infrastructure for water and wastewater exceeds that for energy and transport combined (*Lights! Water! Motion!*, 2007). But water and wastewater infrastructure development has to be seen as part of designing cities of the future (Novotny & Brown, 2007). Within this thinking it is necessary to include sanitation, as opposed to just wastewater, because future decisions will have to consider non-water-based sanitation, even in urban areas. No one approach is likely to dominate, with decisions on the form of sanitation being dependent upon availability of fresh water, opportunities for local water reuse, and operational considerations, alongside solid-waste management and urine-based fertilizer production.

So, investment is required for extending water and sanitation systems, including collection and processing, and for refurbishment of existing water and wastewater systems. Although antiquated treatment systems will require upgrading or replacement, most of the refurbishment investment will be for underground infrastructure. Because of inadequate maintenance, existing systems have deteriorated, resulting in high leakage losses and a backlog of investment. To provide a scale for the refurbishment requirement, the author estimates that if put end to end, existing worldwide water mains (excluding the property-service pipes) would go round the world perhaps as many as 400 times. This also stresses the importance of good-quality installation of durable-material pipes for new or replacement water mains. Although new advances provide more cost-effective means of delivery in other utilities, such as telecommunications, pipes remain the most effective and efficient way of transmitting water. Alternatives for delivering the volumes required are much more expensive in lifetime cost and require more energy. For example, in Ghana, water distribution by road tanker costs 14 times as much as distribution through the pipe networks.

Although infrastructure will provide the physical means of delivering the required service, decisions should not be driven by infrastructure considerations. Infrastructure is the means, not the end. The starting-point has to be 'what service where', so that infrastructure options can be evaluated against service and affordability criteria. On what criteria should policies and planning be based? Despite their limitations with respect to definition and monitoring, the Millennium Development Goals (MDGs) have been effective in giving political focus to water and sanitation (United Nations, 2000). It can be expected that the post-2015 follow-on goals will also be valuable in making progress, especially given that they are likely to be associated with the UN resolution on water and sanitation as a human right (United Nations, 2010). It is appropriate to discuss the post-2015 goals in relation to how they will provide definition for the scale and types of infrastructure needed and in the planning necessary for delivering the water and sanitation services.

Post-2015 development goals and the UN resolution on water and sanitation as a human right

The MDGs of halving the number of people without access to 'improved' water and sanitation by 2015 will be followed by new goals which at the time of writing have yet to be determined. They should be ambitious but realistic. There is no point in setting unobtainable goals which would result in dismissal by governments and disillusionment of people. Consideration has to be given to both the financing and the logistics of what is an immense task, and monitoring measurements must be unambiguous to avoid the 'fudging' of results. The definitions of what is targeted for delivery should be clear, and the UN resolution on the human right to water and sanitation (hereafter, HRWS) has an important role to play here. Its main purpose is non-discrimination in universal access to water and sanitation.

According to the resolution, the General Assembly

1. *Recognizes* the right to safe and clean drinking water and sanitation as a human right that is essential for the full enjoyment of life and all human rights;
2. *Calls upon* States and international organizations to provide financial resources, capacity-building and technology transfer, through international assistance and cooperation, in particular to developing countries, in order to scale up efforts to provide safe, clean, accessible and affordable drinking water and sanitation for all;
3. *Welcomes* the decision by the Human Rights Council to request that the Independent Expert on human rights obligations related to access to safe drinking water and sanitation submit an annual report to the General Assembly, and encourages her to continue working on all aspects of her mandate and, in

consultation with all relevant United Nations agencies, funds and programmes, to include in her report to the Assembly, at its sixty-sixth session, the principal challenges related to the realization of the human right to safe and clean drinking water and sanitation and their impact on the achievement of the Millennium Development Goals.

The link with the MDGs is thus made explicit. The substantive document on which the resolution was based was the Independent Expert's Report (de Albuquerque, 2010, UN A/65/254) to the UN General Assembly dated 3 August 2010. This includes the key normative and cross-cutting elements which 'define' the human rights to water and sanitation. A book on good practice, On the Right Track (de Albuquerque, 2012), followed in March 2012. The key elements are given in Table 1. Extensive work is taking place within a UN framework, with involvement by the International Water Association (a network of water professionals), to produce implementation handbooks. A full discussion on HRWS is outside the scope of this article, but there are some important interpretation issues (Rouse, 2013), some of which will influence service development decisions. Key issues for decisions on urban water infrastructure are continuity, sustainability and affordability. Similar issues for sanitation are considered later in the article.

Continuous water supplies

Generally, in the context of urban water services, the terms 'continuous' and 'sustainable' relate to piped supplies. The rural context may be quite different. On its own, 'continuous' could be interpreted as 'providing sufficient water each day'. Including the key requirement of sustainability has profound implications for continuity of supply. Sustainability means no regression, not only in providing continuous water supplies for the currently unserved but also maintaining supplies for those already connected to a piped supply. This brings into question the need for continuous (24/7) supplies, which, as discussed below, are essential for sustainability quite independently of HRWS. For many years it was believed that given limited water resources, water supplies had to be rationed by hours of day through rotation. It has now been shown (WSP, 2010) that, due to their

Table 1. Key elements in the UN resolution on water and sanitation as a human right.

Normative Elements

Water
　Sufficient, continuous, accessible
　Safe
　Acceptable
　Sustainable
　Affordable

Sanitation
　Sufficient, continuous, accessible
　Physical security
　Safe disposal of excreta
　Sustainable
　Affordable

Cross-cutting elements
　Non-discrimination
　Participation and empowerment
　Transparency
　Accountability

combination of water waste and water-pipe degradation (as a result of pressurization and de-pressurization), intermittent-supply policies result in a greater water resource requirement. In addition, poor levels of service result in unwillingness (quite separate from inability) to pay, with negative consequences for utility income, which is needed to fund maintenance – and a spiral of decline. This has highly important implications for HRWS implementation policy and infrastructure considerations. It means that before systems can be extended to supply either the unserved or the expanding cities, the investment priority has to be refurbishing the existing systems.

A simple policy decision to achieve 24/7 supplies would be to replace the whole distribution system. This approach, which has been valuable in demonstration sites in India, is relatively quick to implement, but expensive. In areas where, perhaps due to specific ground conditions, pipe degradation has been severe, wholesale replacement may be necessary. However, it might be expected that in most areas detailed investigation could result in a more cost-effective approach, based on selective replacement, coupled with local repairs to fix major leaks, and ongoing monitoring and maintenance. Establishing and implementing 24/7 service is a daunting task, but an essential one. There is an urgent requirement for more studies to develop viable infrastructure refurbishment policies, together with investigative and operational procedures.

Bad condition of underground water mains can be compounded by poor construction, with too little attention having been given to the bedding of the pipes in the trenches or to the making of joints and connections. The quality of the original workmanship will influence decisions on replacement. Equally, it is vital that new installations are built to a high standard. This requires specifying appropriately high standards for pipes and fittings, training of installers, diligent overseeing of construction, and both incentives for good work and penalties for poor work built into contracts. This highlights the recognition that progress will require a lot more than just adoption of international targets, with capacity building and training being essential elements.

Sustainable cost recovery

Without sustainable cost recovery, the necessary maintenance and refurbishment of systems is not possible. Sustainable cost recovery is defined by the International Water Association (IWA, 2006) as "costs that are recovered so that a water services undertaking can achieve and maintain a specified standard of service, both for the present and future generations". It is important to recognize that the UN documentation on HRWS stresses that water (and sanitation) services have to be affordable – that does not mean free. Free water for all leads to excessive usage, with subsidies being insufficient for effective maintenance (Rouse, 2013). So, the challenge is to establish charges for good and efficient services, which achieve sustainable cost recovery through tariff mechanisms which also protect the poor. However, the high one-off capital costs of new or replacement systems in some parts of the world would place too high a burden on the 'current' served population, so infrastructure grants, subsidies or long-term, low-interest loans will be required for affordability.

The equivalent issues with sanitation

Clearly, the concept of 'continuous' is different in sanitation from in water. It is the access to the facility which has to be continuous. If installed in a property this is a given, but with public or communal toilets the facilities must be maintained so that they are accessible, safe and acceptable. With a sewer-based system, drainage has to work continuously, whether to a sewer network or to some receptor, such as a septic tank. With dry (separating) toilets, the requirement is for regular collection of faeces and urine at the specified frequency. Latrines have to be emptied to maintain a viable and acceptable service. So, although there is no direct equivalent to the downward-spiral scenario of intermittent piped-water supplies, maintenance is critical to the sustainability of sanitation systems; without this there will be regression of the service. Equally, the cleaning and maintenance of sanitation facilities has to be financed, with a requirement for a charge for the service. Because there is likely to be the same spectrum of affordability in any given location, it is appropriate to consider including the sanitation charge in the 'water' bill, based on affordable tariffs.

Progressive realization and planning

Achieving universal access to water and sanitation services of a required standard will take time. It is a matter not only of financing and building the infrastructure but also of the need for improved governance, capacity building and training to achieve effective operations and maintenance for sustainability. This is recognized in the HRWS resolution through the concept of progressive realization. It applies not only to achieving access to water and sanitation services but also to other aspects such as drinking-water quality. Supplying drinking water free from pathogens and of chemicals at toxic levels should be the priority. Meeting all aspects of the World Health Organization guidelines (WHO, 2004) on drinking-water quality should be a longer-term objective. A phased approach would result in available investment monies being initially spread more widely to give benefit to more people.

Planning is a critical requirement in the delivery of the required infrastructure. Ideally, there would be an outline strategic plan based on a vision for water and sanitation and a mission for its accomplishment. This plan would assign priorities based on progressive realization but with full cognizance of non-discrimination. Periodic 'delivery' plans (perhaps five-yearly) would then be based on those priorities and would take into account water resources, water treatment and distribution, the equivalents for sanitation, and, increasingly, infrastructure for reuse of wastewater. These plans should be integrated with city plans specifically to match city growth expectations.

The importance of information

Planning can only be effective if based on good information. Often, the information on existing systems is poor, particularly with respect to the condition of underground networks. The resources necessary to obtain good baseline data should be built into early plans. This may appear to delay construction but can be expected to accelerate sustainable progress once reliable information is available. Obtaining good data and the establishment of management information systems for operations, asset management and planning are important aspects of capacity building.

Role of regulation – managing planning and benchmarking

It is governments' role to determine policy and that of service providers to deliver services. Policy has to be interpreted in delivery terms, and progress has to be monitored. Often, water service providers, particularly the smaller ones, do not have the management or technical capacity for policy interpretation and planning. An intermediate organization, such as a regulator with the necessary skills, can play an important role in managing the planning process, monitoring progress and providing technical assistance. Regulators tend to be seen as a police force wielding a big stick at recalcitrant service providers, but their role can be much more related to capacity building. A good example of this is ERSAR (Entidade Reguladora dos Serviços de Águas e Resíduos) (Baptiste, 2013), the water and waste regulator in Portugal.

ERSAR was originally established to regulate state-owned and private water companies. In 2009, its remit was extended to include 450 municipal water service providers, many of which are small. It sets performance measures, assists water service providers in improving their system information and information systems, encourages learning from best-in-class benchmarking, and assists in the preparation of improvement programmes. It describes its regulatory approach as "collaborative" and "teaching", with a strong "capacity building role" (Baptiste, 2013). ERSAR is able to provide that vital interpretation of policy objectives into service-performance objectives and to provide the support needed for decision making on infrastructure development.

Regulators provide valuable reviews of infrastructure proposals with respect to whether they are appropriate to meeting specified service-delivery objectives. In Malaysia, infrastructure proposals are reviewed as part of a periodic planning and tariff-setting process, with regulatory approval required for funding. The funding approach has been designed to provide long-term (typically 40-year) low-interest loans through a government organization called in English "Water Asset Co.". With the Malaysian government's credit rating, Water Asset Co. is able to obtain low-interest loans on the international money market. The process is as follows (personal communication, Teo Yen Hua, CEO, Malaysia National Water Services Commission, 2013):

1. As part of the planning process, a water company submits proposals to the National Water Services Commission (Suruhanjaya Perkhidmatan Air Negara, or SPAN). SPAN approves the infrastructure development for funding, which is financed by Water Asset Co.

2. Water Asset Co. owns the new infrastructure; it is leased to the water company at a rate approved by SPAN. The cost to the water company is included in the allowable tariffs which SPAN judges affordable to the water customers. The leasing charge includes a sum for recovery of the capital cost.

3. At the end of the 40-year lease, the capital cost is paid off and the assets transferred to the water company. Water Asset Co. has recovered the capital, which can then be used for other water and wastewater infrastructure developments.

4. This process should provide for sustainability, because the capital funding is part of full cost recovery. It becomes affordable thanks to the ability to spread the infrastructure cost over a long period of time, avoiding the whole cost falling on the 'current' generation.

This is an excellent example of innovation in a governance structure. Innovation in all aspects of water and sanitation governance, management and technology will be necessary to meet the challenges of universal access.

Innovation

Innovation tends to be associated with 'inventions', but it applies to any aspect of life. A general definition of innovation is 'introducing something new'. The Concise Oxford

English Dictionary refers to "bringing in novelties" and "making changes". In the Malaysian example, introducing an affordable approach to funding within a regulatory structure has addressed the problem of affordability of capital for infrastructure development. Of course, hardware innovations are important, but they have to be associated with innovation in governance for successful application. In Singapore, membranes for reverse osmosis have made possible reuse of wastewater, but there has also been innovation in contract management, operations and public information. Also in Singapore, sensor and monitoring technology has been integrated into hydraulic modelling of water distribution networks to provide information in real time for managing leakage (PUB, 2013). The monitoring system also provides for better optimization of distribution systems and development of infrastructure. A Bill & Melinda Gates Foundation (2012) initiative is funding the development of urine-diversion toilets for use in public ablution blocks in informal settlements. The approach is being trialled in the region around Durban, South Africa. The development of the hardware is taking place in the University of KwaZulu-Natal's Pollution Research Group. Successful functioning of the toilet unit is essential, but so is the governance system within which the toilets will be operated. The operating partner in the development is eThekwini Water and Sanitation. Key aspects are the collection systems for urine and faeces.

Infrastructure development: a multi-faceted challenge

Can the infrastructure necessary for universal access of a 'safe' standard be afforded? The simple answer is that the costs of not having access are greater than the investment required to achieve it, so it must be affordable. An update of the global costs of achieving access and the benefits of doing so based on conservative estimates of benefits gives world average benefit/cost ratios of 2:1 for water and 5.5:1 for sanitation (WHO, 2012). Not taking into consideration population growth, it is estimated that the costs of achieving universal access would be USD 20 billion a year for 20 years. An estimate of infrastructure costs for India alone is USD 129 billion (KPMG, 2010). However, the estimates of maintaining access are much higher, amounting to trillions of US dollars, which is in line with the Booz Allen Hamilton estimate of USD 23 trillion made in 2007 (*Lights! Water! Motion!*). Much of the cost for refurbishment of infrastructure is in developed countries with more established and older infrastructure. It is difficult to make accurate assessments of cost, but all the estimates are very large. Yet, it is possible to be confident that the benefits greatly exceed the costs. It is necessary for each country to make detailed assessments of the needs and costs. Even though the financial figures are daunting, the bigger challenge is in policy, planning and delivery. This article has discussed some key aspects for progress: those of policy, goals to give political focus, planning, information, regulation and innovation.

References

Baptiste, J. M. (2013, June). *Regulation of the water services in Portugal: Present challenges.* Presentation at workshop held in Bucharest, Romanian Water Association.

Bill & Melinda Gates Foundation. (2012). *Innovative toilet technology of the 21st century.* Seattle, WA: Bill & Melinda Gates Foundation. Press Release 2012.

de Albuquerque, C. (2010, August 6). *Report of the independent expert on the issue of human rights obligations related to access to safe drinking water and sanitation* (UN A/65/254). Retrieved from www.ohchr.org/Documents/Issues/Water/MDGReportA6524.pdf

de Albuquerque, C. (2012, March). *"On the right track", Good practices in realising the rights to water and sanitation.* Geneva: OHCHR.

Doshi, V., Schulman, G., & Gabaldon, D. (2007). *Lights! Water! Motion!* Houston, TX: Booz Allen Hamilton.

IWA. (2006). *Sustainable cost recovery*. Reference Paper, International Water Association 2006.

KPMG. (2010). *Water sector in India: Overview and focus areas for the future*. PanIIT Conclave 2010. Delhi: KPMG 2010.

Novotny, N., & Brown, P. (Eds.). (2007). *Cities of the future: Towards integrated sustainable water and landscape management*. London: IWA Publishing.

PUB. (2013). Innovation in water, Singapore. An R&D Publication of PUB, Singapore's National Water Agency, Volume 4 April 2013.

Rouse, M. J. (2013). *Institutional governance and regulation of water services: The essential elements* (2nd ed.). London: IWA Publishing.

United Nations. (2000). *Millennium declaration 55/2 8 September 2000*. Retrieved from http://www.un.org/millennium/declaration/ares552e.htm

United Nations. (2010). UN General Assembly Resolution 64/292. The human right to water and sanitation. 3 August 2010. Retrieved from http://www.un.org/en/ga/64/resolutions.shtml

UNDESA. (2011). *World Urbanisation Prospects: The 2011 Revision*. New York: Population Division of the Department of Economic and Social Affairs of the United Nations Secretariat.

WHO. (2004). *Guidelines for drinking water quality*. Geneva: World Health Organisation.

WHO. (2012). *Global costs and benefits of drinking-water supply and sanitation interventions to reach the MDG target and universal coverage*. WHO/HSE/WSH/12.01. Geneva: World Health Organisation.

WSP. (2010). The Karnataka urban water sector improvement project. 24/7 Water Supply is Achievable. Water and Sanitation Program. Field Note, September 2010. WSP New Delhi.

Is water scarcity a constraint to feeding Asia's growing population?

Colin Chartres[a,b]

[a]*International Water Management Institute, Colombo, Sri Lanka;* [b]*eWater, Bruce, Australia*

Growing population and wealth, as measured by per capita GDP, are predicted to put water resources and food production in Asia under increasing pressure over the next few decades. Critical factors include the increasing demand for animal proteins in diets and the growing need for energy. Climate change impacts may further reduce available water resources because of greater evaporation losses in some areas and storms and floods in others. If we are to overcome these significant constraints on food production, we must turn to strategies that are focused around sustainable intensification of agriculture. These include modernization of old irrigation schemes to increase water productivity, innovative concepts that capture and store flood runoff for use in agriculture, much more recycling and reuse of urban wastewater, and other efficiency-improvement techniques. However, these will not happen in a policy vacuum, and it is argued that reforms are needed in water policy, water training and water management institutions across Asia.

Introduction

The 2007–2008 food crisis alerted many governments to the fact that we can no longer take food security for granted. Given the successes of the Green Revolution of the 1960s and 1970s, many people found this surprising, yet, if we look at the reasons for the food crisis, its occurrence and potential recurrence were anticipated by agriculturalists and economists. For example, population grew steadily through the last 50 years as public health care, water supply and sanitation improved and life expectancies increased. At the same time, agricultural land was appropriated for industrial and urban development and water resources came under greater pressure from all users. By 2007–2008 a situation existed where world grain stocks were low, drought inhibited production in some major cereal-growing countries and biofuel production was in competition with food production. As a consequence of these impacts on supply, large consumers like China sought to purchase grains on the international commodity markets, and prices began to rise, rapidly sparking food riots in some countries and export bans in others. Whilst the situation never reached famine proportions, it was inevitably the poor who suffered, with the World Bank estimating that 125 million people were thrown back across the poverty line as a consequence. Given that circumstances similar to those in 2007–2008 could easily recur, a similar food crisis could happen again in the next 10 years. Additionally, leading scientists such as the UK's former chief scientist, Sir John Beddington (2011), argue that as we move into the next 10–20 years, a "perfect storm" is brewing that will create even more severe impacts on food production. This will see climate change impacts combining with continually growing population and the factors mentioned above to create an even more serious food crisis.

Availability of water resources will be fundamental to our efforts to increase food production. However, there are serious concerns that in many Asian countries, water resource utilization is already close to capacity. Furthermore, growing population and wealth mean that we will see more water being diverted from agriculture to industry and urban uses. Similarly, land availability for agricultural expansion is also very low in many countries. These factors are already making governments look at offshore acquisition of land on which to develop agriculture to ensure the security of national food supplies.

During the Green Revolution, the development of new cultivars of the major cereals, combined with access to fertilizers and irrigation water, facilitated the feeding of the growing millions. Indeed, some commentators have argued that Norman Borlaug, known as the father of the Green Revolution, saved one billion people from starvation (World Food Prize website, n.d.). However, whilst innovative plant breeding (with or without genetic manipulation technology), combined with improved agricultural practices, offers scope to further increase crop yields, access to new sources of water will prove more difficult – firstly, because they are generally already being used, and secondly, because hunger for energy means that many unused water supplies are being viewed primarily as sources of hydropower and cooling water for thermal energy production plants. Whilst hydropower and irrigation can coexist, evidence to date in South–East Asia indicates that most hydropower schemes are built and operated primarily from the perspective of energy generation.

These factors collectively mean that we face the challenge of growing more food on less land and with less water than currently. Given the potential forthcoming perfect storm that may seriously impact food production in Asia, the aim of this paper is to examine potential innovative solutions for water management that will allow us to adapt to changing conditions and produce more food from less water.

How much more food and water are required to feed nine billion

An FAO expert consultation (FAO, 2009) argued that globally, by 2050, we will need to produce up to 70% more food to feed the forecast population of nine billion. The reason a population increase of about 30% calls for a 70% increase in food production is that as peoples' incomes grow, their diets change. This creates a much higher demand for animal proteins, including meat and dairy products, which require significant feed inputs. Thus we have to grow more animal feed, in contrast to systems in which cereal production goes directly to human consumption. Modelling done for the Comprehensive Assessment of Water Management in Agriculture (CAWMA) suggested that meat consumption in East Asia in 2050 will be double that of 2010, with a concomitant 63% increase in cereal production, predominantly for animal feed (2007). Population growth is slowing in many Asian countries (Table 1). There are, however, notable exceptions, such as Pakistan, where population is forecast to climb from 169 million to 295 million by 2050. Furthermore, South Asia in particular is home to a very high proportion of people living at or close to the poverty line, who are most likely to be impacted first by food and water shortages.

If we look at the availability of water resources as a whole in Asia (Table 2) and their capacity to grow an increasing amount of food, CAWMA suggested that Asia's total available water resources are plentiful (2007).

However, such statistics can be misleading, because much of the renewable resource is in areas unsuited to agriculture. More recent studies by the Water Resources 2030 Group

Table 1. Population growth for selected regions

	Population (millions)		
	2009	2050	Growth 2009–2050
Africa	1010	1998	98%
Asia	4121	5231	27%
Europe	732	691	−5%
Latin America and the Caribbean	582	729	25%

Source: Based on statistics from UNDESA (2012).

Table 2. Asia's freshwater use in 2000 (after CAWMA, 2007).

	Renewable freshwater resources	Total freshwater withdrawals	Agriculture		Industry		Domestic		Withdrawals (% of renewable resource)
			Amount	share (%)	Amount	share (%)	Amount	share (%)	
Asia	11,594	2378	1936	81	270	11	172	7	20.5

Note: Figures are in cubic kilometres per year unless otherwise stated.

(2009) have demonstrated that India and China face demands 50% and 25% higher than supply, respectively, by 2030. Even then, we know that parts of these large countries have abundant water, but other regions are desperately short, a fact that has seen the commencement of river diversions in China and similar diversions being contemplated in India.

A critical issue in East and South Asia is that most arable and irrigable land is already under production. In South Asia, over 50% of arable land is already under irrigation (CAWMA, 2007). Climate change may bring more northerly lands under production, but at the same time marginal lands in the subtropics may become unsuitable for agriculture.

Chartres and Sood (2013) and the Calouste Gulbenkian Think Tank (2014) have revisited some of CAWMA's scenarios, and their forecasts indicate that consumptive water use in Asia (including the Pacific) could increase from approximately $1600\,km^3$ in 2010 to as much as $4000\,km^3$ by 2050 as a major component of globally growing water demand (Figure 1).

Of this, the largest predicted growth in consumptive water use is for industrial and domestic water. However, under lower GDP growth and moderate population growth, the increases are smaller. Business-as-usual and pessimistic scenarios see global consumptive usage predictions of $5000\,km^3$ and $4000\,km^3$, respectively. Thus, whilst the optimistic scenario for 2050 reported by Chartres and Sood (2013) may not eventuate if economic growth is slower than forecast, it seems clear that water use will increase even under alternative scenarios. It is also important to point out that actual usage of irrigation water requires significantly larger withdrawals, given storage, transmission and evaporative losses. For example, usage of $1800\,km^3$ in irrigation requires withdrawals of about $3000\,km^3$.

Using data from CAWMA (2007), Figure 2 plots predicted irrigation, industrial and domestic water withdrawals globally between 2000 and 2050. This exemplifies the increase in demand from industry and domestic users that we expect to see in future and the fact that irrigation withdrawals will increase only marginally due to competing demand

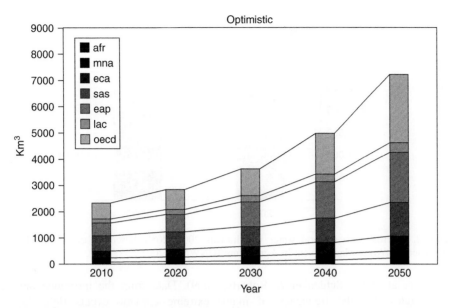

Figure 1.   Global consumptive water use under an optimistic scenario of high GDP and low population growth and full trade. After Chartres and Sood (2013). afr = Africa; mna = Middle East and North Africa; eca = Eastern and Central Asia; sas = South Asia; eap = East Asia and the Pacific; lac = Latin and Central America; OECD = Organization for Economic Development and Cooperation.

from industry and domestic users. The last two withdrawals combined are predicted to increase by 2.2 times.

Irrespective of which global population and economic growth scenarios occur, the data in the comprehensive assessment (CAWMA, 2007) and those of Chartres and Sood (2013) and the Calouste Gulbenkian Think Tank (2014) suggest that global water demand may well be in excess of available supplies in agricultural areas by 2050. Current estimates of global extractable water resources are about $4000 \, km^3$ (CAWMA, 2007). To put this in context, it suggests global water usage in excess of supply by 2050 under business-as-usual scenarios and a serious water shortage over much of Asia under scenarios with rising economic growth and slowing population growth. This is of major concern, and does not take into account other factors such as climate change.

There is an increasing amount of material in the scientific literature examining the potential impact of climate change in Asia and elsewhere on water availability and food production. Chartres and Sood (2013) modelled the potential impact of climate change on water demand based on two future climate scenarios (SRES A2 and SRES B1) developed in the Special Report on Emissions Scenarios (SRES) of the International Panel on Climate Change (IPCC, 2001). SRES A2 represents a future with more focus on global economic growth and SRES B1, one with more emphasis on global environmental sustainability. However, potential evapotranspiration, which is dependent upon temperature, increases, with a much steeper increase after 2040. By 2050, for the irrigated area, the gap between potential evapotranspiration and effective rainfall will be about 17% higher than the baseline for the A2 climate change scenario and about 14% higher for the B1 scenario. This will exacerbate the demand for irrigation water.

Other authors have also demonstrated that increasing temperatures may have a significant impact on the yield of several crops, including wheat, maize and soybeans

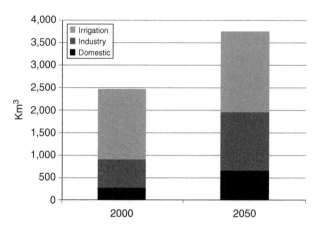

Figure 2. Increases in sectoral water withdrawals 2000–2050, based on the Comprehensive Assessment of Water Management in Agriculture (CAWMA, 2007).

(Lobell et al, 2008; Schlenker & Roberts, 2009). Data from the insurance industry demonstrates that the frequency of major extreme climatic events (hydrological, meteorological and climatological) is increasing and, because of higher population densities, having greater human impact.

In summary, this brief review of the drivers behind water and food scarcity suggests that:

- Asian and global water demands for irrigation are likely to exceed supply by 2050.
- Geographic variability in availability of water resources at the continent and country levels will continue to feature.
- There is limited suitable land for expansion of irrigation in Asia.
- Climate change will potentially increase demand for irrigation water because of higher evapotranspiration rates as temperatures increase. (Whilst there is no clear understanding of future rainfall patterns, increasing variability in the form of droughts and floods is also likely.)

These findings lead to the question: What can be done to avert what could be catastrophic outcomes if we follow a business-as-usual pattern with respect to water and food?

Growing more with less: do we need more infrastructure?

There has always been a tension in the water resources sector between major engineering approaches to dealing with water scarcity and floods and simpler remedies that can be applied at various scales by farmers and water resource managers. A current trend in many Asian countries is focused around major infrastructure developments, particularly for hydropower generation. For example, in Lao PDR three hydropower dams were operational in the early 1970s. By the mid-2000s, this number had increased to 10, and up to 55 more dams are planned (http://www.internationalrivers.org/resources/existing-and-planned-lao-hydropower-projects-3527).

Whilst this may be an inevitable way in which energy demands are going to have to be met, there are many alternative approaches to improving irrigation productivity and (at least to some extent) flood prevention. Some of these approaches use natural infrastructure as a basis for water management, and others are focused on improving water governance and management and farming practices.

Mukherji et al. (2009) suggested that five key strategies need to be followed if Asia is to deal with food security. These are:

1. Modernization of older irrigation schemes
2. Support for farmer-led innovation
3. Looking beyond conventional participatory irrigation management and irrigation management transfer methodologies
4. Expansion of capacity and knowledge
5. Investment outside of the irrigation sector.

Irrigation schemes in much of Asia were developed 30 to 40 years ago, and many have reached the stage in their life where further reinvestment in the infrastructure is required. This actually allows scope for the introduction of more modern technologies for canal management, water-use metering and a range of water-efficiency gains that could help protect farmers against increasingly variable climate and assist with demand, as opposed to supply-based water delivery to farmers. Revitalization of canalized irrigation schemes also provides some opportunity for water management authorities to look at water allocations to competing users and to consider environmental water needs.

In much of South Asia, the last 30 years have seen an unprecedented increase in smallholder-led irrigation based on small pumps and groundwater. Shah (2009) has described this "groundwater irrigation revolution" as atomistic and anarchic because of the millions of pumps scattered across the landscape, with users paying little heed to the sustainability of the resource. Consequently, major declines in groundwater have been observed in Indian states like the Punjab. Elsewhere, farmers have "scavenged" wastewater for fodder and vegetable production, with concomitant risks to their own and food consumers' health. However, there are lessons to be learned from these opportunistic uses of water by smallholder farmers in terms of both what works well for them and what could be improved in terms of food safety and environmental issues.

Participatory irrigation management and irrigation management transfer to farmer groups were hailed as major policy successes when implemented across several Asian countries 20 to 30 years ago. However, a recent study by Mukherji et al. (2009) suggested that many schemes have not been as successful as previously thought. Whilst well-documented evidence on "success" factors was hard to come by, it appeared that many schemes failed when the "priming" support of a government or non-governmental agency was withdrawn. Similarly, there has been a lack of reform in many countries' irrigation agencies, which has not helped the situation. The key question for the future is: Are there ways in which we can enhance collective responsibility for irrigation schemes through outsourcing of irrigation services, creation of public–private partnerships, or provision of incentives for officials to initiate beneficial reform? While food remains relatively cheap, there are doubts as to whether these reforms can be achieved; but as water comes under more competition from other users they may become imperative for food security.

In terms of expanded capacity and knowledge in the irrigation sector, there is considerable scope for improvement. This is imperative if we want to attract investment in the agriculture sector. It means closely examining and reforming university curricula, investing in staff training and attracting new talent into the irrigation industry. Particularly important will be the reform of existing institutions to build a cadre of staff interested in innovation, productivity increases, water-use efficiency and environmental conservation, as opposed to moribund departments that base their activities around licensing and regulation – in some cases illegal licensing and extraction of water, driven by bribery and other forms of corruption.

Lastly, Mukerji et al. suggested that we need to look beyond the irrigation sector at Asia's wider political economy and its drivers. Policies and programmes related to trade, water use and environment may all have both beneficial and negative impacts on the agricultural sector. These need to be understood and factored in to regional planning processes if we are to develop more vibrant and responsive irrigation systems.

Whilst the need for energy will undoubtedly continue the push for large dams, there are many ways that smaller-scale infrastructure can be important in meeting growing water demands. Rainwater harvesting, small reservoirs and tanks, and the artificial recharge of groundwater systems with runoff and partially treated wastewater are all important options for consideration. A recent study by Pavelic et al. (2012) demonstrated the possibility of capturing and storing, underground, potentially damaging floodwaters in the Chao Praya River basin of Thailand and then utilizing this water for dry-season irrigation. As the 2011 floods demonstrated, Thailand's naturally high seasonal endowment of water resources brings with it the regularly experienced problems associated with floods during the wet season and droughts during the dry season. The government response usually focuses on downstream engineering solutions to address flooding. These are critical, but do not necessarily capture the potential for basin-scale improvements to water security, food production and livelihood enhancement. Pavelic and his co-authors suggested that managed aquifer recharge could be applied to capture, store and recover episodic extreme flood events in Thailand. They estimated that in the Chao Phraya River basin, surplus flows recorded downstream above a critical threshold could be harvested and recharged within the shallow alluvial aquifers in a distributed manner upstream of flood-prone areas without significantly impacting existing large and medium storages or the gulf and deltaic ecosystems. Capturing peak flows approximately one year in four by dedicating around $200 \, km^2$ of land to groundwater recharge would reduce the magnitude of flooding and socio-economic impacts and generate around USD 250 million per year in export earnings for smallholder rainfed farmers through dry-season cash cropping without unduly compromising the demands of existing water users. The authors proposed that farmers in upstream riparian zones could be co-opted as flood harvesters and thus contribute to improved floodwater management through simple water management technologies that enable agricultural lands to be put to more productive use. Local-scale site suitability and technical performance assessments would be required, along with revised governance structures. Depending on further feasibility studies, it is probable that such an approach could also be applicable to a number of similar environments in Thailand and potentially throughout Asia.

Asia is also becoming an increasingly urbanized continent. The move to the cities will create challenges for both agricultural and urban communities. In some agricultural regions, urban migration may halt the trend of further fragmentation of land holdings and perhaps offer opportunities for consolidation. Similarly, there may be opportunities for the development of more integrated market and supply chains, which may also be beneficial to farmers. However, the growth of urban communities will inevitably increase the demand for water. This water may have to be appropriated from agriculture, which puts further pressure on farmers to become more efficient. However, large cities also generate very significant amounts of urban runoff and wastewater. These present opportunities for recycling of runoff within the city and reuse of the wastewater in agriculture. A key challenge here is to develop water management and treatment systems that minimize health and pollution risks to the agricultural water users, consumers and the environment.

The final question that we must ask about water and agriculture in Asia relates to the current efficiency of both rainfed and irrigated systems. Clearly, whilst the efficiency of agricultural systems in Asia has been improving steadily over the last 50 years, there is still room for further improvement (Johnston et al., 2010). The critical issue will be whether there can be sustainable intensification of agriculture to deliver the required food and fodder. To do this requires considerable rethinking about water productivity and also much more focus on how agriculture interacts with the environment in terms of sustaining critical ecosystem services. In particular, these include reducing the runoff of agricultural wastewater (containing pesticides and nutrients), protecting groundwater systems, and also reducing erosion and sedimentation. Johnston et al. listed a large number of agricultural management practices that will need to be adhered to in the Greater Mekong Region if it is to become more productive and also sustainable. They include introduction of new varieties, crop diversification, improved water productivity, restoration of degraded forest lands, and better integration of fishery and agricultural systems. Many of these are equally applicable across many other regions of Asia. As in the case of irrigation revitalization (Mukherji et al., 2009), these changes will not necessarily happen without government, policy and institutional reform and support.

Conclusions

If water and food shortages are to be averted, the scenarios of water demand need more detailed analysis at the country level to allow improved policy and strategy formulation. The evidence presented here indicates that Asian countries have a major challenge ahead of them to remain food and water secure. Whilst dam building will continue to be driven by ever increasing demands for energy, there are many ways in which agriculture can become more productive without being totally reliant on large dams for irrigation. These include greater reliance on local water harvesting and management schemes, managed aquifer recharge, a suite of agronomic and policy measures that will enhance water productivity and water-use efficiency, and the safe reuse of urban wastewater. A critical challenge will be the extent that food production can be increased in greater harmony with the environment.

References

Beddington, J. (2011). Food, energy,water and the climate: A perfect storm of global events? Retrieved from http://www.bis.gov.uk/assets/goscience/docs/p/perfect-storm-paper.pdf

Calouste Gulbenkian Think Tank. (2014). *Water and the future of humanity*. New York, NY: Springer.

CAWMA. (2007). *Water for food, water for life: A comprehensive assessment of water management in agriculture*. London: Earthscan/Colombo: International Water Management Institute.

Chartres, C. J., & Sood, A. (2013). The water for food paradox. *Aquatic Procedia, 1*, 3–19.

FAO. (2009). *How to feed the world in 2050*. Proceedings of the Expert Meeting on How to Feed the World in 2050. Rome: Food and Agricultural Organization of the United Nations.

Höppe, P., & Löw, P. (2012). Characteristics of the extreme events in 2011 and their impact on the insurance industry. In C. Courbage & W. R. Stahel (Eds.), *Extreme events and insurance: 2011 annus horribilis*. The Geneva Reports: Risk and Insurance Research. Retrieved from https://www.genevaassociation.org/media/200995/ga-2012-geneva_report[5].pdf

IPCC. (2001). *Special report on emissions scenarios*. Retrieved from http://www.grida.no/publications/other/ipcc_sr/?src=/climate/ipcc/emission/094.htm.

Johnston, R., Hoanh, C. T., Lacombe, G., Noble, A., Smakhtin, V., Suhardiman, D., & Sze, C. P. (2010). *Rethinking agriculture in the greater Mekong Subregion: How to sustainably meet food needs, enhance ecosystem services and cope with climate change* (p. 26). Colombo: International Water Management Institute.

Lobell, D.B., Burke, M.B., Tebaldi, M.D., Falcon, W.P., & Naylor, R.L. (2008). Prioritizing climate change adaptation needs for food security in 2030. *Science*, 319, 607–610.

Mukherji, A., Facon, T., Burke, J., De Fraiture, C., Faurès, J-M., Füleki, B., & Shah, T. (2009). *Revitalising Asia's irrigation: To sustainably meet tomorrow's food needs.* Colombo: International Water Management institute. Rome, Italy: Food and Agricultural Organisation of the United Nations.

Pavelic, P., Srisuk, K., Saraphirom, P., Nadee, S., Pholkern, K., Chusanathas, S., & Smakhtin, V. (2012). Balancing-out floods and droughts: Opportunities to utilize floodwater harvesting and groundwater storage for agricultural development in Thailand. *Journal of Hydrology, 470–471*, 55–64.

Schlenker, W., & Roberts, M.J, (2009). Nonlinear temperature effects indicate severe damages to U.S. crop yields under climate change. *Proceedings of the National Academy of Sciences, 106* (37), 15594–15598.

Shah, T. (2009). *Taming the anarchy: Groundwater governance in South Asia* A co-publication of Resources for the Future, (p. 310). Washington, DC: International Water Management Institute. Colombo, Sri Lanka.

Water Resources Group 2030. (2009). *Charting our water future.* London: McKinsey & Co. http://www.2030waterresourcesgroup.com/water_full/Charting_Our_Water_Future_Final.pdf

UNDESA. (2012). *Population and vital statistics report. Statistical papers series A.*Vol. LXIV. New York : United Nations Department of Economic and Social Affairs. Retrieved from unstats.un.org/unsd/demographic/products/vitstats

World Food Prize website. (n.d.). Retrieved from www.worldfoodprize.org/en/dr_norman_e_borlaug/full_biography/

Water services industry reforms in Malaysia

Yen Hua Teo

National Water Services Commission Malaysia, Cyberjaya, Malaysia

Concerted efforts to reform and transform the water industry in Malaysia began in 2006. It was a visionary effort by the federal government to ensure an adequate supply of clean water to the public and industry. A policy and institutional framework was created to re-invent and transform the water services industry into an efficient and sustainable sector that will play a pivotal role as one of the major components of economic growth. Though minor adjustments may be needed during its implementation, the overall policy direction is pragmatic and viable and has started to produce tangible outcomes.

Introduction

Many developing countries are undertaking reform in the water services industry as a pre-emptive move to ensure adequate water supplies for current and future needs. The economic growth experienced in most developing countries as they are integrated into the inter-dependent economies of globalization is the major driver for such a reform, because increased consumption will deplete the limited water resources. Growing population, rapid urbanization and industrialization, as well as unquenchable consumerism, are straining the supply of water. Coupled with the threat of climate change, the future outlook portends more frequent shortages of water and severe droughts that could cause political instability if left unresolved.

Unfortunately, most reforms in the water services industry in developing countries are not comprehensive and tend to focus on certain localities; the predicaments and problems faced by the majority of the population are not being addressed. Reforms should be nationwide, but to undertake such an exercise is a daunting task. It involves numerous consultations with various stakeholders to convince them of the benefits of the reforms, monitoring performance and fulfilling not only the economic demand but also the social needs of the whole population. In addition, reforms in developing countries very often do not give sufficient emphasis to sanitation services. There is plenty of rhetoric about providing sanitation services, but few regulatory reforms undertaken to make sanitation affordable and sustainable.

In Malaysia, the concerted effort to reform and transform the water industry which began in 2006 was undertaken in the absence of any imminent water crisis. Rather, it is a visionary effort by the federal government to transform the water industry to ensure that it can continue to supply adequate clean water to the public and industry. The Malaysian government has put in place comprehensive policies covering both water supply and sewerage services. In fact, it has been widely acknowledged that Malaysia is amongst the few countries that are embarking on an ambitious quest to create the policy and institutional framework to reinvent and transform the water services industry into an efficient and sustainable sector that will play a pivotal role as one of the major components of economic growth. Though minor adjustments may be needed during its implementation, the overall policy direction is pragmatic and viable and has started to produce tangible outcomes.

The role of the Suruhanjaya Perkhidmatan Air Negara (SPAN) or National Water Services Commission

The journey towards regulatory reforms in Malaysia began with amendments to the federal constitution which transfer water services and supplies from the "state list" to the "concurrent list" and two acts, i.e. the Water Services Industry Act (WSIA) (2006) and the National Water Services Industry Act (SPAN Act) (2006), that enable the federal government to regulate water services and govern the water services industry while water sources remain within the purview of the state governments.

The introduction of the two pieces of legislation was done after extensive consultations as the federal government declassified the draft bills and made them available online for public feedback. Briefings to specific stakeholders were also carried out before the two bills were tabled in Parliament for approval.

SPAN was established in February 2007 to implement and enforce the WSIA. The role of SPAN is to govern the water services industry from the treatment of raw water to the discharge of wastewater. The functions of SPAN are, inter alia, to advise the minister on national policy objectives, to monitor and regulate water supply services and sewerage services activities, and to review and recommend tariffs.

One of the objectives of the WSIA is to establish a framework for regulatory intervention to promote the national objectives for the water supply and sewerage services industry. These objectives are:

(1) To establish a transparent and integrated structure for water supply and sewerage services that delivers effective and efficient service to customers
(2) To ensure long-term availability and sustainability of water supply, including the conservation of water
(3) To contribute to sustainability of watercourses and the water catchment areas
(4) To facilitate the development of competition to promote economy and efficiency in the water supply and sewerage services industry
(5) To establish a regulatory environment which facilitates financial self-sustainability amongst the operators in the water supply and sewerage services industry in the long term
(6) To regulate for the long-term benefit of the consumers
(7) To regulate tariffs and to ensure the provision of affordable services on an equitable basis
(8) To improve the quality of life and environment through the effective and efficient management of the water supply and sewerage services
(9) To establish an effective system of accountability and governance between operators in the water supply services and sewerage services industry
(10) To regulate the safety and security of the water supply and sewerage systems

In a nutshell, SPAN is entrusted to develop the industry model that will transform the water services industry into a well-regulated industry that strives for better water conservation and efficiency through the right pricing of water services, coupled with innovative financing instruments to secure funding to finance the cost of upgrading and replacing aging assets as well as the construction of new infrastructure. The management of water facilities must be improved to generate revenue and cash flow to ensure the viability and long-term sustainability of the water services industry.

Industry structure

Malaysia has a land area of 330,803 km^2 and a population of 28.334 million (as of 2010). In 2012, 94.7% of the population had access to piped water (96.9% of the urban population and 90.7% of the rural population) (MWIG, 2013). As for sanitation, based on the Global Environmental Performance Index Report (Yale Centre of Law and Policy, 2012),[1] 94.5% of the Malaysian population has access to sanitation services. The water infrastructure in Malaysia is mostly developed by the government through allocations provided under the five-year Malaysian development plans. Some treatment facilities have been constructed by the private sector, in states that have privatized their water service. The development of sewerage systems has been private-sector-driven since the 1970s; the government has only implemented central sewerage systems in selected cities and towns with a population greater than 100,000. Currently, there are 21 water operators in Peninsular Malaysia and the Federal Territory of Labuan; 13 are involved with distribution and treatment, 1 with distribution only and 7 with treatment only. Sewerage services in Peninsular Malaysia were privatized to Indah Water Konsortium (IWK) in 1994 and subsequently taken back by the government in 2000, except in the north-eastern state of Kelantan, where services are being provided by Majaari Sevices Sdn. Bhd., a state-owned company.

Undoubtedly, the Malaysian water services industry is better than those found in most other developing countries. However, the industry structure is fragmented, and the inconvenient truth is that the country's present water services industry is definitely not sustainable in the long run. There are a plethora of issues that need to be tackled and resolved. The current infrastructure of the water services industry is old and poorly maintained, hampered by lack of funds. Some water-treatment plants and distribution networks that were constructed in the 1900s are still in operation today. Consequently, the water industry suffers a huge loss of revenue from leakage and other causes, with non-revenue water (NRW) at about 36% (MWA, 2013).

The pricing structure is not based on full cost recovery; tariffs are below costs and thus not sustainable over the long term. Full cost recovery means that the tariffs imposed are sufficient to meet both operational and capital expenditures without any government or non-governmental support. In reality, the revenue collected by the water service industry can barely cover total operating expenditures. The inability or reluctance to revise tariffs has resulted in the revenue collected by some service providers being able to cover only operating and maintenance costs.

These problems are due mainly to lack of uniform policy and planning. The industry is fragmented; each state within the federation has its own legal and policy framework. Before the amendments to the federal constitution which paved the way for the federal government to regulate water services, matters related to water services and supplies were under the state list. What this means is that water supply was under the sole jurisdiction of the respective state governments; the federal government could not set policy or regulate the industry. However, as most of the state governments were unable to meet the financial resources required to fund new water facilities or to replace aging infrastructure, the federal government had to extend interest-free loans to all state governments. Most of these state governments were unable to service their loan repayments. This has resulted in many state governments having huge outstanding loans. The total outstanding loans of state governments and IWK amounted to MYR 7.6 billion as of the end of 2006 and MYR 2 billion as of June 2012, respectively. The era of a fragmented industry is characterized by non-uniform legislation, procedures and key performance indicators (KPIs), as well as different levels of service standards, non-uniform tariff-setting frameworks and the use of varying material standards.

Asset-light model

One of the strategic thrusts behind the Malaysia government's reforms for the sector is to adopt an asset-light model. This also entails an expeditious transfer of loans and assets from state governments to the federal government through Pengurusan Aset Air Berhad (PAAB), a company wholly owned by the federal government. Its main purpose is to enable water supply service providers to focus on providing services to consumers without having to be burdened by the issue of funding and major infrastructure procurement. Under this model, service providers operate and maintain the facilities while the tasks of funding and development of major infrastructure such as treatment plants, intake facilities and the replacement of distribution networks are the responsibility of PAAB. Facilities planning for new infrastructure or for upgrading, refurbishment or asset renewal has to be approved by SPAN. This is done through three-year rolling business plans for all service providers, which have to be submitted to SPAN for license renewal.

Whilst the long-term goal for the sector is towards full cost recovery, in the immediate and medium terms it would be quite impossible for the sector to fund its requirements through conventional financing facilities, i.e. through government allocation, which has its limitations, or private initiatives premised on high funding costs and short-tenure borrowings.

Under the asset-light approach, PAAB will lease these existing assets back to the service providers at reasonable and affordable rates. At the same time, service providers are required to plan and submit their facilities requirements to SPAN under the 30-year master plan and 3-year business plan. Once approved, service providers will then submit applications to PAAB for funding and procurement. The assessment of needs by SPAN will be done on the basis of demand projection, impact on tariffs and funding availability. PAAB being a government-backed facility owner with a AAA credit rating, it will be able to raise financing at much lower cost than any private companies or operators and optimize its financial resources through borrowing on longer tenures to match asset life.

Progress achieved

Migration to new regime

The progress achieved so far has produced tangible results. Five out of the 11 states (Johor, Melaka, Negeri Sembilan, Penang and Perak) have restructured their loans and asset holdings by adopting the asset-light model. One more state (Perlis) has signed the loans and assets transfer agreement but has yet to effect the transfer as the process of corporatization has not been completed. It is federal government policy that any service provider must be corporatized and not operating as a governmental organization.

At the same time, the service providers operating in these five states have also migrated to the new licensing regime under the WSIA, whereby three-year licenses were issued. They worked hard to achieve their respective KPIs. As a result of the requirement to comply with the KPI targets, the five licensees improved their overall management and technical performance. They reduced NRW, a major source of loss and wastage for service providers. For example, NRW for Melaka dropped from 30.1% in 2008 (MWA, 2009) to 23.8% in 2012 (MWA, 2013). Similarly, for Johor, it dropped from 31.2% to 27.8%, and for Negeri Sembilan, from 50.5% to 40.4%, over the same period (MWA, 2009, 2013). As for Penang and Perak, which only migrated in 2011 and 2012, respectively, improvements are beginning to be seen. The progress in NRW is attributable to a concerted effort undertaken to embark on a holistic NRW-reduction programme, including active leakage control, replacing faulty meters and creating district metering zones and better asset-management practices, as well as the replacement of old pipes. Water quality has been enhanced by the setting up of an accredited central laboratory and implementation of scheduled monitoring and checking of water tanks and mechanical and electrical equipment. Increased efficiency in billing had led to higher revenue, while the setting up of a customer service centre has improved service to customers.

Impacts of corporatization

One of the policies adopted by the Malaysian government in its efforts to transform the water services industry is to empower water operators through corporatization. Previously, the respective state government decided on its own the structure and organizational set-up of their water supply entity. Some preferred it to be in the form of a state-level department, whilst other, created water boards. Two states (Selangor and Johor) proceeded to privatize all their water supply operations, in both treatment and distribution. In order to effect a systematic transformation process, the federal government, after extensive study and stakeholder consultations, decided that all states that had yet to corporatize their water supply department must do so under the WSIA. This policy was adopted because it was noted that an entity empowering to operate based on corporate practices and principles would be more nimble in structure and thus able to respond quickly to consumers' needs without being hampered by public agency bureaucracy.

Thus far, the corporatization policy has indeed brought tangible results. The success of Syarikat Air Negeri Sembilan Sdn. Bhd. (SAINS), a state water supply corporation, is a good example. Revenue for SAINS increased by over 41%, from MYR 123.3 million in 2008 (MWA, 2009) to MYR 173.9 million in 2012 (MWA, 2013), though tariffs remained unchanged. This was mainly due to the more efficient billing and collection system, as well as intensified enforcement actions against illegal connections. As a state-government-owned company, SAINS is run as a corporate entity and given the necessary financial and management autonomy, but with full accountability. Similar successes have been recorded by Syarikat Air Melaka Bhd. in Melaka and Syarikat Air Darul Aman Sdn. Bhd. in Kedah.

Tariff adjustment

One of the biggest challenges facing the water industry in many countries is the difficulty of effecting price adjustments. Water supply is capital intensive and with long payback period as access to water is universally accepted as a human right. Thus, governments are reluctant to increase tariffs. Yet, countries cannot contain the cost of water supply, especially given the increases in energy prices, which form a major component of operating expenditure. Since the enforcement of the WSIA in 2008, SPAN has received and reviewed applications for tariff adjustments for six service providers in the states of Kedah, Penang, Melaka, Negeri Sembilan, Johor, Kelantan and the Federal Territory of

Labuan. The federal government approved tariff reviews for the states of Kedah, Penang, Johor, Melaka and Kelantan, and the new rates were published in the federal government gazette under Water Services Industry (Rates for Water Supply Services) Regulations 2010 (Government of Malaysia, 2010). The new tariff adjustments have improved the financial position of service providers, leading to better service for all consumers.

Licensing

The underlying purpose of licensing is to ensure that service providers comply with all the provisions in the WSIA. This includes obligations in terms of ability to supply water to consumers, efficient billing and revenue collection systems, proper maintenance and operation of water facilities, undertaking proper planning to meet demand requirements, efficient management of resources, etc. It is a requirement in Malaysia that the supply of treated water to consumers meets the standards imposed by the World Health Organization and that wastewater is properly disposed of in order to protect the environment and water sources from contamination. This involves the whole supply chain, inclusive of both public and private water systems. Thus far, SPAN has licensed 14 service providers of public water supply, 1 sewerage service provider, 835 private system owners and operators (where 60 are owners of private water supply systems and 355 of private sewerage systems and 61 are operators of private water supply systems and 359 of private sewerage systems), and 16,609 permit holders who are involved with the operation, construction, connection, modification or repairs to private water supply and sewerage systems (MWA, 2013). For water supply, a license has been granted to all 11 states except for Perlis and Selangor and the Federal Territory of Labuan. These licensees and permit holders are being monitored with respect to water quality, effluent standards and quality of works (among other parameters). Enforcement action will be taken against any owners or operators found to be violating the provisions in the WSIA (2006) and its subsidiary legislations.

Enforcement

SPAN is committed to strict enforcement of the rules and regulations under the provisions of the act. Strict enforcement will send a signal to industry players and the public that SPAN is serious and any failure to comply with the law will be prosecuted accordingly. This will not only act as a deterrent but also create public awareness that there are existing laws to regulate the water services industry. This is to ensure that all service providers and the public at large comply with the regulations. To date, SPAN has opened investigation papers on 384 cases; 48 have been convicted, and the rest are under investigation or awaiting hearing by the courts (MWA, 2013). Even though water supply is a natural monopoly, SPAN believes that it must be well regulated to protect the interest of all consumers.

Key challenges

Resistance to change

As in any other country, the transformation of the Malaysian water services industry has encountered resistance, including from the state governments because of lack of understanding of the asset-light model. Some have misconstrued the efforts of the federal government as loss of ownership and control over their water assets. To allay these fears, a ring-fencing mechanism was put in place whereby restrictions are placed on the land on which the assets are located, such as prohibition from utilizing it for any purpose other than water supply. Under such an arrangement, lands which are no longer needed for water infrastructure can only be disposed of with the consent of state governments. After numerous road shows and discussions with the relevant stakeholders, there is now better acceptance and understanding of the restructuring model. As mentioned earlier, since the enforcement of the WSIA in 2008, 6 of the 11 states have signed the asset-transfer agreement with PAAB. The remaining states have also officially accepted the restructuring model, though implementation and negotiations have not been concluded. This includes the state of Selangor, where the state government has officially accepted the concept of the asset-light model but maintains its position of acquiring the equity interest of all the existing concessionaires. The federal government has targeted to complete the whole exercise by 2013.

Tariff-setting mechanism

Under the water services reform initiatives that began with the enforcement of the WSIA in early 2008, the need to establish a tariff-setting mechanism that is transparent and fair forms an integral part of the overall transformation plan for the water services industry. The regulatory accounting framework, which is in the process of being established, will be an integral element in shaping the mechanism for setting tariffs in the future. Licensees are required to submit their regulatory accounting information, which basically is a system for establishing information integrity and transparency. This is to allow SPAN to work with a uniform and reliable information set to monitor the performance of licensees. The challenges expected before the regulatory accounting framework could be fully realized and used as a tool for tariff setting include accounting separation (i.e. cost allocation for each stage of the supply chain), developing specific indicators for performance measurement, optimizing operations by lowering costs and improving key business processes, and setting defined standards of serviceability and operating capability for water-based assets. It requires input to carry out benchmarking, inter alia, to compare and analyze costs and performance metrics, to review activity-based costing of operations for cost efficiency, to identify performance improvements in reducing wastage and improving service level and to set benchmark costs which are the regulatory costs applied for tariff setting. A tariff-setting framework that is transparent and fair, coupled with tangible improvements in service delivery, will make future tariff hikes more palatable.

Capital expenditure and delivery

The current low tariffs mean that service providers have no incentive to invest in upgrading their infrastructure which is capital intensive. The role of the federal government via PAAB is vital in seeking funding. Capital expenditures required to invest in new infrastructure will smooth out project implementation and delivery on time and at value-for-money prices. Projects may need to be fast-tracked, but their implementation must comply with policies and procedures that have been set. Balancing affordability with requirements, i.e. development of new infrastructure, refurbishment and upgrading of existing assets, are very much desired but cannot be sustained by the existing tariffs.

Since the reforms were introduced in 2008, water infrastructure assets (except for development of water resources) are being developed and financed by PAAB, whose funding is from the capital market. Some of the major water infrastructure projects that have been undertaken by PAAB are shown in Table 1.

Addressing non-revenue water leakages

One of the greatest sources of waste is leakage, or more specifically the physical-loss portion of NRW, which ranges from 18% to 66% depending on the states. The national target is to reduce NRW to 25% by 2020. There is an urgent need to address the problem in a holistic way. Success in NRW reduction is becoming an increasingly important aspect of meeting demand, particularly in areas where water resources are limited. Reducing NRW is not a purely technical issue but actually an issue of good management and governance. Aside from wasting scarce resources and investments, high NRW rates also mean that consumers are paying for the inefficiencies of water utilities. NRW reduction will not only lead to more optimized water use and distribution but also reduce the demand for water, which immediately translates into cost savings on utilities' operations and maintenance. The federal government is in the midst of restructuring the sewerage industry along the approach of an asset-light model and finally integrating water and sewerage services.

Asset management

In Malaysia, amongst other assets, there are 473 water-treatment plants, 6050 public sewage plants, 2474 private sewage-treatment plants, 134,495 km of water pipelines and 16,721 km of sewer networks (MWA, 2013). The replacement costs associated with

Table 1. Major water infrastructure projects undertaken by PAAB.

State of Johor
1 Upgrading, Rehabilitation and Extension of Existing Semangar Water-Treatment Plant, Kota Tinggi
2 New Buluh Kasap Water-Treatment Plant
3 Distribution Improvement Works for Endau, Mersing
4 Sludge-Treatment Works for Yong Peng 2 & 3 Water-Treatment Plants and Distribution Improvement Works in Johor
5 Distribution Main from Yong Peng to Sg. Berlian Batu Pahat, supply improvement Seluyut, Kota Tinggi and improvement of water supply to Parit Sulung area, Batu Pahat

State of Melaka
1 Bertam DAF Phase 2 Water-Treatment Plant, Durian Tunggal
2 Design and Build of Water Supply System to Rembia Industrial Estate at Alor Gajah
3 Trunk Main Replacement and Upgrading Works and New Distribution System in Melaka, Parcels 1 and 2

State of Negeri Sembilan
1 Extension of Kuala Jelai Water-Treatment Plant
2 Upgrading of Jempol Water-Treatment Plant and main pumping pipe from Jempol Water-Treatment Plant to Taisho and Kompleks Serting
3 Upgrading of distribution system, i.e. pipe replacement and rehabilitation programme
4 Upgrading and rehabilitation works of Water Treatment Plants Lakai and Pantai

Source: Database of National Water Services Commission, Malaysia (2013).

pipelines and treatment plants far exceed that which service providers can realistically afford, given constrained water and sewerage prices. To increase their useful life, assets must be managed in a proactive and strategic manner, a prerequisite which will become increasingly important under the regulatory environment.

Currently, the culture of maintenance is not given priority by some of our service providers. SPAN has impressed on them to put greater emphasis on total asset management. Asset management is not a one-year or even a five-year project but rather a continuous and fundamental change in the way infrastructure assets are maintained and managed. A change in the management culture is imperative for understanding that all asset decisions are investment decisions while focusing on continual improvement driven by results (sustainability). Expertise would be employed to help service providers implement successful asset-management programmes. This would include facility audits to provide current data on the actual usage of existing facilities and an asset-management plan with a commitment to:

- spending the time and money to implement the programme
- focusing on making cost-effective asset decisions
- providing a sustainable level of customer service for the community

Development of efficient sewerage infrastructure

Since the 1970s, the private sector has been the prominent developer of sewerage systems. The capital expenditures of sewerage systems were built into the selling price of properties. Policy reviews and strategies towards realizing efficient sewerage infrastructures at affordable costs and meeting development goals are being continuously undertaken by the federal government. Starting from 1980, all developments with population equivalent of 150 (30 houses) or more are required to construct a sewage-treatment plant and sewer system to cater to the development areas (Indah Water Konsortium, 2007). As a result, premises connected to the public sewer increased from 743,375 in 1997 (based on IWK's database) to 3,165,616 in 2012 (MWA, 2013). To date, Peninsular Malaysia has 16,721 km of sewer networks, 6050 public treatment plants, 4380 communal septic tanks, 1,298,207 individual septic tanks and 894,859 pour-flush facilities (MWA, 2013). The percentage-of-population equivalent by sewerage systems is 59.3% public treatment plants, 7.3% private treatment plants and 31.9% septic tank or pour flush facilities (MWA, 2013). The main challenge for the sewerage services in Malaysia is to have a tariff mechanism that better reflects the cost of providing the service. Currently, the federal government has to provide subsidies to IWK because its revenue is not sufficient to cover operating expenditure.

Integration of water and sewerage services

Sewerage cannot be operated as a business on its own but must be bundled as part of the value chain of providing holistic water services. This is evidenced by the operating deficit suffered by IWK, the holder of the concession for privatized sewerage services, which is now wholly owned by the federal government mainly due to the inability to raise sewerage tariffs and fully collect the bills issued. There is great resistance from consumers to paying for sewerage service, yet services cannot be disconnected as in the case of water for delinquent consumers. IWK has embarked on extensive public education on the need for its services, achieving some degree of success but not enough to turn the company around. The integration of water and sewerage is imperative because the demand for sewerage services is highly correlated with the demand for water services. The management of both services needs to be done in a holistic manner across the entire value chain. This is recognized by the federal government, and the integration of water and sewerage services as well as initial efforts towards an integrated water and sewerage tariff have been included in the water services industry roadmap under the 10th Malaysian Plan (2011–2015) (EPU, 2010).

Conclusion

The progress and achievements to date have been impressive; they should galvanize all stakeholders to continue with the efforts, because there is still an unfinished agenda to complete. Over the last five years or so, SPAN has developed a regulatory framework that includes the strategic direction which describes the approaches being adopted and the tasks to implement the regulatory functions. Based on SPAN's short experience, there are many challenges to address, though new opportunities have also been created in the transformation process. A successful reform will also encompass a range of dynamic approaches through the transformation of legal, organizational, institutional and financial frameworks, which will redefine new ways of providing these basic services as well as creating new opportunities that will enhance the efficiency and quality of the water service industry.

Note

1. EPI for Malaysia (epi.yale.edu) is a joint research between the Yale Center for Environmental Law & Policy (Yale University), the Center for International Earth Science Information Network (Columbia University), and Universiti Teknologi Malaysia.

References

EPU (Economic Planning Unit, Prime Minister Department). (2010). Tenth Malaysia plan (2011-2015). Retrieved December 10, 2013 from http://www.epu.gov.my/epu-theme/RMKE10/rmke10_english.htm

Government of Malaysia. (2006). National Water Services Industry Act (SPAN Act) 2006. Retrieved from http://www.span.gov.my

Government of Malaysia. (2006). Water Services Industry Act (WSIA) 2006. Retrieved from http://www.span.gov.my

Government of Malaysia. (2010). Water services industry (rates for water supply services) regulations 2010. Retrieved from http://www.federalgazette.agc.gov.my. i. Kedah [P.U. (A) 332.], ii. Kelantan [P.U. (A) 333.], iii. Penang [P.U. (A) 334.], iv. Johor [P.U. (A) 371.] and v. Melaka [P.U. (A) 372.].

Indah Water Konsortium Corporate Sustainability Report 2007. Retrieved from http://www.iwk.com.my/pdf/Sustainability%20Report.pdf

Malaysian Water Association (MWA). (2009). Malaysia Water Industry Guide (MWIG). Kuala Lumpur.

Malaysian Water Association (MWA). (2013). Malaysia Water Industry Guide (MWIG). Kuala Lumpur.

Yale Centre of Law and Policy. (2012). Global environmental performance index. Retrieved from http://epi.yale.edu./epi2012

Water infrastructure in China: the importance of full project life-cycle cost analysis in addressing water challenges

Shuping Lu

Xylem, Shanghai, P.R. China

To address serious wastewater challenges, the government of China is investing in the rapid building of new treatment plants across the country. However, current practice often favours both cost- and energy-inefficient designs and implementation, especially in smaller cities and towns. Combining a full life cycle costing (LCC) approach with financing innovations and the identification and implementation of new technologies can reduce such inefficiencies by 50% or more. One general and two wastewater-specific case studies of new approaches to efficient infrastructure design are discussed.

Background

Across the globe, a growing number of people are facing increasingly severe water challenges as sources of water in many regions become increasingly depleted or polluted, or inaccessible due to inadequate infrastructure. The Organisation for Economic Co-operation and Development (OECD) estimates that the number of people living in areas of high water stress will rise to 3.9 billion by 2030 if current trends continue. At the same time, energy production consumes significant amounts of water, while pumping, moving and treating water consumes a large share of the world's energy (OECD, 2009; World Policy Institute, 2011).

As the world's largest and most rapidly developing nation, the People's Republic of China is at the front lines of both the global water and energy crises. Over the past 30 years, China has experienced unprecedented economic growth, with a sustained double-digit rate of GDP increase for decades (Kahrl & Roland-Holst, 2008). In 2010, China overtook Japan as the second-largest economy in the world, after the United States (Liping, 2013).

While China's growth has yielded marked improvements in standard of living for its population, the associated increases in pollution and consumption of resources raise serious questions about the long-term sustainability of the current growth trajectory (*China Daily*, 2012a, 2012b). Among the most serious potential resource limitations is that of water (Liu & Diamond, 2008).

The state of China's water today

Today, most regions of China suffer from water scarcity – understood as "the lack of access to adequate quantities of water for human and environmental uses", and encompassing interlinked problems of pollution, resource depletion and inadequate infrastructure to meet demand. (Lall, Heikkila, Brown, & Siegfried, 2008).

China has nearly 20% of the global population but only 7% of the world's freshwater resources. As in many parts of the world, to meet demand the nation increasingly relies on groundwater pumping to meet crop irrigation needs, resulting in rapidly falling water tables in many places. For example, from 1974 to 2000, water tables in the North China Plain, which holds most of the country's arable land, have been falling by as much as 1 m per year (Qiang, Wanfang & Liang, 2011; Zhang, 2011).

Pollution of existing water resources is a major challenge as well. Today, at least 70% of the surface water in the country is unfit for human consumption, while in the most populated parts of the country 90% of groundwater is polluted, 60% seriously so (Ebenstein, 2012; Qiang et al., 2011).

Access presents another ongoing challenge, with some 300 million rural residents still lacking a source of clean water (Liu & Yang, 2012). As in other parts of the world, enormous quantities of water are lost through leaks from aging water infrastructure. According to China's *Global Times*, total tap-water losses from leaks may be as great as $6\,km^3$ per year (Beibei, 2011).

Finally, while on a percentage basis China's non-agricultural water demand currently represents a small percentage of total energy consumption, this share is set to increase with the planned expansion of water-treatment facilities and the building of more hydraulic infrastructure. (Kahrl & Roland-Holst, 2008).

In spite of these challenges, however, the per capita water footprint of the average Chinese citizen is $1071\,m^3/y$, compared to the US average of 2842 m3/y (UNESCO-IHE, 2011). This suggests that without conservation, if living standards in China were to reach developed-world levels, consumption of water would put much greater pressure on resources that are already severely stressed throughout the country.

China's water future

To address these enormous challenges, in the last two years, the government of China has unveiled a series of new regulations and standards aimed at improving water treatment, conservation and infrastructure. In January 2011, the government signalled that it would be putting water at the top of its agenda by dedicating its "No. 1 Document" (a policy paper that traditionally lays out the highest official priorities) to water issues and announcing that it would invest RMB 4 trillion over 10 years to combat water pollution and increase water access (China to invest 4 trillion in water resources, 2011). In January 2012, the government released a document asking the entire country to limit water exploration, cut water pollution and improve water-use efficiency; in July, it increased the number of drinking-water quality indicators from 35 to 106, almost on a par with the European Union (*China Daily*, 2012a, 2012b).

In addition, China is now in the beginning stages of implementing its 12th Five-Year Plan (2011–2015), in which it laid out ambitious goals to cut water consumption per unit of value-added industrial output by 30%, to increase the water-efficiency coefficient of agricultural irrigation to 0.53 and to significantly reduce major water pollutants, including cutting chemical oxygen demand by 8% and ammonia nitrogen pollution by 10% (Jones Lang LaSalle, 2012).

Current status and trends of China's waste water treatment

China currently operates 3243 wastewater-treatment plants, for a capacity of 139 million tons per day. The country is also building another 1300 plants, adding 26 million tons per day (Ministry of Housing and Urban-rural Development, 2012). However, urban wastewater-treatment utilization remains relatively low. While 640 out of 647 cities and 73.3% of counties have wastewater-treatment facilities, some 377 wastewater-treatment plants built over one year have not met national requirements, and the average operating rate is less than 60%. (Ministry of Housing and Urban-rural Development, 2012). Wastewater discharge standards are low: only 12% of wastewater-treatment plants reach Grade 1A standards. (Ministry of Housing and Urban-rural Development, 2012).

While China is rapidly adding wastewater-treatment capacity by building a significant number of treatment plants, this growth has often come at the expense of operational efficiency; but an increasing number of public–private partnerships could alter this pattern. Most public–private partnerships are conducted as variations of build-operate-transfer (BOT), in which a private company receives a concession to build a utility and recover its costs by charging to operate the plant. For BOT models, project owners are responsible for the construction and operation of projects for 15–20 years. Overall, BOT contracts have higher operating efficiencies and display better long-term performance than alternative investment models. Energy consumption is the area with the greatest potential for significant operational savings, as plants financed through BOT contracts typically use up to 50% less electricity than plants financed by other methods (China Greentech Initiative, 2011).

Going forward: wastewater treatment for the 12th Five-Year-Plan and beyond

Observers predict that rapid, ongoing urbanization in China will generate at least RMB 1 trillion in annual investment opportunities in public utilities, including heating, water supply and waste treatment. Furthermore, according to Global Water Intelligence, China plans to invest RMB 380 billion in urban wastewater infrastructure, maximizing "the potential of under-utilized assets" (2012; see also Jing, 2009).

In its five-year plan for sewage treatment, the nation aims to improve its treatment of wastewater to 85% in urban areas, 70% in smaller cities and counties and 30% in towns by 2015. Over that period, China plans to invest at least RMB430 billion in sewage treatment and will be encouraging more private investment in the sector. By the end of 2015, the plan calls for more than 15% of treated sewage to be reused (Chow, Lee, & Lu, 2012).

Issues and barriers to sustainable water management

In spite of this stated commitment to invest in and enforce more sustainable water management, China's wastewater initiative faces a number of issues and barriers.

First, in spite of the predominance of state-owned treatment plants, experts believe that with respect to water infrastructure, government investment alone is inadequate. The government plans to meet this challenge through marketization reforms that are expected to address water shortages, insufficient infrastructure, water pollution and other problems (Zhong, Mol, & Fu, 2008).

In addition, the construction of urban wastewater-treatment plants has been skewed geographically and in favour of larger cities. As of 2011, according to an Asian Development Bank (2011) report, 106 cities, mostly in the north-west and central-western provinces, still were not operating wastewater-treatment plants, and wastewater treatment was "essentially non-existent" in 65% of county towns.

Part of the reason for this is that whereas larger cities and towns have access to a variety of funding options, including public–private partnerships and BOT contracts, in smaller municipal areas, such arrangements have been much less common. Private investors may be discouraged from investing in these smaller projects for a number of reasons, ranging from governance constraints to financial and technical issues, to concerns about the sharing of investment and operation responsibilities with local government. As a result, small cities and towns have access to a smaller range of financial resources. The Asian Development Bank reported that results of a survey in a sample of small cities showed that O&M contracts with limited capital investment were more easily implemented than BOT contracts, but the report emphasized that there is no "one size fits all" financing model (2011). In addition, the government has sent mixed signals regarding private-sector participation. (China Greentech Initiative, 2011).

Because infrastructure and equipment are largely financed by pubic funds, the fact that revenues collected from users do not recover the cost of services is an issue as well. The Asian Development Bank (2011) listed several potential reasons for the lack of full cost recovery, including environmental and public health externalities, and the fact that people are not accustomed to paying for the full cost of services (or politicians perceive them not to be) and therefore raising rates to do so is considered politically sensitive and socially unacceptable.

Technological challenges are tightly intertwined with these financial issues. In a sector that struggles with inefficient operation, "state operated plants are often reluctant to adopt technologies with higher initial investment requirements", even when those technologies could yield significant long-term cost and environmental savings. (China Greentech Initiative, 2011).

Treatment of sludge lags far behind that of wastewater, with fewer than 25% of wastewater-treatment plants having stable sludge-treatment facilities. Nearly 76% of sludge currently ends up in landfills, and 14% is improperly discharged into the environment, causing secondary pollution. (China Greentech Initiative, 2011).

The critical importance of life-cycle cost accounting for public utility construction in wastewater treatment

A growing number of experts across disciplines today emphasize the critical importance of life-cycle costing (also known as whole-life costing) when procuring infrastructure, particularly when such infrastructure is associated with significant ongoing operational costs.

Life-cycle cost is defined as "the total cost of ownership of machinery and equipment, including its cost of acquisition, operation, maintenance, conversion, and/or decommission". Life-cycle costing is a way of estimating the total costs of a project from inception to disposal with a goal of choosing the most cost-effective approach among a number of alternatives (Barringer, 2003).

In addition to allowing for a more accurate lifetime cost assessment, life cycle costing is often regarded as a necessary (though not necessarily sufficient) component of environmental decision making, as it takes into account factors such as energy costs, demolition and recycling that are typically outside the boundary of traditional accounting systems. Examples of data inputs typically used to perform a life cycle cost analysis include building costs, administration, type of building, site costs, energy, nature of design, design fees, location, demolition costs, maintenance and energy consumption (Gluch & Baumann, 2004); see Table 1.

In spite of the significant amount of research and study on of life cycle costing, it is not commonly applied, even in developed European countries. Instead, procurement costs

Table 1. Examples of input data needed to perform life-cycle costing for a building.

Investment cost data	Operation and maintenance data	Project-specific data
• Building costs • Site costs • Design fees • Salvage value • Demolition costs • Other	• Administration • Energy • Water • Wastewater • Material • Cleaning • Maintenance • Insurance • Rates • Taxes • Other	• Type of building • Type of design • Type of building material • Location • Lifetime periods • Other specific data

Source: Gluch and Baumann (2004).

based on a simple payback period are often used as the primary or only criteria for equipment and system selection. Without life-cycle analysis, however, it can be difficult to demonstrate that the operational savings of a particular investment are sufficient to justify the investment costs (Davis Langton Management Consulting, 2007).

There are many potential reasons for this gap. According to the Whole Life Cost Forum, life-cycle costing (or whole-life costing) requires a different perspective and approach to cash, assets and cash flow, with capital and revenue costs understood as coming from the same "pot". Further, there is a common misconception that life-cycle analysis will always appear to give higher capital costs (NPV, DCF & IRR, n.d.).

Like many other utilities, the Chinese government often pursues a lowest-price bidding principle when it comes to infrastructure procurement. However, such an approach may not adequately capture the full economic and environmental life-cycle costs, especially when procuring energy-intensive infrastructure like a wastewater-treatment plant. Without adequate life-cycle cost accounting, seemingly low-cost procurement in the present can lead to greater costs and outright failures later.

Common weaknesses of current practice include: using artificially high design capacity to receive more up-front funding from local government; use of low-cost and unskilled labour to install equipment; the adoption of process technology with lower up-front costs and simpler operation; and a focus on low-cost bid price with little attention to total life-cycle costs. These errors can lead to much higher overall operating costs, lower operational facility, increased repair costs, inflexible response to changes in wastewater quality, frequent breakdown and repair costs, and higher electricity costs for greater treatment times (China Greentech Initiative, 2011); see Table 2.

On the other hand, according to the Alliance to Save Energy, a non-profit group supporting energy efficiency, application of water and energy-efficiency principles to municipal water infrastructure (for both service and treatment) repays itself quickly and yields many other benefits, including immediate improvements in service and more revenue (Barry, 2007).

Pumping systems in general account for an enormous percentage of global energy use: nearly 20% of total electricity consumption around the world. In industrial-plant operations, pumping often consumes a much larger share, anywhere from 25–50% (Hydraulic Institute, Europump, and the US Department of Energy, 2001). Energy costs in the wastewater industry are also rising for various reasons. Implementation of stricter effluent requirements (including enhanced removal of nutrients and other emerging

Table 2. Today's practices affect tomorrow's water-treatment operating costs.

	Current practice	Operating-cost impact
• Design	• Using artificially high design capacity to receive more up-front funding from the local government	• Inaccurate design capacity may result in a low treatment rate and lower operational facility
• Construction	• Using low-cost and unskilled labour for plant construction and equipment installation	• Inexperienced labour may lead to increased repair costs and lower operational facility
• Process technology	• Adopting process technology with lower up-front costs and simple operation	• Process technologies selected may not be flexible for changes in quality of water treated
• Equipment	• Focus on low-cost bid price, with minimal attention to total lifecycle coats	• Acquisition of unsuitable equipment may lead to frequent repair due to breakdown; may also lead to higher electricity costs due to longer treatment time required

Source: Zheng, Xingcan et al., Municipal Wastewater Treatment – Technology Selection and Case Study (Beijing, China: China Construction Press, 2007)

contaminants) sometimes requires more energy-intensive technologies. At the same time, aging wastewater-collection systems result in additional inflow and infiltration, which can lead to higher pumping and treatment costs. Finally, increases in electricity rates have an impact (EPA, 2010).

Given projected increases in electricity demand and corresponding prices, taking electrical consumption into account is of particular importance for energy-intensive sectors. According to an article in Xinhua (China electricity consumption to almost double by 2020, 2010), the China Electricity Council is projecting that China's electricity consumption will almost double over the next decade, with a year-on-year price hike of 3%. Quoting the council's vice president, Wei Zhaofeng, the article suggested that these estimates were based on analysis of discussions of electricity price reform, rapidly rising thermal coal prices and electricity companies' average 8% return on net assets.

According to the 12th Five-Year Plan's industry report on energy saving and emissions reduction, the Chinese economy is especially vulnerable to energy price hikes because its energy consumption per unit of GDP is more than twice the world average (19.3% of the world's energy consumption but only 8.6% of its GDP). Reasons cited for continued lags in efficiency included imperfect energy-saving standards and delayed measurement of energy consumption and pollutant emissions. The report called for strengthened monitoring and surveillance capabilities as well. All of these initiatives suggest an increasing role for life-cycle costing in procurement, especially when focusing on energy costs (State Council on the Issuance of Energy Conservation 'Twelve five year plan' notice, 2012).

As mentioned previously, the average operating rate of wastewater-treatment plants is less than 60%. Only 12% of wastewater-treatment plants meet Grade 1A standards. Given the stated goals of the 12th Five-Year Plan to raise discharge standards and reduce environmental impacts, a full assessment of the reliability, safety and effectiveness of wastewater-treatment-plant technology is critical (Ministry of Housing and Urban-rural Development, 2012).

In spite of these challenges, Chinese government and industry have expressed strong support for sustainability initiatives in various sectors, suggesting significant opportunities to lessen environmental impacts, improve efficiency and lower life-cycle costs both generally and in the wastewater-treatment sector specifically.

Following are three case studies highlighting these potential opportunities. The first outlines the effort to make the new Shanghai Hongqiao airport as energy-efficient as possible, thus demonstrating the potential of a high-profile project broadly focused on sustainability.

The other two case studies highlight new wastewater applications from the Xylem corporation that provide examples of how new technology can yield large improvements in efficiency and potentially have a dramatic impact on total life-cycle costs.

Case studies

Shanghai Hongqiao airport

Until the completion of Pudong International Airport in 1999, Hongqiao was Shanghai's primary airport, serving both domestic and international flights. After the completion of Pudong, officials undertook a major renovation and expansion of Hongqiao, which was in turn completed in 2010. It included a new runway and a new Terminal 2, four times the size of Terminal 1.

As part of the renovation, the engineers redesigned numerous systems to operate more efficiently and to save energy. In doing so, the airport provides a high-profile example of how accounting for full life-cycle costs can both save money and conserve resources over the long term.

The airport is adjacent to Shanghai Hongqiao Railway Station. The station itself recently became an example of integrated renewable energy with the opening of the world's largest stand-alone integrated photovoltaic project. The project began transmitting electricity to the Shanghai grid in 2010. The 6.68 MW project is estimated to produce 6.3 million kWh of electricity per year, enough to power 12,000 Shanghai homes, and will reduce coal consumption and carbon emissions by 2245 and 6600 tons, respectively. It has 20,000 solar panels, covering a roof area of 61,000 m^2 (Huge solar station starts operation in Shanghai, 2010).

The redesign of the airport itself integrated a number of efficiency measures, including advanced lighting and water management systems. As a result of these innovations, in 2012, the airport won the KNX Award for Energy Efficiency in Frankfurt, Germany. KNX is an open international intelligent building control standard for commercial and residential buildings. The standard enables the integration and programming of products from diverse manufacturers using a single software tool, resulting in lower operating costs and significant energy savings, according to the KNX trade association. Using the tool, lighting and heating are switched on only when needed.

The award was given to the Shanghai Longchuang Control Automation System Company for its demand-oriented, highly efficient lighting-control system for the airport's 6000 lighting circuits. According to the association, the design focused on ensuring optimal lighting conditions throughout the day, "which the KNX building control components do by controlling the lights according to the amount of available daylight, flight schedules, and other key lighting-relevant criteria" (KNX Association cvba, 2012).

The Flygt Experior energy-efficient pump

Industrial pumps are used for a wide variety of applications in diverse sectors, including agriculture, municipal water and wastewater services, industrial food processing, and the chemical, petrochemical, pharmaceutical and mechanical industries. Given the huge amount of energy these pumps consume (as much as 20% of global electricity consumption), it follows that identifying and applying the most energy-efficient pumping technology for a given application is a key step toward a more operationally and energy-efficient, sustainable industrial model (Hydraulic Institute, Europump, and the US Department of Energy, 2001). In addition, the large energy consumption of industrial pumps provides an important example of how applying full life-cycle cost analysis is necessary to provide an accurate picture of the cost-effectiveness and operational efficiency of a given infrastructure project.

Fortunately, the latest industrial pump technology can dramatically reduce operating costs and energy consumption while increasing service life and improving profitability (Pauly, 2011). Furthermore, within municipal water and wastewater-treatment applications, "the pumping system is all important, since every liter of water that passes through the system represents a significant energy cost", according to the Alliance to Save Energy.

In 2011, the ITT Corporation (itt.com), one of the largest manufacturers of engineered industrial components, announced the release of a new wastewater-pumping system, the Flygt Experior. In the same year, the corporation split into three companies, assigning its water and wastewater business (including the Flygt line) to the newly created Xylem corporation (xyleminc.com). According to the company, the Flygt Experior can achieve up to 50% energy savings over other pumps. This efficiency is achieved through a synergy of several components of the pumps (Flygt, 2011).

First, the pump motor itself is optimized for wastewater pumping, with lower motor temperatures. Secondly, self-cleaning technology uses an impeller that moves axially to eliminate clogging and allow large detritus to get through, while the hydraulic system pushes detritus from the centre to the perimeter of the inlet. This new impeller design significantly improves on the anti-clog function of the earlier Flygt N pump series.

Finally, advanced controls offer the potential for greatly improved efficiency. It is well known that variable-speed operation can save significant amounts of energy. In fact, if the speed of a pump is halved, the flow rate will be halved, but the power requirement will be reduced to one-eighth. Thus, designing pumps that can operate dynamically at different speeds with changing pressures can save a great deal of energy (Olsson, 2011).

The pump's SmartRun pre-programmed control has been designed to capitalize on the benefits of variable-speed drives while reducing the need for maintenance by preprogramming important parameters to both optimize pumping for the specific plant and make the control system more user-friendly (Flygt, 2011).

The Flygt Experior therefore illustrates how new technology is continuing to emerge that can help wastewater-treatment plants cut energy use, operating costs and (by extension) plant life-cycle costs dramatically.

Case study: conserving wastewater energy consumption through new approaches to aeration

In conventional wastewater-treatment processes, the aeration process is used to push air into a liquid, creating an aerobic environment to help beneficial microbes break down organic matter. Aeration both mixes the wastewater, so that the microorganisms come into contact with dissolved and suspended organic matter, and supplies the oxygen required by those metabolizing microbes. The aeration system consumes anywhere from 25% to 60% of the net power demand for a sludge wastewater-treatment plant, making it a significant component of operational costs and an important variable in full life-cycle cost analysis for wastewater-treatment plants (EPA, 2010).

In August 2012, the Xylem corporation released the results of a study from a wastewater-treatment plant in Sweden showing that by using more efficient equipment and improved systems, the plant could reduce its energy consumption by 65%. Results of the study suggest that the cost of the new systems would have a four-year payback, and that the new system would decrease the plant's total energy consumption by 13%.

According to the study, biological secondary treatment is the most energy-intensive step in a plant's wastewater-treatment process. In spite of this, most wastewater-treatment plants still use outmoded aeration systems such as proportional-integral-derivative controllers, a feedback mechanism widely used in industrial control systems for most of the last century, even as the literature presents more and more advanced approaches.

The new Aeration Control System (ACS) is a software system designed for advanced monitoring and control of the aeration process within secondary treatment. The object of the process is to maximize overall energy efficiency while maintaining the desired levels of dissolved oxygen (DO) in aerated basins to preserve good treatment. The DO cascade control consists of an inner and an outer loop that control airflow and DO concentration, respectively.

The ACS also makes use of most-open-valve logic (MOVL) to decrease system pressure losses by keeping valves as open as possible (up to 95%). Based on valve status, the MOVL calculates pressure set points for blower control, allowing the system to run blowers at lower air pressure, thereby saving energy.

The treatment plant used to test the new system was built in 1997 and designed for 26,000 population equivalents. The typical conventional pre-dentrification activated-sludge plant contains two treatment lines, each with anaerobic, anoxic and aerobic basins.

To evaluate the potential for energy savings, researchers designated the first line as a test line which would use the ACS system, along with new Sanitaire Silver Series low-pressure fine bubble diffusers and a new screw-type blower. The second line was used as a reference line, using the current system with a simple DO control, old fine bubble tube diffusers and old lobe blowers.

The new equipment was implemented over three evaluation periods, from April to November of 2011, with adjustments, fine tuning and new components added after the first two periods.

During the first period, operation of the test line saved 34% of the energy used by the reference line, which researchers primarily attributed to the installation of a new blower. During the second period, energy savings rose from 34% to 57%. The additional savings were attributed to the higher oxygen transfer efficiency of new diffusers, which reduced needed airflow by 20%.

For the third period, researchers fine-tuned the DO cascade control, added a new DO profile and activated the MOVL system, which allowed the blower to work at lower air pressure and decreased pressure losses over the valves. Taken together, the changes yielded total energy savings of 65%. The test line achieved its highest weekly energy savings during the second evaluation period, during two peak-load weeks.

As the main goal of the project was to decrease energy consumption without affecting treatment efficiency, it was necessary to compare water quality as well. The study found that BOD_7 removal efficiency was almost exactly the same (96% versus 97%) for both treatment lines, while the NH_4 reduction was good in both lines (99%) for Periods 2 and 3. During the first period, with only two weeks of data, NH_4 reduction was lower in the test line (71%) than in the reference line (88%).

Overall, by changing the aeration system, the plant's total energy consumption was reduced by 13%. If these savings were applied to the whole plant, it would save approximately €21,000 per year, leading to a payback period of 4 years. Analyzing payback times for different components showed that the cost of adding new diffusers alone would pay for itself in only 1.5 years. Finally, by upgrading both lines, total payback would be reduced to 3 years, as some components, such as the control system, could be used for both treatment lines. Annual savings would be €46,000 (Lazie, Larsson, & Nordenborg, 2012).

Conclusion

Globally, water stress, whether from absolute scarcity, degradation of water quality or lack of access, is a growing problem, with experts estimating that the number of people living under water stress will rise to 3.9 billion by 2030.

The connections between water use, depletion, pollution and energy have also drawn increasing attention in recent years. The production of energy, especially conventional energy, usually requires a significant amount of fresh water. At the same time, pumping and transporting water for municipal, agricultural and other uses consumes significant amounts of energy, as does moving and treating wastewater.

The People's Republic of China stands at the forefront of these issues, facing serious water challenges, including groundwater depletion and wide-spread water pollution, as well as continuing shortages of infrastructure, both to provide safe water access and to adequately treat wastewater. Continued rapid economic development is expected to stress water resources and treatment capacity even further, even as it consumes a greater share of the nation's energy, especially in the urban setting.

These challenges are particularly apparent in the area of wastewater treatment. In order to curb increasing pollution challenges associated with rapid industrialization and urbanization, China has set out ambitious goals for treating wastewater across the country, as expressed in its most recent five-year plan and other policy initiatives. However, providing this treatment efficiently at the necessary scale and the desired quality levels will require substantial innovation in financing, operating procedures and technology.

Currently, there are significant inefficiencies in the standard practice of wastewater treatment, in terms of both energy and operational costs, especially in smaller cities, towns and rural areas. In general, these inefficiencies are most pronounced at state-operated plants; privately operated facilities contracted as build-operate-transfer or related public–private arrangements are on average 50% more efficient. However, public–private partnerships account for fewer treatment plants than public-owned facilities, especially in smaller cities and towns. Potential reasons for the small share of public–private partnerships in some areas include a lack of financing options for smaller projects, technical issues and governance constraints.

Given China's ambitious wastewater-treatment goals and the imperative to conserve energy for both operational cost and environmental reasons, it is important to explore new financing and technological approaches. Appropriate life-cycle costing in the procurement stage is one potentially critical tool for evaluating a variety of different options. Life-cycle costing is an accounting approach that considers a much wider range of parameters than traditional accounting, including the total cost of ownership and equipment, from acquisition, through operation and maintenance, to decommission. However, in spite of the large amount of research and study of the impact of the methodology of life-cycle costing, it is not commonly applied, even in developed European countries. Instead, procurement costs based on a simple payback period are often used as the primary or only criteria for equipment or system selection.

By using a systems approach and applying appropriate new technologies, total life-cycle costs, including for operations and energy, can be greatly reduced in wastewater treatment as well as other public utilities. To support this conclusion, three illustrative case studies were presented.

First, the recent renovation of the Shanghai Hongqiao airport provides a high-profile case study of a large installation that has been designed using a number of efficiency measures, including an intelligent software tool to provide a demand-oriented, highly efficient lighting system for the airport's 6000 lighting circuits, and saving an estimated RMB 1.2 million in energy consumption per year.

Regarding the potential for wastewater-treatment-specific energy savings, two innovations were described. First, the Flygt Experior pump provides an example of a new generation of pumping technology that significantly reduces energy consumption in pumping by combining highly efficient motors, intelligent controls and advanced self-cleaning technology. The combination of these innovations can save up to 50% in typical pump energy consumption, according to the company.

Finally, a new aeration system for wastewater treatment was described. Tested at a wastewater-treatment plant in Sweden, the new approach showed that a plant could reduce its aeration energy consumption by 65% by combining upgrades in fine bubble diffusers, a new screw-type blower and an advanced control system. If applied to the whole plant, the upgrade would yield a 3-year payback period.

The successful rapid deployment of new wastewater-treatment facilities in China to address endemic wastewater and pollution issues will require broad cooperation between different levels of government and the private sector, especially if energy and operations costs and their environmental externalities are to be contained. Selecting the most appropriate and efficient suite of technologies for a given location will require sophisticated systems engineering and cost accounting. In particular, life-cycle costing is a necessary analytical step in identifying the most efficient approach. Combining such an approach with financial innovations, partnerships and openness to new technological innovations in a rapidly evolving industry is the most effective way to lower costs, improve treatment and reduce environmental damage.

References

Asian Development Bank. (2011). *People's Republic of China: Urban wastewater and solid waste management for small cities and towns*. Philippines: Author.

Barringer, P. (2003, May 20–23). *A life cycle cost summary*. Paper presented at the International Conference of Maintenance Societies (ICOMS®-2003), Perth, Australia.

Barry, J. A. (2007) *WATERGY: Energy and water efficiency in municipal water supply and wastewater treatment*. Washington, DC: Alliance to Save Energy.

Beibei, Ji. (2011, May 30). Vast amounts of resources are being lost to leaky pipes. *Global Times*. Retrieved from http://www.globaltimes.cn/china/society/2011-05/660331.html

China Daily. (2012a, April 10). Majorities in China feel living standard improving. *China Daily*. Retrieved from http://www.chinadaily.com.cn/business/2012-04/10/content_15011072.htm

China Daily. (2012b, April 10). China to boost sewage treatment industry. *China Daily*. Retrieved from http://www.chinadaily.com.cn/business/2012-04/10/content_15011072.htm

China electricity consumption to almost double by 2020: China Electricity Council. (2010, December 21). *Xinhua*. Retrieved from http://www.globaltimes.cn/business/industries/2011-01/618577.html

China Greentech Initiative. (2011, April). *The China Greentech report 2011: China's emergence as a global Greentech leader* (19, 25, 173–179). China: Author. Retrieved from http://www.china-greentech.com/

China to invest 4 trillion in water resources in next 10 years. (2011, January 30). *Global Times*. Retrieved from http://www.globaltimes.cn/business/industries/2011-01/618577.html

Chow, V., Lee, S.H.Y., & Lu, I. (2012, May 7). *China solid waste and water: 12th FYP supports our OW on CEI and bullish view on WTE*. China Solid Waste and Water, New York, NY: Morgan Stanley Research.

Davis Langton Management Consulting. (2007, May). *Life cycle costing (LCC) as a contribution to sustainable construction: A common methodology*. (5) London: Author.

Ebenstein, A. (2012, February). The consequences of industrialization: Evidence from water pollution and digestive cancers in China. *Review of Economics and Statistics*. *94* (1): 186–201 doi: 10.1162/REST_a_00150

EPA. (2010, September). *Evaluation of energy conservation measures for wastewater treatment facilities*. Washington, DC: Author.

Flygt, a Xylem Brand. (2011). *Flygt experior. Inspired by you. Engineered by us* [Brochure]. White Plains, NY: Author.

Global Water Intelligence. (January 2012). *Chinese Change*. Vol 13, Issue 1 (January 2012). Oxford. Retrieved from http://www.globalwaterintel.com/archive/13/1/need-to-know/chinese-change.html

Gluch, P., & Baumann, H. (2004). The life cycle costing (LCC) approach: A conceptual discussion of its usefulness for environmental decision-making. *Building and Environment*, *39*, 571–580. doi:10.1016/j.buildenv.2003.10.008

Huge solar station starts operation in Shanghai. (2010, July 19). *Xinhua*. Retrieved from http://news.xinhuanet.com/english2010/china/2010-07/19/c_13403958.htm

Hydraulic Institute, Europump, & the US Department of Energy. (2001). *Pump life cycle costs: A guide to LCC analysis for pumping systems*. Washington, DC: Author. Retrieved from http://www1.eere.energy.gov/manufacturing/tech_deployment/pdfs/pumplcc_1001.pdf

Jing, F. (2009, August 27). China's cities to receive massive influx. *China Daily*. Retrieved from http://www.chinadaily.com.cn/china/2009-08/27/content_8621552.htm

Jones Lang LaSalle. (2012, February). *Global sustainability perspective: Urbanization and sustainability: Focus on Asia*. 3 Chicago, IL: Author.

Kahrl, F., & Roland-Holst, D. (2008). China's water – energy nexus. *Water Policy*, *10* (S1): 51–65. doi:10.2166/wp.2008.052.

KNX Association cvba. (2012). Glittering KNX Awards Ceremony 2012 attended by winners, nominees and more than 1500 guests from 76 countries [press release]. Retrieved from http://www.knx.org/news-press/press-room/

Lall, U., Heikkila, T., Brown, C., & Siegfried, T. (2008). Water it the 21st Century: Defining the elements of global crises and potential solutions. *Journal of International Affairs*, *61*(2), 1–17.

Lazie, A., Larsson, V., & Nordenborg, A. (2012). *Energy savings potential of a new aeration system: Full scale trials* Xylem (2012). New York, NY: White Plains.

Liping, H. E. (2013). China as the world's second largest economy: Qualifications and implications. In Peng Er Lam (Ed.), *China and East Asia: After the Wall Street crisis*, 33 New Jersey, London: World Scientific.

Liu, J., & Diamond, J. (2008). Revolutionizing China's environmental protection. *Science*, *319*, 37–38. doi: 10.1126/science.1150416

Liu, J., & Yang, W. (2012). Water sustainability for China and beyond. *Science*, *337*: 649–650. doi: 10.1126/science.1219471

Ministry of Housing and Urban-rural Development, 2012. (2012). Document #112 [2012] of urban construction department of the ministry. Retrieved from http://www.mohurd.gov.cn/zcfg/jsbwj_0/jsbwjcsjs/201209/t20120907_211338.html

NPV, DCF, IRR. (n.d.) Retrieved November 12, 2013 from http://www.wlcf.org.uk/page25.html

OECD. (2009). Managing water for all: An OECD perspective on pricing and financing. Retrieved from http://www.oecd.org/env/42350563.pdf

Olsson, G. (2011). Water and energy nexus. *Encyclopedia of sustainability science and technology*. Germany: Springer Verlag.

Pauly, C. (2011). Driving down operating costs. *World Pumps*, *2011*, 35–37.

Qiang, W., Wanfang, Z., & Liang, Z. (2011). China's environment: Challenges and solutions. *Environ Earth Sci*, *64*, 1503–1504. doi: 10.1007/s12665-011-1380-6

State Council on the Issuance of Energy Conservation "Twelve five year plan" notice (August, 2012). Retrieved November 12, 2013 from http://www.gov.cn/zwgk/2012-08/21/content_2207867.htm

UNESCO-IHE. (2011). National water footprint accounts: The green, blue and grey water footprint of production and consumption. (5). Value of Water Research Report Series No. 50. Retrieved from http://www.unesco-ihe.org/Value-of-Water-Research-Report-Series/Research-Papers

World Policy Institute. (2011, March 18). The water-energy nexus: Adding water to the energy agenda. (3). Retrieved from http://www.worldpolicy.org/policy-paper/2011/03/18/water-energy-nexus

Zhang, J. (2011). China's success in increasing per capita food production. *Journal of Experimental Botany*, 1–5. doi:10.1093/jxb/err132.

Zhong, L., Mol, A., & Fu, T. (2008). Public-private partnerships in China's urban water sector. *Environmental Management, 41* (6), 863–877. doi: 10.1007/s00267-008-9070-1

Water infrastructure for the Hindu Kush Himalayas

David James Molden, Ramesh Ananda Vaidya, Arun Bhakta Shrestha, Golam Rasul and Mandira Singh Shrestha

International Centre for Integrated Mountain Development, Kathmandu, Nepal

The Hindu Kush–Himalayan region is the source of 10 major rivers serving over 1.3 billion people. In spite of this abundance, mountain people have limited access to water for food, households and energy. Climate change is increasing the uncertainty about water availability and the frequency of extreme weather events. To buffer seasonal variations and address growing water demand, properly planned, developed and managed infrastructure and related institutional capacities are required. They should also recognize mountain-specific issues. Priority areas include transboundary water governance, cross-border information systems, an improved knowledge base for mountain regions, and benefit sharing between mountain and downstream communities.

Introduction

The Hindu Kush–Himalayan region

The mountainous region of Asia consisting of the Himalayas and associated mountains contains more ice and snow than any other region outside the North and South Poles and is sometimes known as the Third Pole. Within the Third Pole, the Hindu Kush Himalayas (HKH) are the source of 10 major rivers and their numerous tributaries, which provide sustenance, livelihoods and prosperity to more than 1.3 billion people living in the 10 river basins (Figure 1). The Hindu Kush Himalayas, the focal area of this paper, are vital for water, energy, food, and ecological security for much of Asia; yet, more attention is required to understand and better manage the water resources and water infrastructure there.

The Hindu Kush–Himalayan region depends heavily on water resources for food production, domestic water supply and sanitation, health, energy, tourism, industry and the functioning of ecosystems. All countries in the region face difficult challenges to meet the growing demand for water for food, energy and economic activities. Although the region is rich in water, mountain farmers have limited access to water for irrigation. Despite the huge hydropower potential, they also have limited access to energy in one of the world's energy-deficit regions. Shortage of power is crippling many economic activities in the region and affecting the lives and livelihoods of the mountain people. Climate change is further increasing the uncertainty of water availability and water security through changes in temperature, precipitation, monsoon patterns and water regime; an increase in extreme events such as drought and flood; and accelerated melting of the Himalayan glaciers

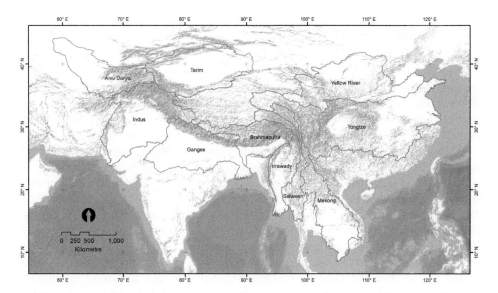

Figure 1.   The Hindu Kush-Himalayan (HKH) region and associated 10 major river basins.

(Eriksson et al., 2009). During the monsoon, huge amounts of water trigger floods and other hazards causing significant economic and environmental damage; yet, insufficient water in the dry season causes problems in irrigation, navigation, and maintaining a minimum environmental flow in the rivers (Ahmad, Biswas, Rangachari, & Sainju, 2001).

To buffer the shocks of seasonal variation of water availability and address the growing demand for water, the Himalayan region needs appropriate infrastructure and institutional capacities to manage it. Water infrastructure refers to both constructed systems (e.g. reservoirs and retention systems; piped collection and distribution systems; and treatment systems) and natural infrastructure (e.g. watersheds; forested land; stream buffers; flood-plains and hydrological networks; and wetlands) (Clements, D'Amato, & Taylor, 2010). Water infrastructure, both physical and natural, provides mechanisms for dealing with climate variability which, if planned and managed properly, can improve water security, agricultural productivity, and adaptive capacity. Water infrastructure can fuel economic growth and make an important contribution to safeguarding livelihoods and reducing rural poverty. Inadequate investment in water infrastructure over decades has undermined the capacity of this region to meet the growing water demand, mitigate the impacts of floods and droughts, and adapt to the impacts of climate change. However, despite a growing interest in water infrastructure, so far little effort has been made to understand the role of infrastructure and critical factors that constrain investment in water infrastructure in the Hindu Kush–Himalayan region. It is also important to recognize that different considerations are required for mountain infrastructure than for infrastructure in plains and coastal areas, in view of fragile environments and socio-economic marginalization.

The objective of this paper is to assess the role of water infrastructure in addressing the challenges of livelihoods, poverty reduction, economic growth and environmental protection in the Hindu Kush–Himalayan region and downstream, and the current status of infrastructure in irrigation, hydropower and flood risk reduction in the region. It examines several key considerations with respect to developing water infrastructure in the region, and provides some recommendations on sustainable infrastructure development.

Water availability and demand

Given the importance of the Hindu Kush Himalayas in generating water, and the increasing demand for this water, it is vital to better understand the present and future availability of water (see Table 1 for features of the Hindu Kush–Himalayan River systems). Spatial and temporal variability of precipitation are high, with more than 80% of the annual amount falling during the monsoon. Heavy south-westerly monsoon rains often cause rivers to overflow their banks, sometimes annually, bringing devastation to the people living in the floodplain areas, while in the remaining months there are acute water shortages.

While the annual runoff generated in the highlands is of great magnitude, the runoff generated per capita is quite low in many countries. With the high seasonality of flow, water scarcity is common in the dry season. For example, Cherrapunji, the location with the world's highest annual rainfall at an average of 11,987 mm (Murata, Hayashi, Matsumoto, & Asada, 2007), is sometimes referred to as a 'wet desert' because of the difficulty in accessing water in the dry season. Many of the river basins in the western Himalayas are physically water scarce (Molden, 2007), with more than 75% of river flows withdrawn for agriculture, industry and domestic purposes and supply barely able to meet demand. Some, like the Ganges, Brahmaputra, Salween and Irrawaddy basins, are considered 'economically water scarce', with less than 25% of flow withdrawn for human purposes but with significant improvements in water infrastructure needed to make the existing resources available for use.

Table 1. Characteristics of the river basins originating in the Hindu Kush–Himalayan region. Source: updated from Eriksson et al. (2009).

	River		River basin			
Name	Annual mean discharge (m³/sec)[a]	Glacier melt in river flow[b] (%)	Total area (km²)	Population density (persons/km²)	Population (thousands)	Water availability (m³ per person per year)
Amu Darya	1376[a]	n/a	534,739[c]	39	20,855	2,081
Brahmaputra	21,261[a]	~12	651,335[d]	182	118,543	5,656
Ganges	12,037[a]	~9	1,016,124[e]	401	407,466	932
Indus	5,533	<50	1,081,718[f]	165	178,483	978
Irrawaddy	8,024	n/a	413,710[g]	79	32,683	7,742
Mekong	9,001[a]	~7	805,604[h]	71	57,198	4,963
Salween	1,494	~9	271,914[i]	22	5,982	7,876
Tarim	1,262	<50	1,152,448[j]	7	8,067	4,933
Yangtze	28,811[a]	~18	1,722,193[k]	214	368,549	2,465
Yellow	1,438[a]	~2	944,970[k]	156	147,415	3,08

[a] The data were collected by the Global Runoff Data Centre from the most downstream stations of the river basins: Chatly (Amu Darya); Bahadurabad (Brahmaputra); Farakka (Ganges); Pakse (Mekong); Datong (Yangtze); and Huayuankou (Yellow).
[b] Estimation of the meltwater contribution is difficult and varies between upstream and downstream situations; approximate values are given here.
[c] Tajikistan, 72.8%, Afghanistan, 14.6%; Uzbekistan, 8.5%; Kyrgyzstan and Turkmenistan together, 5.5%.
[d] China, 50.5%; India, 33.6%; Bangladesh, 8.1%; Bhutan, 7.8%.
[e] India, 79%; Nepal, 14%; China, 7%.
[f] Pakistan, 52%; India, 33%; China, 8%; Afghanistan, 7%.
[g] Myanmar, 91%; China, 5%; India, 4%.
[h] China, 21%; Laos, 25%; Thailand, 23%; Cambodia, 20%; Vietnam, 8%; Myanmar, 3%.
[i] China, 52%; Myanmar, 44%; Thailand, 4%.
[j] China, 97%; Kyrgyzstan, 2%; Tajikistan, 1%; Pakistan and Afghanistan together, <1%.
[k] China, 100%.

Changes due to climate change – in moisture inputs in the form of snow and rainfall, and temporary storage in the form of glaciers, ice, permafrost, snow, groundwater and wetlands – will have a profound effect on the flow regimes of the major rivers and need to be taken into consideration for future infrastructure development. Monsoon rains are the predominant source of moisture, particularly in the eastern and central Himalayas (Figure 2). The river-flow hydrographs generally peak during spring or summer, coinciding with runoff generated by summer monsoon precipitation (Figure 3). Changes in monsoon patterns are of significant concern for infrastructure development, yet not well understood.

The next important source of water for Himalayan rivers is the cryosphere (snow, glaciers and permafrost). For centuries millions of people have benefited from the glacial melt water that feeds the rivers downstream. However, surprisingly little is known about the extent or changes in water storage in the Himalayan cryosphere. An inventory of glaciers in the greater Himalayan region (Bajracharya & Shrestha, 2011) revealed more than 50,000 glaciers, with a total area greater than 60,000 km^2, Representing about 30% of the total glaciated mountain area of the world. This baseline needs close future monitoring.

The recession of Himalayan glaciers is a matter of great concern, particularly after the release of the Fourth Assessment Report by the Intergovernmental Panel on Climate Change (IPCC, 2007), when there was insufficient data to reach reliable conclusions, leading to global scientific controversy. Several recent studies (e.g., Armstrong, 2010; Bolch et al., 2012; Cogley, Kargel, Kaser, & van der Veen, 2010; Immerzeel, Beek, & Bierkens, 2010; Miller & Rees, 2011) indicate that although glacial retreat in the HKH region is occurring, the rates of retreat are less than those originally suggested by the Fourth Assessment Report.

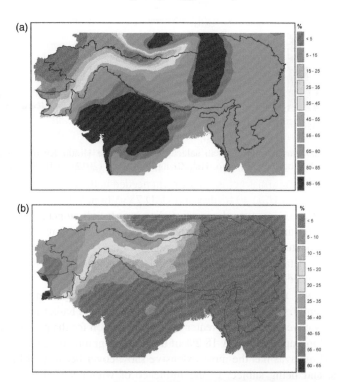

Figure 2.   Fraction of annual precipitation contributed by (a) monsoon and (b) winter precipitation. The outline shows the Hindu Kush–Himalayan region. Source: New, Lister, Hulme & Makin (2000).

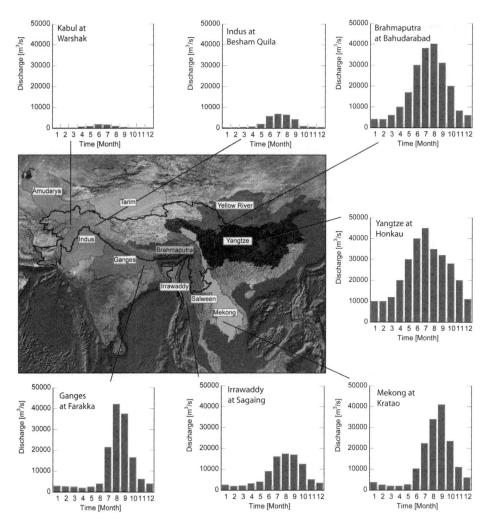

Figure 3. Seasonal variation in flow in selected rivers in the Hindu Kush Himalayan region. Sources: Ali and De Boer (2007), Guo, Hu, Zhang, and Feng (2012), A.B. Shrestha (2008), and Webby et al. (2007).

Miller and Rees (2011) compared recent studies on glaciers, together with the relative confidence levels for the measurement methods. Their summary, shown in Figure 4, shows that of the glaciers studied across the HKH region, more glaciers are retreating than are advancing; yet, the data remain incomplete. Clearly, more objective and transparent analysis of the evidence is needed.

Snow cover was not assessed in the Hindu Kush Himalayas in a comprehensive manner until recently. Gurung, Amarnath, Khun, Shrestha, and Kulkarni (2011) estimated the average snow cover area in the greater Himalayan region for the period 2000–2010 to be 0.76 million km^2, approximately 18.2% of the total geographical area. The western part of the greater Himalayas has the most extensive snow cover because of high elevations, high latitudes, and being subject to the influence of winter westerlies (Bookhagen & Burbank, 2010). The long-term dynamics of snow cover in the HKH region are still not known, with different studies showing different results in both magnitude and direction

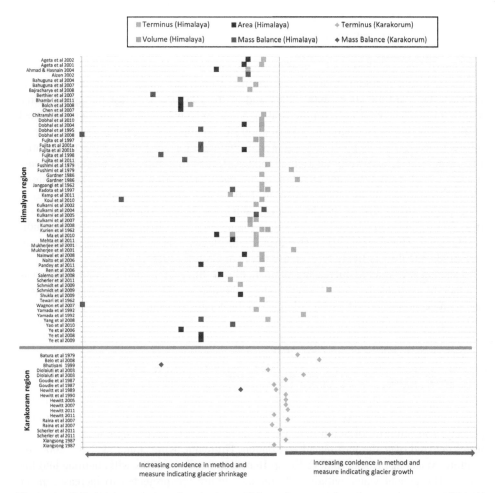

Figure 4. Relative assessment of reviewer confidence in reported study outcomes according to method employed, clarity of reporting and measurement type. Source: Miller et al. (2011).

(e.g. Gurung et al., 2011). It is clear that the historical data are still insufficient to generate statistically significant results. Böhner and Lehmkuhl (2005) used climate-model studies to predict that the snow cover of the Himalayan regions will decrease by 43–81% by 2100 if the annual mean temperature at higher elevations in Asia increases by 1–6°C as predicted by the IPCC. Similarly, the status and change of permafrost and its relative contribution to runoff are poorly understood, but could also be significant.

The impact of changes in glaciers, snow and permafrost on river flows is not yet clear. The effects of changes in glacier melt, as summarized by Miller and Rees (2011), suggest that the glacial melt that occurs in the monsoon-dominated eastern and central parts of the Himalayas does not contribute significantly to annual river discharge downstream. It is estimated that glacial melt accounts for only 10% of the annual river flow, on average, of the Ganges. Estimates vary between 2% and 20% for other basins. However, the percentage contribution of glacial melt to low flows of rivers has not been adequately assessed. Furthermore, glacial melt is an important source of water for both agriculture and vegetation in the upper reaches, especially during dry periods. In the rivers of the eastern region, the large volume of rainwater dwarfs the contribution of meltwater for contribution to total runoff. The groundwater contribution to the annual water budget of Himalayan river basins can be quite substantial, and for the eastern Himalayas it can be more significant than the contribution of glaciers (Andermann et al., 2012). In contrast, glacial melt contributes significantly to water discharge in areas of low rainfall such as the Indus.

Overall, model studies indicate that the mean upstream water supply will decrease between the two time slices 2000–2007 and 2046–2065 by 8.4% for the upper Indus, 17.6% for the Ganges, 19.6% for the Brahmaputra, and 5.6% for the Yangtze (Immerzeel et al., 2010). In rivers where the contribution of snowmelt is negligible, an increase in upstream water yield is predicted (e.g. a 9.5% increase for the Yellow River). Recently, Immerzeel (2011) used fully distributed models, forced by a full range of global climate models, which paid particular attention to the parameterization of future glacial extent. These projections show an increase in both temperature and precipitation and a concomitant steady decline in glacial area, which would lead to a significant increase in river flows. This kind of trend has also been suggested in the Niyang River basin in south-east Qinghai (Zhang et al., 2011). However, as the glacier masses decline and cross certain thresholds, the flow is likely to decrease (Rees & Collins, 2006).

Demand for water is increasing dramatically in the region, and a major concern is whether the available water will be able to meet this demand. Based on various geophysical and socioeconomic indicators, including groundwater abstraction, Immerzeel and Bierkens (2012) suggested that the Amu Darya and Indus River basins are the most vulnerable to changes in water availability. Water resources in these basins provide the basis for a substantial part of the region's total GDP and important environmental services, which are also of importance beyond the region (Niou, 2002; Penland & Kulp, 2005; Woodroffe, Nicholls, Saito, Chen, & Goodbred, 2006). On top of the climatic changes, the region is undergoing remarkable socio-economic transformation. China and India are today experiencing economic growth, growing international importance and a rapid reduction in poverty. The countries of South Asia and China have experienced a significant increase in water demand over the past decades (Condon, Hillmann, King, Lang, & Patz, 2009; de Fraiture, Wichelns, Rockström, & Kemp-Benedict, 2007), and this will continue into the future. The annual water withdrawals for agriculture are projected to increase, under IWMI's comprehensive assessment scenario, by 9% in South Asia and 16% in East Asia from 2000 to 2050, compared to a global average of 13% (de Fraiture et al., 2007). For non-agricultural uses, the withdrawals have been projected to increase much more quickly – at an average annual rate of 3.3% for South Asia and 2.9% for East Asia, compared to the global rate of 1.6% (de Fraiture et al., 2007).

These projections imply that the gap between water availability and demand may be a potential problem in the HKH countries in the future. To this end, wise investments in physical water infrastructure can help in building resilience by augmenting water availability when there is too little of it and regulating it when there is too much of it.

Simultaneous investments in institutions will be necessary to promote the development and construction of water infrastructure as well as for the efficient, equitable, and sustainable governance and management of water-related services (Frederick, 1997; Lam, 1998). The type and relative importance of the level of institutional infrastructure depends on the type of physical infrastructure. For large-scale hydropower regulation and energy markets, national-level institutions are required, while for smaller-scale water storage, catchment-level or irrigation-system-level institutions are needed, and those for flood risk reduction may have to be largely at a community level. Although we touch on some of these issues here, more attention is required on the cross-scale and complex institutional and governance arrangements required for infrastructure investments.

Water storage for mountain communities

Because of the seasonal variation in water availability and the steep topography, it is challenging for mountain communities to store water so that it is available for use in the dry season for agriculture and domestic uses. Traditionally, mountain people have built terraces to store water in the soil profile and reduce erosion; they have also built small-scale irrigation systems using spring water or tapping into streams. The number of dams and reservoirs in the hills and mountains of the region is quite limited, although many villages have developed small-scale water ponds to serve domestic and agricultural needs. Large-scale reservoirs have been developed during the last six decades to serve large-scale irrigation, especially in locations where the hills transition to plains and there is potential for more large-scale storage.

The Hindu Kush–Himalayan region is blessed with a host of natural systems of water storage. First, the region has the largest bodies of ice outside the polar caps. Second, there is the snow cover and permafrost. Third, there are 8790 glacial lakes in Bhutan, China (Ganges sub basins within China), India (Himachal Pradesh and Uttarakhand), Nepal, and Pakistan (Indus river basin) with a cumulative area of about $802 \, km^2$ (Ives, Shrestha, & Mool, 2010). Fourth, the Himalayan wetlands located in the headwaters assist in the flow of rivers, feed groundwater aquifers, trap sediments, recycle nutrients and maintain the quality and quantity of the water cycle. High-altitude wetlands account for 16% of the total area of the greater Himalayan region (Trishal & Kumar, 2008). Finally, groundwater aquifers in the region are literally large underground reservoirs; these include the aquifers in the unconsolidated Bhabar zone and the Terai Plains, south of the Siwalik Range in the Himalayas (WECS, 2002). Groundwater in the hills supplies many local springs, but there is increasing anecdotal evidence that springs are drying up across the foothills of the Himalayas. These natural storage systems hold an important but underappreciated key to future water needs.

Transforming natural systems of water storage into planned active systems is no easy task. This will require improved knowledge on the dynamics of glaciers and snow, improved understanding of the vulnerabilities of wetlands, and more knowledge about aquifer systems. There is a need to explore the potential of using natural lakes for storage and of harnessing and storing glacial and snow meltwater at high altitudes (Schild & Vaidya, 2009). Equally important is the recognition of the potential of natural infrastructure within policy and implementation institutions.

Water investments to support hill and mountain people

There is already a wealth of water knowledge that mountain people have developed over millennia that should provide important insights for future water development. The farmer-managed irrigation systems of Nepal, for example, are modes of well-managed common-pool resources that rely on strong locally crafted rules as well as evolved norms (Lam, 1998; Pradhan, 1989). Ostrom's (1990) eight design principles for successful common-pool resource governance explain the success of farmer-managed irrigation systems very well. Traditional water harvesting from glaciers is common in certain areas of the Himalayan region, especially in the Chitral and Hunza districts of Pakistan. Water harvesting from glaciers in the Spiti Valley of Himachal Pradesh in India uses diversion channels to tap distant glaciers for water to supply water to villages (Agarwal & Narain, 1997). More recently, in the Leh district of Ladakh, India, "artificial glaciers" were created by capturing autumn flows and allowing the water to freeze during winter; when melted, it could be used as a source for irrigation in spring (Sudhalkar, 2010).

Soil moisture plays a vital role as a natural system of water storage, and management of the abundant rainfall in the Himalayas requires active management (Molden, 2007; Rockstrom et al., 2010). Watershed management, through improved land-cover and water-conservation practices, can help to maintain soil moisture and support water harvesting, improve infiltration for groundwater recharge and keep the mountain springs flowing. For example, in the *zabo* (which means 'impounding water') system, a holistic approach to watershed management practised in Kikruma Village of Nagaland, India, the catchment area at the top of the hill slope is kept under natural vegetation. Ponds with earthen embankments are dug below the catchment area to harvest water for irrigation and livestock. Cattle yards fenced with ordinary branches or bamboo are maintained below the ponds, and the pond runoff water used for cleaning the yards. Finally, the cleaning water, enriched with manure, flows into rice terraces at the lowest level of the slope (Agarwal & Narain, 1997). These systems have important positive externalities, including reduced erosion and short-term water storage for downstream users, and preservation or accumulation of biomass, an important climate change mitigation measure. However, these externalities are undervalued, and typically not compensated. One constraint on these mountain land and water management systems is their high cost relative to returns. The introduction of higher-value products or of policies that compensate for ecosystem services could help mountain people maintain healthy lifestyles in a healthy environment.

Mountain water for hydropower

With growing demand for energy in mountain regions and elsewhere, plus growing environmental concerns, there is a need to transform energy supplies. Traditional biomass fuels remain the major source of energy in the Hindu Kush–Himalayan region, with the dependence rate on these fuels at more than 80% in Afghanistan, Bhutan and Nepal and about 15% in all of India (ADB, 2011). With the rising environmental concerns of deforestation and air pollution, there is a need to carefully consider the role of hydropower. The contribution of hydroelectricity to total commercial energy is about 50% in Bhutan, 17% in Nepal, 13% in Pakistan, 6% in India and 4% in Afghanistan (ADB, 2011), and to the total electricity supply it is about 100% in Bhutan, 92% in Nepal, 74% in Myanmar, 33% in Pakistan, 17% in India, and 16% in China (Hydropower and Dams World Atlas, 2009).

The hydro-energy potential of the greater Himalayan region is more than 500 GW (Vaidya, 2012), but the actual capacity harnessed is only a small fraction of this. As a result, there is a severe electricity shortage in the region: the demand–supply gap is more than 15% in Pakistan and about 10% in India and Nepal. Furthermore, the demand is expected to grow at an annual rate of 10% in Nepal, 9% in India, 6% in Pakistan and 5% in Bhutan (ADB, 2011).

In terms of installed capacity, China is the leader in the region and the world, with 213.4 GW of installed capacity in 2010, or 39% of its exploitable capacity of 542 GW (Cheng, Shen, Wu, & Chau, 2012). Of the potential capacity, 272 GW, or 50%, lies in the four Himalayan provinces of Qinghai, Sichuan, Tibetan Autonomous Region, and Yunnan (Vaidya, 2012). The large (at least 1000 MW) hydropower plants currently located in the hydropower bases in the Himalayan provinces of Qinghai, Sichuan and Yunnan account for more than 90 GW of the installed capacity (Cheng et al., 2012). The installed capacity is projected to reach 300 GW by 2020: 75 GW in small plants (50 MW or less) and 225 GW in medium and large plants (Zhao, Lu, Lu, Jieyu, & Xiaomeng, 2012).

Large hydropower plants already built in the region include Tala in Bhutan; Ertan (Sichuan), Manwan (Yunnan) and Dachaosan (Yunnan) in China; Bhakra and Tehri in India; and Tarbela and Mangla in Pakistan. In contrast to other countries in the region, Nepal's hydropower industry does not have large plants, but has a diverse structure in medium (defined in Nepal as 300 MW or less), small (25 MW or less) and micro hydro plants (100 KW or less). Of the installed capacity, 28% is from small plants and 72% from medium-sized plants; 28% is under private ownership; and 97% is grid-connected (NEA, 2010).

Nepal and Pakistan have rich experience in micro hydropower plants, especially in relation to community involvement in planning, construction and operation, and including a significant industrial base for producing electro-mechanical equipment. Hydropower plants of 150 kW or less were introduced in 1990 by the Aga Khan Rural Support Programme in the remote mountain valleys of Gilgit, Baltistan and Chitral in northern Pakistan as a community-led development initiative. By 2005, these communities had built 240 such plants, with a total capacity of more than 10,000 kW. A project was registered with the Clean Development Mechanism Executive Board in October 2009 to develop 103 new micro and mini hydropower plants in Pakistan, with a total capacity of 15 MW, at a cost of USD 18 million (Hunzai, 2011). Medium, small and micro power plants help fill the gap for mountain communities, especially in view of the challenges of realizing large hydropower facilities.

Issues related to environmental barriers to hydropower development

Changes in glacier, snow and ice melt and increasing use of water need to be taken into consideration when planning hydropower development. A modelling study of climate change impacts on the flow regimes of rivers in Bhutan concluded that the contribution to streamflow from glacier meltwater will remain unchanged until about 2050 but will start to decline thereafter (Beldring and Vokso, 2011). In China, it has been suggested that as the scale of hydropower development increases in its Himalayan provinces of Sichuan and Yunnan, the impact of uncertain runoff will be more significant. The impact of extreme events on the operation of hydropower stations will be even more significant, as demonstrated by the drought of 2008 (Cheng et al., 2012), and uncertainty in design becomes more important. More intense rainfall events in the future may lead to increased floods and sedimentation, leading to increased siltation for hydropower infrastructure to contend with. Improved watershed management, with compensation to watershed communities, is an important potential solution.

The frequency and magnitude of glacial lake outburst flood (GLOF) events may increase, threatening downstream hydropower development. According to the recorded history of glacial lake outburst events, there have been 34 GLOF events in Bhutan (4), the Tibetan Autonomous Region of China (16), and Nepal (14) (Ives et al. 2010). This is especially important in the Koshi Basin, which has a potential hydropower capacity of about one-fourth of the technically feasible capacity in Nepal but also a large number of potential GLOF sites. GLOF risks provide a new challenge in planning and managing existing and future hydropower. Many GLOF events occur across national boundaries, again highlighting the need for transboundary cooperation.

Social, technical, financial, and environmental issues of hydropower development

Delivering electricity to isolated mountain communities is both a social and a technical concern. Socio-economic development calls for poor rural communities to benefit from electricity. But providing distribution networks connected to power-grid networks is a major technological constraint. First of all, the hydropower plants are remote from developed areas. In China, for example, hydropower resources in its Himalayan provinces are far from its industrial belts. Second, the lack of a domestic construction industry able to undertake such projects is a major concern in India in relation to small-power-plant construction, despite its well-developed construction industry. Third, the less industrialized countries in the region need to trade power with the more industrialized ones; thus, cross-border grid interconnections are vital. Power trade and exchange between the Himalayan region and the core industrial belts of China and India could improve the capacity utilization factor of the power plants in the Himalayan region, thus enabling the countries in the region to supply power at a price affordable to their households.

Addressing social and environmental concerns will be critical for the sustainable development of hydropower. Rigorous scientific studies with a focus on the potential effects of hydropower development on terrestrial biological diversity in the region have appeared only recently (Pandit & Grumbine, 2012). It has been reported that several projects are currently stranded at different stages in the north-eastern states of India because the states are revisiting their plans in view of local resistance and ecological concerns. Sikkim has also cancelled a number of planned projects (Economic Times, 2012). The success of reservoir projects, therefore, lies in well-conceived and implemented rehabilitation and resettlement plans in addition to addressing environmental concerns (World Commission on Dams, 2000). A participatory approach should be adopted involving the stakeholders, and the basic rules of the game should be set and agreed upon right at the outset of the project (Gopalakrishan, 2012). In addition, it has been suggested that society at large has to be involved by providing correct information through the media.

The indirect benefits of hydropower projects are often underappreciated. According to a World Bank study, the Bhakra Dam project generated significant indirect benefits in the Punjab state of India: every rupee returned in direct economic benefits was accompanied by 0.9 rupees of indirect economic benefits (Bhatia, Cestti, Scatasta, & Malik, 2008). However, particular attention needs to be given to the population who benefit: as mountain people do not necessarily receive such benefits. The challenges in making a prudent selection of hydropower projects lie, therefore, in developing a methodology that accounts for the indirect costs as well as the indirect benefits, in mitigating negative social and environmental costs, and in ensuring equitable distribution of benefits.

To increase the pace of the development of multipurpose projects, institutional mechanisms have to be crafted for benefit sharing, and sometimes cost sharing, between the upstream and downstream communities affected by storage projects, often across national borders. A common complaint of mountain and hill people is that the benefits of hydropower largely benefit downstream populations, with local hill and mountain people bearing the bulk of the social and environmental costs; the electrical supply does not reach mountain people, and jobs are given to outside labourers.

Raising funds at a reasonable rate to privately finance power projects is a major concern, not only in Nepal, where infrastructure finance is at an early stage of development, but also in China, a country with a well-developed infrastructure finance system. This is true especially for small power projects. The major challenge is to raise funds from financial markets at a cost that allows power plants to sell power at affordable prices to its consumers. There are a number of reasons: first, the need to realize project returns commensurate with the project risks; second, the low load factor (i.e. the ratio of average demand over the year to peak demand) on power plants in the region because of its small industrial base; and third, high non-technical system losses, because of the utility company's inability to prevent power theft through illegal hook-ups during distribution. For private financing, funds invested in the project are backed by the cash flows and assets of the project only, with little recourse to the underlying balance sheet of the sponsors. The return required by investors, therefore, depends primarily on the level of risk of the project, and not on the financial status of the sponsor (Head, 2000). Major project risks include hydrological and construction risks, environmental risks, market risks, financial risks such as exchange-rate risk, and political risks such as changes in laws (Patramanis, 2006). The governments in the region have realized that hydroelectricity is not wholly a private good, because it involves harnessing a natural resource (with property rights that often belong to the state) and transmitting power over networks (also a public good). Public-private partnership between the government and the private sector, where each party manages the type of risk it can handle best – and shares risk as and when needed – may be the best way forward for attracting private financing for hydropower development in the region.

The landscape of hydropower development is changing. Construction companies in China and India have rich experience in hydropower development. They have also been helping develop hydropower plants in Bhutan and Nepal. India has had successful experience developing the Chukha (336 MW) and Tala (1020 MW) hydropower plants in Bhutan (PTC India, 2010) and has started construction of a storage-reservoir project on the Punatsangchhu River. The Indian initiatives are led by its public-sector hydropower company, the National Hydroelectric Power Corporation. China's public-sector hydropower company, The Three Gorges, have signed an agreement to build and operate the West Seti project (750 MW) in Nepal in partnership with the Nepal Electricity Authority. Furthermore, the government of India has formed a Cabinet Committee on Investment for project investments over IRS. 10 billion (about USD 180 million), to provide single-window clearance to large projects (The Hindu, 2012).

Infrastructure for flood risk reduction

In the period 1976–2005, 41% of global flood disasters, accounting for 65% of people killed and 96% of those affected, happened in Asia. South Asia accounted for 33% of the floods in Asia, 50% of those killed, and 38% of those affected. During the past three decades (1976–2005), the reported number of natural disasters in South Asia was 943, with 332 (35%) caused by floods (M. S. Shrestha, 2008), primarily in the Indus, Ganges and Brahmaputra basins. The global percentage of disasters caused by flooding is 30%. The IPCC (2012) indicated that economic losses from climate-related disasters have increased, albeit with large spatial and interannual variability. The 2010 floods in Pakistan killed 2000 people and left 20 million homeless, with a financial loss of USD 10 billion (FFC, 2010); the 2007 floods in India and Bangladesh killed more than 3000 people and left millions homeless. Clearly, reduction of flood risks has to be high on the list of infrastructure needs for the greater Himalayas.

Several studies have indicated that the intensity of rainfall in the region has increased (despite a decrease in the total number of rainy days), resulting in severe floods and landslides (Goswami, Venugopal, Sengupta, Madhusoodanan, & Xavier, 2006; Mirza, 2002). IPCC has warned that floods of the kind that hit Pakistan may become more frequent and more intense in the same region and in other parts of the world because of climate change plus high exposure and vulnerability. A study conducted by Mirza and Dixit (1997) on the effects of global warming on future flooding in Bangladesh, with a 2°C rise in global mean temperature and a 10% increase in precipitation, showed that the average flood discharges for the Ganges, Brahmaputra and Meghna could be as much as 19%, 13% and 11% higher, respectively. Climate-related extremes are also likely to produce large impacts on infrastructure (IPCC, 2012).

An integrated flood management approach, including structural and nonstructural measures, is being increasingly adopted, taking into consideration both the benefits and adverse impacts of floods (WMO, 2009). Structural measures such as dams, dykes, embankments, retention basins and channel modifications can reduce flood risks (Shrestha, GC, Adhikary, & Rai, 2012). A large number of multipurpose dams have been built, and more are planned, for hydropower production, flood protection, and water for irrigation and domestic use. Interestingly, water infrastructure for hydropower performs better if infrastructure for flood protection is properly developed, because of their common concern with respect to sedimentation. At the community level, a series of check dams can significantly control erosion and reduce flooding downstream, as shown for example in the Begnas Tal–Rupa Tal watershed management project in Nepal (Bogati, 1997).

Some conventional structural measures used to protect against floods have at times proved insufficient. Lessons can be learned, for example, from the breach of the Koshi Embankment in Nepal in August 2008 (Dixit, 2009). Reliance on a structural embankment created a false sense of security for the people living across the border in downstream Bihar, India. There was no flood preparedness or early-warning system in place. The Koshi flood broke through the embankment without warning and affected more than 70,000 people in Nepal and 3.5 million in Bihar. It is clear that transboundary cooperation for early warning and protection is needed. While embankments are the most common infrastructure, different approaches should be sought, including for example non-structural measures for flood risk reduction.

Effective national systems are required, including early-warning systems comprised of multiple actors from national and sub-national governments, the private sector, research institutions and civil society, playing different but complementary roles to manage risk according to their accepted functions and capacities (IPCC, 2012). These systems can take immediate advantage of technological advances made in forecasting. Medium-term forecasts can better equip farmers with information for improved agricultural production, while short-term forecasts provide early warning to people living in flood-prone areas, helping with timely evacuation and preparedness. Implementation of an effective flood forecasting and early-warning system involves the establishment of a real-time observation network, efficient data transmission and acquisition, accurate forecasting, decision support, dissemination, and coordinated action and enhanced regional cooperation where river basins extend across several countries. For example, the World Meteorological Organization, the International Centre for Integrated Mountain Development and its member countries in the region are working together on the implementation of a regional flood information system. The project aims to provide a total end-to-end system that will function as a decision-support tool enabling decision-makers to alert vulnerable communities in a timely fashion.

Conclusion and recommendations

The Hindu Kush Himalayas contain vast reservoirs of water in the form of snow, ice and glaciers and are the origin of 10 major rivers and many of their tributaries. Although the region is rich in water resources, access to water for economic use in mountain areas is made difficult by the high degree of intra-annual rainfall variability and lack of water-storage facilities. Furthermore, climate change is likely have a serious impact on the hydrological regime and on water availability in the region. Water scarcity on one hand, and flooding on the other, will pose a serious challenge to the approximately 1.3 billion people living in the 10 river basins. Sound development of infrastructure for water storage, flood protection, irrigation, water supply and energy is urgently needed to buffer the present growth and potential future variability in the flow regime, to reduce uncertainty in water availability, to reduce flood and drought risks and to improve access to water to support economic growth. Better care and use of natural infrastructure offers opportunities to address the significant infrastructure requirements.

Knowledge gaps with respect to present and future hydrology pose a serious constraint for infrastructure development. Changing hydrology will pose special challenges to the design, planning and management of Himalayan infrastructure. There is increasing evidence that glaciers are shrinking; less clear, however, is the impact on downstream water sources from changes in the cryosphere and monsoon patterns. There is less information about the role and changing nature of monsoons, snow cover, permafrost, glacial lakes, wetlands and groundwater – all essential if we are to get a handle on future water availability. Natural systems of water storage such as wetlands, glaciers, mountain lakes and soil moisture serve as reservoirs for dry-season water. These need to be transformed into planned active systems. This requires improved knowledge on the cryosphere and the biosphere – and recognition of the importance of these systems within the planning community.

To expedite infrastructure development, issues outside of engineering must be addressed. Social and environmental concerns are of special concern given the fragile environment and the fact that the marginalized rural mountain men and women often do not reap the benefits of infrastructure development. These mountain people are the caretakers of a range of ecosystem services essential for downstream people, such as water and sediment yields, yet mechanisms for compensation of these services are limited, constraining the development of practices such as watershed management. With increasing water use and changing water availability, the linkages between upstream and downstream are increasing, calling for more benefit sharing and cost sharing.

Ultimately, the effectiveness of infrastructure will be determined by water governance and management mechanisms. There are some good examples at the community level displayed by farmer-managed systems, but more and different institutional arrangements across scales are needed, given the increasing interaction between upstream and downstream users. For example, a mix of structural and non-structural arrangements like flood forecasting and early-warning systems are required for effective flood risk mitigation; this requires integrated management arrangements. Institutional arrangements for improved financing are required. While there are more calls for private-sector involvement, there are limits to this approach. Public–private partnership between the national government and the private sector, where each party manages the type of risk it can handle best, needs to be encouraged to attract private financing for hydropower development in the region. For example, the national governments would be in the best position to take the lead in managing political risks, as well as risks due to streamflow variability, sediment-load changes, and potential GLOF events.

Transboundary river-basin governance and management arrangements are essential to reap the potential benefits, but these are difficult given the geopolitical environment. Nevertheless, even without ideal transboundary arrangements, important steps can be made in this direction. These include knowledge-sharing efforts between research and management communities; setting up joint information systems for early warning on floods; and encouraging dialogue between scientists and influential personalities in different countries.

Sustainable and equitable infrastructure development for mountain areas needs urgent investment to build resilience, reduce disasters and contribute to economic growth. Mountainous regions require different infrastructure consideration from plains and coasts, given the fragile environment, the marginality of many mountain people and the transboundary nature of many of the rivers emanating from the mountains. New approaches to address socio-economic, environmental and transboundary concerns are required to overcome the controversies surrounding infrastructure development at the scale and pace required.

References

Agarwal, A., & Narain, S. (Eds.). (1997). *Dying wisdom: Rise, fall and potential of India's traditional water harvesting systems State of India's environment, A citizen's report 4.* New Delhi: Centre for Science and Environment.

Ahmad, Q. K., Biswas, A. K., Rangachari, R., & Sainju, M. M. (Eds.). (2001). *Ganga-Brahmaputra-Meghna region: A framework for sustainable development.* Dhaka: The University Press Ltd.

Ali, K. F., & De Boer, D. H. (2007). Spatial patterns and variation of suspended sediment yield in the upper Indus river basin, Northern Pakistan. *Journal of Hydrology, 334,* 368–387.

Andermann, C., Longuevergne, L., Bonnet, S., Crave, A., Davy, P., & Gloaguen, R. (2012). Impact of transient groundwater storage on the discharge of Himalayan rivers. *Nature Geoscience, 5,* 127–132.

Armstrong, R. L. (2010). *The glaciers of the Hindu Kush–Himalayan region: A summary of the science regarding glacier melt/retreat in the Himalayan, Hindu Kush, Karakoram, Pamir, and Tien Shan mountain ranges.* Kathmandu: ICIMOD.

Asian Development Bank. (2011). *Energy trade in South Asia: Opportunities and challenges.* Mandaluyong: Asian Development Bank.

Bajracharya, S. R., & Shrestha, B. (Eds.). (2011). *The status of glaciers in the Hindu Kush-Himalayan region.* Kathmandu: ICIMOD.

Beldring, S., & Voksø, A. (2011). *Climate change impacts on the flow regimes of rivers in Bhutan and possible consequences for hydropower development* (Report No. 4). (S. Beldring, Ed.). Oslo: Norwegian Water Resources and Energy Directorate.

Bhatia, R., Cestti, R., Scatasta, M., & Malik, R. P. S. (Eds.). (2008). *Indirect economic impacts of dams: Case studies from India, Egypt and Brazil.* New Delhi: Academic Foundation for the World Bank.

Bogati, R. (1997). A case study of people's participation in Begnastal and Rupatal (BTRT) watershed management in Nepal. Case studies of people's participation in watershed management in Asia. Retrieved from http://www.fao.org/docrep/X5669E/x5669e04.htm

Böhner, J., & Lehmkuhl, F. (2005). Environmental change modelling for central and high Asia: Pleistocene, present and future scenarios. *Boreas, 34,* 220–231.

Bolch, T., Kulkarni, A., Kaab, A., Huggel, C., Paul, F., Cogley, J. G., & … Stoffel, M. (2012). The state and fate of Himalayan Glaciers. *Science, 336,* 310–314.

Bookhagen, B., & Burbank, D. W. (2010). Toward a complete Himalayan hydrological budget: Spatiotemporal distribution of snowmelt and rainfall and their impact on river discharge. *Journal of Geophysical Research, 115,* 25.

Cheng, C. -T., Shen, J. -J., Wu, X. -Y., & Chau, K. (2012). Operation challenges for fast-growing China's hydropower systems and respondence to energy saving and emission reduction. *Renewable and Sustainable Energy Reviews, 16,* 2386–2393.

Clements, T., D'Amato, V., & Taylor, T. (2010). Integrating water infrastructure in a new paradigm for sustainable, resilient communities. *Proceedings of the Water Environment Federation, Cities of the Future/Urban River Restoration,* 801–825.

Cogley, J. G., Kargel, J. S., Kaser, G., & van der Veen, C. J. (2010). Tracking the source of glacier misinformation. *Science, 327,* 522–522.

Condon, E., Hillmann, P., King, J., Lang, K., & Patz, A. (2009, June). *Resource disputes in South Asia: Water scarcity and the potential for interstate conflict.* Paper presented at the Workshop in International Public Affairs, Wisconsin, USA.

De Fraiture, C., Wichelns, D., Rockström, J., & Kemp-Benedict, E. (2007). Looking ahead to 2050: Scenarios of alternative investment approaches. In D. Molden (Ed.), *Water for food, water for life: A comprehensive assessment of water management in agriculture* (pp. 91–148). Colombo: Earthscan, London and International Water Management Institute.

Dixit, A. (2009). Kosi embankment breach in Nepal: Need for a paradigm shift in responding to floods. *Economic and Political Weekly, 44*, 70–78.

Economic Times. (2012). Hochtief scouting for hydropower projects. 14 September, p. 3.

Eriksson, M., Xu, J., Shrestha, A. B., Vaidya, R. A., Nepal, S., & Sandström, K. (2009). *The changing Himalayas: Impact of climate change on water resources and livelihoods in the greater Himalayas*. Kathmandu: ICIMOD.

Federal Flood Commission. (2010). *Annual flood report*. Islamabad: Ministry of Water and Power, Government of Pakistan.

Frederick, K. D. (1997). Adapting to climate impacts on the supply and demand for water. *Climatic Change, 37*, 141–156.

Gopalakrishnan, M. (2012). Resettlement and rehabilitation lessons from India. In C. Tortajada, D. Altinbilek, & A. K. Biswas (Eds.), *Impacts of large dams: A global assessment* Series on Water Resources Development and Management, (pp. 357–378). New York: Springer.

Goswami, B. N., Venugopal, V., Sengupta, D., Madhusoodanan, M. S., & Xavier, P. K. (2006). Increasing trend of extreme rain events over India in a warming environment. *Science, 314*, 1442–1445.

Guo, H., Hu, Q., Zhang, Q., & Feng, S. (2012). Effects of the three Gorges Dam on Yangtze river flow and river interaction with Poyang Lake, China: 2003–2008. *Journal of Hydrology, 416–417*, 19–27.

Gurung, D. R., Amarnath, G., Khun, S. A., Shrestha, B., & Kulkarni, A. V. (Eds.). (2011). *Snow-cover mapping and monitoring in the Hindu-Kush Himalayas*. Kathmandu: ICIMOD.

Head, C. (2000). *Financing of private hydropower projects, discussion paper WDP 420*. Washington, DC: The World Bank.

Hunzai, I. A. (2011, August). *Renewable energy development through community ownership and management in the remote mountain valleys of Northern Pakistan*. Case study presented at the Regional Sharing Workshop on Assessment of Challenges and Opportunities in the Asia-Pacific Region for Rio+20 of ICIMOD, Kathmandu, Nepal.

Hydropower and Dams World Atlas. (2009). Cited in world hydro-potential and development. Norwegian Renewable Energy Partners (INTPOW). Retrieved from http://www.intpow.com/ index.php?id=487&download=1

Immerzeel, W. (2011, August). *Climate change impacts on the water resources of the Hindu Kush Himalayas*. Paper presented at the Authors' Workshop for the Regional Report on Climate Change in the Hindu Kush–Himalayas: The State of Current Knowledge of ICIMOD, Kathmandu, Nepal.

Immerzeel, W. W., Beek, L. P. H., & Bierkens, M. F. P. (2010). Climate change will affect the Asian water towers. *Science, 328*, 1382–1385.

Immerzeel, W. W., & Bierkens, M. F. P. (2012). Asia's water balance. *Nature Geosciences, 5*, 841–842.

IPCC. 2007. *Climate change 2007: The physical science basis. Contribution of Working Group I to the Fourth Assessment Report of the Intergovernmental Panel on Climate Change*. [S. Solomon, D. Qin, M. Manning, Z. Chen, M. Marquis, K.B. Averyt, M. Tignor and H.L. Miller (Eds.)]. Cambridge: Cambridge University Press.

IPCC. (2012). Summary for policymakers. In C. B. Field, V. Barros, T. F. Stocker, D. Qin, D. J. Dokken, K. L. Ebi, M. D. Mastrandrea, K. J. Mach, G. -K. Plattner, S. K. Allen, M. Tignor, & P. M. Midgley (Eds.), *Managing the risks of extreme events and disasters to advance climate change adaptation* A Special Report of Working Groups I and II of the Intergovernmental Panel on Climate Change. Cambridge: Cambridge University Press.

Ives, J. D., Shrestha, R. B., & Mool, P. K. (2010). *Formation of glacial lakes in the Hindu Kush-Himalayas and GLOF risk assessment*. Kathmandu: ICIMOD.

Lam, W. F. (1998). *Governing irrigation systems in Nepal: Institutions, infrastructure, and collective action*. Oakland, CA: ICS Press.

Miller, J., & Rees, G. (2011, August). *Water availability: River discharge and glacial hydrology*. Paper presented at Authors' Workshop of ICIMOD for the Regional Report on Climate Change in the Hindu Kush Himalayas: The State of Current Knowledge, Kathmandu, Nepal.

Miller, J. M., Warnaars, T., Rees, H. G., Young, G., Shrestha, A. B., & Collins, D. C. (2011). *What is the evidence about glacier shrinkage across the Himalayas?* (Technical Report No. 201642).

Retrieved from Department for International Development: http://www.dfid.gov.uk/r4d/Project/60764/Default.aspx

Mirza, M. M. Q. (2002). Global warming and changes in the probability of occurrence of floods in Bangladesh and implications. *Global Environmental Change, 12,* 127–138.

Mirza, M. M. Q., & Dixit, A. (1997). Climate change and water resources in the GBM basins. *Water Nepal, 5,* 71–100.

Molden, D. (Ed.). (2007). *Water for food, water for life: A Comprehensive assessment of water management in agriculture.* London: Earthscan and Colombo: International Water Management Institute.

Murata, F., Hayashi, T., Matsumoto, J., & Asada, H. (2007). Rainfall on the Meghalaya plateau in northeastern India—one of the rainiest places in the world. *Natural Hazards, 42,* 391–399.

Nepal Electricity Authority. (2010). *Fiscal year 2009–2010: A year in review.* Kathmandu: Nepal Electricity Authority.

New M., Lister, D., Hulme, M. & Makin, I. (2002). A high-resolution data set of surface climate over global land areas. *Climate Research, 21,* 1–25.

Niou, Q. Y. (2002). *2001–2002 report on Chinese metropolitan development.* Beijing: Xiyuan Press (in Chinese).

Ostrom, E. (1990). *Governing the commons: The evolution of institutions for collective action.* Cambridge: Cambridge University Press.

Pandit, M. K., & Grumbine, R. E. (2012). Potential effects of ongoing and proposed hydropower development on terrestrial biological diversity in the Indian Himalaya. *Conservation Biology, 26,* 1061–1071.

Patramanis, T. (2006). *Structured finance for hybrid infrastructure models.* (Master's thesis) Engineering Systems Division, Massachusetts Institute of Technology, Cambridge MA.

Penland, S., & Kulp, M. A. (2005). Deltas. In M. L. Schwartz (Ed.), *Encyclopaedia of coastal science* (pp. 362–368). Dordrecht: Springer.

Power Trading Corporation India. (2010). *Eleventh annual report 2009–2010.* New Delhi: Power Trading Corporation India Limited.

Pradhan, P. (1989). *Patterns of irrigation organization: A comparative study of 21 farmer managed irrigation systems.* Colombo: International Irrigation Management Institute.

Rees, H. G., & Collins, D. N. (2006). Regional differences in response of flow in glacier-fed Himalayan rivers to climatic warming. *Hydrological Processes, 20,* 2157–2169.

Rockström, J., Karlberg, L., Wani, S. P., Barron, J., Hatibu, N., Oweis, T., & … Qiang, Z. (2010). Managing water in rainfed agriculture—the need for a paradigm shift. *Agricultural Water Management, 97,* 543–550.

Schild, A., & Vaidya, R. A. (2009). The evolving role of ICIMOD in the development of water storage capacity. *Water storage: A strategy for climate change adaptation in the Himalayas, sustainable mountain development no. 56, special issue.* Kathmandu: ICIMOD.

Shrestha, A. B. (2008). *Resource manual on flash flood risk management: Module 2: Non-structural measures.* Kathmandu: ICIMOD.

Shrestha, A. B., GC, E., Adhikary, R. P., & Rai, S. K. (2012). *Resource manual on flash flood risk management Module 3: Structural measures.* Kathmandu: ICIMOD.

Shrestha, M. S. (2008). Impacts of floods in South Asia. *Journal of South Asia Disaster Studies, 1,* 85–106.

Sudhalkar, A. A. (2010). *Adaptation to water scarcity in glacier-dependent towns of the Indian Himalayas: Impacts, adaptive responses, barriers, and solutions.* (Master's thesis). Massachusetts Institute of Technology, Cambridge, MA, USA.

The Hindu. (2012, December 13). It's cabinet panel on investment now. *The Hindu.* Retrieved from http://www.thehindubusinessline.com/industry-and-economy/government-and-policy/its-cabinet-panel-on-investment-now/article4196598.ece

Trishal, C. L., & Kumar, R. (2008). *Integration of high altitude wetlands into river basin management in the Hindu Kush Himalayas.* New Delhi: Wetlands International, South Asia.

Vaidya, R. (2012). Water and hydropower in the green economy and sustainable development of the Hindu Kush-Himalayan region. *Hydro Nepal: Journal of Water, Energy and Environment, 10,* 11–19.

Water and Energy Commission Secretariat. (2002). *Water resources strategy – Nepal.* Kathmandu: Water and Energy Commission Secretariat.

Webby, R. B., Adamson, P. T., Boland, J., Howlett, P. G., Metcalfe, A. V., & Piantadosi, J. (2007). The Mekong—applications of value at risk (VaR) and conditional value at risk (CVaR) simulation to the benefits, costs and consequences of water resources development in a large river basin. *Ecological Modelling*, *201*, 89–96.

Woodroffe, C. D., Nicholls, R. J., Saito, Y., Chen, Z., & Goodbred, S. L. (2006). Landscape variability and the response of Asian megadeltas to environmental change. In N. Harvey (Ed.), *Global change and integrated coastal management: The Asia-Pacific region* (pp. 277–314). New York: Springer.

World Meteorological Organization. (2009). *Integrated flood management concept paper* (WMO – No. 1047). Geneva: Associated Programme on Flood Management (APFM). Retrieved from http://www.apfm.info/pdf/concept_paper_e.pdf

World Commission on Dams. (2000). *Dams and development: A new framework for decision-making*. Report of the World Commission on Dams. London: Earthscan.

Zhang, M., Ren, Q., Wei, X., Wang, J., Yang, X., & Jiang, Z. (2011). Climate change, glacier melting and streamflow in the Niyang River basin, southeast Tibet, China. *Ecohydrology*, *4*, 288–298.

Zhao, Z., Lu, L., Lu, L., Jieyu, W., & Xiaomeng, L. (2012). A critical-analysis on the development of China hydropower. *Renewable Energy*, *44*, 1–6.

The Gujarat State-Wide Water Supply Grid: a step towards water security

Andrea Biswas-Tortajada

Water and Sanitation Management Organisation, Gandhinagar, India

Gujarat is one of India's economic powerhouses, but its geographical conditions mean that most of the state's districts face water deficits. In 2002, emergency arrangements to meet water shortages were replaced with a longer-term strategy: the construction and management of the State-Wide Water Supply Grid. This scheme moves towards connecting 47 million people to safe, potable water supplies. It has also positioned Gujarat as a pioneer in India in terms of moving towards water security and conservation, a policy choice that has boosted economic growth and made important strides towards human development.

Introduction

Though it is one of India's industrial and agricultural powerhouses, Gujarat is also one of the most water-scarce states in the country, with a water availability of around 900 m^3 per capita per year, which is only 58% of the national average of 1545 m^3 (WASMO, 2013). More importantly, the state's topographical, hydrological, climatic and soil conditions result in large regional variations in the availability of water, leaving most of Gujarat's districts with water deficits. This situation seems to have worsened in the last 40 years: 3 to 5 years in every decade have been marked by drought, and with each episode, the communities' coping resources are further strained (Dass, 2006).

Up until 2002, this situation called for yearly crisis management and emergency arrangements, including a financial cost of INR 1250 million to1500 million (1 USD is equivalent to INR 55) to send water tankers to the regions facing temporary and recurrent shortages. Added to this, and even without accounting for social and environmental costs, the Gujarat Water Supply and Sewerage Board (GWSSB) (2003) estimated that households were spending around INR 7000 million to 8000 million (USD 127.27–145.45 million) every year to secure water supplies, mostly in purchases from private vendors. The annual social cost of water scarcity is put conservatively at INR 20,000 million (around USD 363.63 million) (GWSSB inaugurated technical support unit, 2013). These past measures were been temporary and costly, and urged Gujarat's government to reform its water sector (Parul, 2006).

Over the last decade, Gujarat has emerged as a pioneer in the country in the move towards water security and the efficient management of water resources. The highest priority has been awarded to drought-proofing the state via investments in water infrastructure, the implementation of an inclusive and long-term water policy, and the involvement of rural communities in managing local infrastructure and water supply services. Since 2002, the state's water sector has been building a State-Wide Water Supply Grid to address absolute and relative water scarcity as well as issues of access equity. From the moment the first elements of the State-wide Water Supply Grid were constructed, with the Sardar Sarovar Canal Based Drinking Water Supply Project at its core, the rural and urban landscapes began to change. (The Sardar Sarovar Canal is also known as the Narmada Canal.) The scheme, to be completed in 2013–2014, makes bulk water transfers from water-surplus to water-scarce areas, a policy that can potentially bring about substantial development benefits for at least 47 million people in this Indian state.

The government of Gujarat has stopped diverting resources in relief works to mitigate the socio-economic impacts of weather inclemencies and taking ad hoc measures to address latent water-scarcity issues. Instead, it has started investing in a series of infrastructure developments designed to recharge depleting aquifers, improve water quality, mitigate the burden poor water quality imposes on human health, and encourage new productive activities. These efforts could turn into an engine for human development. The grid, a combination of bulk water transmission pipelines, water treatment plants, service reservoirs and the longest water distribution network in the world, brings water to the state's most remote and fraught areas.

Gujarat's water profile

The wide heterogeneity in Gujarat's topography, hydrology, climate and soil conditions results in a geographical imbalance in water resource endowment. In fact, 70% of the state is arid or semi-arid and prone to droughts (Patel, 1997). Rainfall is unevenly distributed, as clearly reflected in the annual rainfall patterns observed over the last 35 years and summarized in Table 1.

At least once in every three years, Gujarat experiences a deficit in rainfall. In regions where water availability is heavily dependent on annual rainfall, drought has caused severe drinking-water shortages. Scanty and unpredictable rainfall, intensified irrigation and saline soil formations compromise water security in North Gujarat, Saurashtra and Kachchh. This is aggravated by a salinity ingress rate of 2 km per year along 1600 km of coastal aquifers (Gupta, 2001; WASMO, 2013). Further challenges arise from the fact that groundwater can only be extracted in 34% of the land area (see Table 2).

By the turn of the millennium, Gujarat had lost about 27% of its groundwater resources. Unsafe and unsustainable exploitation of groundwater sources affected 90% of the state's area, and 87% of the municipal corporations that depended on groundwater sources (Kumar & Singh, 2001). Indiscriminate groundwater mining has meant that any shortfall in rainfall almost immediately generates a 'drought condition' and water scarcity for agricultural activities and drinking water in certain regions. This has also contributed to

Table 1.   Rainfall trends.

Region	Average annual rainfall (mm)	Rainy days
South Gujarat	>1100	120
Central Gujarat	800–1000	30–70
Saurashtra	400–800	20–30
Kachchh	<400	10–20

Source: Gujarat Water Supply and Sewerage Board (2013).

Table 2.   Regional water resources availability.

Region	Total water resources (MCM)	Surface water (MCM)	Groundwater (MCM)
Central and South Gujarat	35,700	31,759	3,950
Kachchh	11,000	650	450
North Gujarat	5,300	2,000	3,300
Saraushtra	7,900	3,600	4,300

Source: Narmada, Water Resources, Water Supply and Kalpasar Department (2013).

the grave deterioration of water quality in at least 25% of Gujarat's habitations and caused extensive health damages (WASMO, 2013; Gurajat Jalseva Training Institute (GJTI), 2013).

Drought and acute water shortages also resulted in heavy setbacks in health, nutrition, education and the environment. These challenges intensified as population exploded, lifestyles turned more urban, dietary habits changed, the socio-economic profile of the state changed, and agriculture intensified around the production of water-intensive crops. In response to this scenario, Gujarat has sought to overcome some of the development challenges posed by physical water scarcity.

A paradigm shift

Gujarat's vision of achieving water security is based on tapping new water catchment areas, transferring bulk water by interlinking water-scarce and water-abundant basins, recycling wastewater and desalination. It mainly relies on the multi-state, multi-purpose Sardar Sarovar river-valley project. With this, the water sector in Gujarat is trying to push for a significant paradigm shift away from dependence on groundwater towards intensifying the utilization of surface water from the Narmada River to attain water security. This project has been built to address absolute and relative scarcity and make better use of existing water endowments. At the same time, water harvesting projects, conservation initiatives and supply and demand management practices have conjointly been put in place to increase the reach and scope of the grid, and the benefits it can bring to the population.

On the supply side, the grid includes reservoir construction; the conjunctive use and conservation of groundwater; re-use and recycling of wastewater; the construction of check dams and pond deepening with the Sardar Patel Participatory Water Conservation Scheme; and building and augmenting infrastructure to make bulk water transfers from surplus to deficit areas. On the demand side, initiatives include community-based, participatory irrigation management projects; prevention of salinity ingress; and the protection of arable lands from erosion and floods.

The grid includes 387 projects making inter-basin water transfers from areas with surplus surface water to water-scarce and quality-affected areas. It includes works based on the Sardar Sarovar Canal, the Sujalam Sufalam Yojana initiative for river inter-linkages and some 179 Rural Regional Water Supply Schemes. In its entirety, the grid aims at connecting 75% of Gujarat's population, approximately 47 million people, to safe and potable water sources. Some of the benefited 15,009 villages and 145 towns are tail-enders, 700 km away from the command area (Gupta, 2004; GWSSB inaugurated technical support unit, 2013).

To reach the most scorched regions of Saurashtra, Kachchh, and Central and North Gujarat, 51 bulk pipeline projects oversee the construction of 3250 km of bulk water transmission mains. By April 2013, 2654 km had already been built and 37 projects completed. These mains have connected 72.65% of the households in Central and North Gujarat, 82.88% in Saurashtra, 96% in Kachchh and 35.57% in South Gujarat to the State-Wide Water Supply Grid (Singh, 2013). Additionally, 2654 km of bulk water transmission pipelines, 156 water filtration and treatment plants, 120,769 km of distribution networks, 11,640 elevated service reservoirs and 11,365 underground reservoirs have been completed. Responsible for storing up to 3.86 billion litres of water, treating 2.81 billion litres and ultimately supplying almost 3 billion litres per day, these works have been at the technical forefront of the state's efforts to enhance water security (Gujarat Water Supply and Sewerage Board, 2013a, 2013b). By May 2013, 25.6 million people in 11,235 villages and more than 13.4 million urban dwellers in 131 towns were already part of the grid, totalling 39 million beneficiaries (see Table 3).

In 1990–91, Gujarat's ninth five year plan incorporated the government's decision to use water from the Narmada River to supply drinking water to Kachchh, North Gujarat, Saurashtra and Panchmahals (Planning Commission, 1990). The Drinking Water Supply Master Plan, based on the Narmada Main Canal, allocates 0.86 million acre-feet (1060 million cubic meters) of water to meet domestic consumption in 131 urban centres and 9633 villages (Sardar Sarovar Narmada Nigam Ltd, 2013b). The Narmada Main Canal has come to be known as the lifeline of Gujarat. At 458 km, it is the longest irrigation canal in the world. It was designed to transport more than 11.5 km^3 every year (Bunsha, 2006). The system includes 634 structures: 289 for communication, 114 for water control, and 231 for drainage (Sardar Sarovar Narmada Nigam Ltd, 2013a).

The aggregate length of the grid's entire distribution system is estimated to be 120,769 km. On its own, the canal network of the Sardar Sarovar Canal–based Water Supply Project, the grid's main component, will be 75,000 km long. Construction of the branch canals, distributaries, minors and sub-minors is still underway; the Narmada Main Canal was completed in 2008. As of December 2012, progress had made in over a quarter of all envisioned works: 30 out of the 38 branch canals had been built; 2233 km of tributaries finalized (44%); 32% of the 18,413 km of scheduled minors installed; and 21% of the 48,058 km of sub-minors constructed. It is expected that the entire Narmada Canal distribution system will be completed in 2014–2015 (Sardar Sarovar Narmada Nigam Ltd, 2012).

Largely thanks to the Narmada-based component of the grid, natural water endowments are no longer conditioning people's access to water in the arid regions of Kachchh and Saurashtra. Off-taking at km 385.814 of the Narmada Main Canal, the Kachchh Branch Canal runs for 360 km to secure water for these severely water-stressed regions. Through this connection, 801 villages and 8 cities in that district were receiving an average of 220 million litres per day (MLD) as of May 2013. The Maliya station also supplies 360 million litres daily to 1045 villages and 23 towns in the districts of Rajkot, Jamnagar and Probandar. Management practices can still be considerably improved to minimize losses, but the increases in water availability already represent a pivotal development for these regions.

In July 2008, people in Kachchh had to make do with 44 litres of water a day. By April 2013, the amount of water delivered had tripled, to 122 litres per capita per day. Furthermore, it is expected that upgrading works in 36 pumping stations will secure additional water supplies to Saurashtra and Kachchh. The capacity of the pumping stations at the head works in Navda was enlarged from 350 MLD to 440 MLD in August 2012.

Table 3. State-Wide Water Supply Grid, scheme progress.

	Planned schemes and foreseen coverage				
	No. of bulk pipeline projects	Length (km)	Distribution systems	Villages covered	Towns covered
Sardar Sarovar/Narmada Canal	51	3,250	123	9,633	131
Rural Regional Water Supply Schemes	–	–	198	5376	14
Total	51	3,250	321	15,009	145

	Completed schemes				
	No. of bulk pipeline projects	Length (km)	Distribution systems	Villages covered	Towns covered
Sardar Sarovar/Narmada Canal	37	2,654	85	7,455	118
Rural Regional Water Supply Schemes	–	–	181	3,852	14
Total	37	2,654	266	11,307	132

	Progress		
	Schemes	Villages	Towns
Sardar Sarovar/Narmada Canal	28	1,763	7
Rural Regional Water Supply Schemes	21	738	0
Total	49	2,501	7

Source: Sardar Sarovar Narmada Nigam Ltd (2013a, 2013b).

In April 2013, an even larger pumping station was habilitated and began supplying 600 MLD, of which 170 ML is transferred to 2325 villages and 38 towns in Bhavnagar, Rajkot, Junagadh and Porbandar. At these head works, 19 pumps operate at an average capacity of 26,526 m^3/h. In addition, investments of INR 1.7 billion are planned to strengthen and enhance water facilities in Saurashtra and Kachchh. A new parallel bulk pipeline has been envisioned to cover the segments of Chavand−Porbandar, Budhel−Kadiyali, Navda− Gadhada−Chavand, Amreli−Visavadar and Chavand−Amreli (Gujarat Water Supply and Sewerage Board, 2013a, 2013b).

Even with the reassurance Kachchh has obtained from having been connected to the grid, local sources have dried up to such an extent and water become so limited that emergency measures have had to be put in place. This year alone, 130 villages and 30 habitations (groups of families living close together) were included as part of a contingent master plan to drill 72 tubewells and deploy 48 tankers. As of May 2013, 59 bore wells had already been drilled and water supplied by tanker to 12 villages and 28 habitations. It ought to be mentioned that this still-challenging situation is already an improvement over the critical scenario faced in 2001−2002, when 298 villages in Kachchh had to be supplied by tankers (Gujarat Water Supply and Sewerage Board, 2013a, 2013b).

The hard engineering works behind the Narmada Canal and the overall grid have helped mitigate water scarcity in dry areas across Gujarat and are responsible for supplying half of the 3000 MLD that flow across the state's drinking-water taps. However, infrastructure alone cannot deal with the communities' pressing water needs. Local utility offices are being created in the municipalities encountering the most acute difficulties and where branches of the water supply board have not been yet established. Since February 2013, a new zone technical unit is operating in Saurashtra and Kachchh and in the districts of Porbandar, Junagadh, Amreli and Bhavnagar. This office has been specially staffed with technicians and engineers from the GWSSB to address the water-scarcity challenges that emerge in these regions during summer (Sandesh, 2013).

Particularly in the hot summer months, or at times of delayed or insufficient monsoon rains and prolonged periods of drought, farmers resort to drawing water directly from the main and branch canals. When such illegal activities are widely carried out, they can compromise the service delivered to villages at the tail of the pipeline. The taps are there, but drinking water fails to flow as a large number of pumping sets are sunk into the Narmada Canal, air valves tampered with, pipelines broken and water extensively drawn out. Damaged infrastructure jeopardizes, on the one hand, drinking-water security and safety, and on the other, the delivery system farmers themselves rely on for their livelihoods. Moreover, the limited water resources available in the state call for use prioritization (awarding utter importance to drinking water) and improved management practices. In this manner, economic and environmental activities can improve as progress is achieved in human development.

Starting in 2013, 32 teams have been deployed all across Gujarat to obtain first-hand information on the status of the pipelines, cross-check water accounting recordings and identify the sources of intended and unintended nonrevenue water. These groups patrol the pipelines and canals and protect the engineering works that deliver water to the most water-scarce areas in the state. Each of the teams in this task force is constituted by two members from the GWSSB, one officer from Gujarat Water Infrastructure Limited, one representative from the local office and three policemen. In addition, institutional efforts are being put into obtaining real-time information on the ground situation and gathering feedback on how to regularize and strengthen the management of the canal and the water distribution network.

Tapping the benefits

Water is a prerequisite for a minimum standard of health and the sustaining of productive activities. It is also a multifaceted social, cultural, economic, religious and political resource that facilitates or leads to the creation of a range of capabilities that condition an individual's ability to function and interact with his or her environment. This sheds light on the potential role water has not only as an important development indicator but also as a key driver of human development and a medium to create human capabilities.

Unfortunately, in places where water security cannot be assured, resource management often conditions the overall status of human health, education, and social and economic activities. It also influences the standing of certain demographic and gender groups and the state of the environment. This in turn restricts access to opportunities and their realization, compromising development at the individual, household, community and macro levels. In contrast, running water within the household premises is often a prerequisite for a better quality of life; it can open up social, educational and employment opportunities for men and women, improve health, and enhance incomes. In Gujarat, the role water can play as a development engine has now been acknowledged, and it is informing policy choices.

From 2001 to 2012, the government invested financial, physical and human resources worth INR 115.93 billion towards balancing water demand and supply. In present value, this amount is more than thrice that of the INR 34.65 billion spent the previous decade, from 1991 to 2000, and four and half times the INR 25.75 billion allocated for water throughout the 1980s (Narmada, Water Resources and Water Supply Department, 2013). The priority Gujarat has given to its water-supply sector has also surpassed allocations at the national level for drinking water and sewerage development in percentage terms. Between 2002–03 and 2011–12, state investments in the water sector represented 4.96% of the total budget, 2.7 times the 1.86% allocation made at the national level (Gujarat Water Supply and Sewerage Board, 2013b).

The creation of the State-Wide Water Supply Grid highlights the potential linkages between improved, timely and reliable access to water, in terms of quality and quantity, and poverty alleviation, overall socio-economic development and enhanced quality of life. This work constitutes an important departure from some of the traditional approaches that have limited water access to only certain selected urban centres. In that regard, the implementation of the Narmada Canal-Based Water Supply Project and the continuous execution of Rural Regional Water Supply Schemes have made relevant progress. The grid has mostly aimed at reaching many remote and far-flung rural communities, mainly benefiting villagers and people outside major urban centres. The GWSSB estimates that out of the more than 39 million inhabitants covered by this initiative as of March 2013, 26 million reside in rural areas, whilst the remaining 17.7 million are urban dwellers (Figure 1).

The availability of water has positively impacted on many aspects of individual, household and community well-being in a large number of villages and towns in Gujarat. This process has taken place thanks to improved public policies and institutions. A prosperous region and society can thus not afford to overlook the mutually reinforcing links connecting poverty and access to water. It has been estimated that every INR 55 (1 USD) spent in the water sector brings about productivity gains and health cost reductions averaging INR 440 (8 USD) (United Nations Development Programme (UNDP), 2006). Regarding the agricultural sector, the Narmada Canal has created positive externalities and productivity multipliers, as discussed by Kumar, Jagadeesan, and Sivamohan (2014) in this issue.

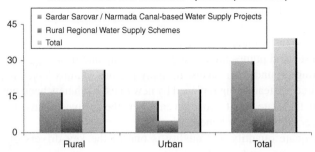

Figure 1. Addressing rural–urban divides in access to drinking water. Source: GWSSB records. Elaborated by the author.

An initial way of assessing the compounded effect that Gujarat's socioeconomic transformation has had over the last decades, and most particularly from 2001, onwards is partially reflected in the United Nations Human Development Index (HDI). According to India's Human Development Report (HDR), Gujarat has made consistent improvements in this measure (Planning Commission, 2001). In 1991, the HDI was 0.431 (Kumar, 1991); 10 years later it was 0.479 (Hirway & Mahadevia, 2004). By 2007–08, this index had seen a dramatic rise of 0.048, reaching 0.527 (Joshi, 2009). Two years later, in 2009–10, the index had increased to 0.688 (Debroy, 2013; Ministry of Finance, 2011–2012).

These gradual HDI improvements capture reductions in school absenteeism, the inclusion of women in remunerated economic activities, and improvements in health, especially in rural areas. There, the developmental gains from investments in drinking-water supply have opened up a wide array of opportunities to dwellers and contributed to general family welfare. Back in 2002, only 22% of the state's households had water connections. By 2010, domestic taps were available in 58.67% of households, and merely a year after, the coverage had reached 69%. Already at the beginning of 2013, this figure had jumped to 76.73%, more than double the national level of 34%.

In terms of basic household amenities, India's 2011 HDR shows the state performing slightly better than the 91% national average, with at least 93% of the households having access to an improved source of drinking water (Planning Commission, 2011). In urban areas, 95.6% of households had access to an improved source of drinking water by 2008–09, a benefit also extending to 91.4% of rural households. In Gujarat, 69% of the households receive tap water, 11.6% obtain their water through a hand pump, 9.6% from a tubewell, 7.1% from a well and the remaining 2.6% from springs, rivers, canals, tanks, ponds, lakes or other sources.

Varying local conditions call for locally feasible alternatives. In the tribal and hilly areas, where the population is scattered in small hamlets across vast areas, tailored solutions have many times been proposed by the communities themselves. These arrangements have varied from tapping spring water (when that source has been available) to developing gravity-based systems that operate without electricity, modifying standard pumps to suit local conditions, installing solar water pumps and hand pumps, building cluster storage systems and operating some 7527 mini pipe schemes.

During the 1980s, 38,426 hand pumps were installed, and 71,465 more during the following 10 years. From 2001 to 2012, more than 100,310 such devices were set up, almost as many as those installed in the previous two decades together. As a result of these efforts, 42.55% of households in the tribal areas now have connections (Gujarat Water Supply and Sewerage Board, 2013a, 2013b). Nationally, there is one hand pump for every 250–300 inhabitants. In Gujarat, there are currently 152,036 hand pumps in the tribal belt alone, each one serving around 41 persons (James, 2011). However, it is to be assessed how many of these hand pumps are actually functioning and how the installation of these devices is affecting groundwater levels. In many regions, pumps have broken down and been left unrepaired, instead being replaced by new ones. Each new hand pump adds to the maintenance bill the state has to foot, even when these investments do have positive development externalities in the benefited areas.

Water in adequate quantity and quality is one of the key drivers of public health. Improved water sources and water in adequate quantity generate important synergies in human development outcomes and outputs. Though water quality significantly deteriorated in 2000 and again in 2002–03, the Gujarat Jalseva Training Institute recorded a decrease in the number of villages facing problems due to excessive fluoride in 2011–12 (GJTI, 2013). The affected habitations totalled 1226, less than one-third of the 4341 dealing with these issues 10 years before; and 1215 settlements registered high levels of nitrate, compared to 1336 in 2000. Over the last decade, all these previously affected habitations and villages have been supplied with alternate and safe sources, as a result of which the health situation has improved substantially. The town of Ganeshpura, for example, recorded a fluoride concentration of 3.35 mg/L in February 1997, and when tested again in December 2010 this had fallen to 1.0 mg/L (Sim & Leong, 2011).

Water from the Narmada is good in quality and does not show any significant signs of bacteriological or chemical contamination. Since industrial development in the Narmada basin has been less intensive than in other major basins, the river faces fewer pollution problems even when discharge of untreated sewage is bound to degrade water quality (Banerjee, 2007). This suggests that areas incorporated into the grid and relying on water from this surface source are less likely to experience previously faced health problems due to high nitrate and fluoride concentrations. Moreover, water flowing from the Narmada River is considerably lower in total dissolved solids and salinity than most of the local groundwater sources upon which many villages and urban centres entirely relied before. In many Rural Regional Water Supply Schemes, water from local sources is blended with Narmada water to comply with drinking-water quality standards (Sharma, Dixit, Jain, Shah, & Vishwakarma, 2008, 2011). Key industrial players in the state have also acknowledged the good quality of water coming from the river. Industrial plants are able to use it without having to undertake major treatment processes (Adani Group, personal communication, 8 May 2013).

To reinforce and further all the progress already attained, the GWSSB has developed 156 filtration and treatment plants, with an aggregate daily capacity of 2.810 billion litres. This way, water is made potable at the distribution point in 10,937 villages. These plants use a series of effective technologies to tackle various quality problems, for example, filtration, sedimentation, reverse osmosis, aeration, chlorination, etc. Furthermore, when quality problems are too severe or are identified in very remote areas, reverse-osmosis plants are built as a last resort. The existing 278 facilities award priority attention to coastal and tribal areas and are for the community to build, own, operate and transfer (BOOT). With time, it is expected that local populations will develop the capacities to take full responsibility for the operation of the reverse-osmosis plants installed in their communities. Thanks to all these measures, households have reported ample health gains from enhanced access to safe water and the adoption of simple practices (for instance, chlorination) to assure that water is fit to drink (WASMO, 2013).

With 76.16% of villages chlorinating their water sources, common ailments have become less prevalent, especially amongst infants and children, who are usually the worst affected by outbreaks of water-borne diseases. Since the grid's first pipe was laid, the death rate by infectious and parasitic diseases in Gujarat has gradually dropped, from 17.3% in 2002 to 14.91% in 2011. In 2005, 470,675 cases of diarrhoea resulted in 15 deaths. By 2011, the number of cases had fallen to 367,450 and no deaths were reported (Commissioner of Health, Medical Services and Medical Education, 2013). At present, 12,030 ultraviolet plants and 550 reverse-osmosis installations are operating in schools around the state. By 2007–2009 more than 87% of schools in the state had drinking-water facilities (WASMO, 2013).

Healthier people incur lower medical costs; they also avoid the associated expenses of seeking treatment, buying drugs and commuting to the health care facilities, and the forgone time spent being ill and receiving care (Jain, 1996). Healthier children miss fewer days at school, contributing to the overall educational attainment Gujarat has seen in the last decade. Similarly, healthier adults do not interrupt their engagement in productive activities carried out in the household as well as in the formal and informal employment sectors. Even in the absence of detailed studies quantifying the impact of improved access to water on health and income in the state, it can be confidently stated that with such progress, household incomes have become less vulnerable to health shocks.

As taps reach Gujarat's villages and distribution works expand to reach their many households, the burden of fetching water and attending to rudimentary sanitation is greatly alleviated from women and girls (World Health Organisation, United Nations Children's Fund, 2010). In predominantly agrarian and pastoral communities, women and young girls sometimes have to walk up to 8 km and spend up to 3 hours everyday collecting water (Jhabvala & Bali, 1991; Vyas & Gupta, 2001). Access to water is thus a springboard to foster their development, education, health, income opportunities, empowerment and overall societal standing. Equally important, the institutionalized participation of women in community-level water management bodies, (*pani samitis*) has helped overcome the social barriers restricting their involvement in public and decision-making activities.

The long distances separating households from water sources also affect the time the female groups of a society have at their disposal to undertake any other activity and condition the volume of water they are able to secure on a given day. In Kachchh, Surendranagar and many of the tribal areas, this time frame may be considerably extended especially during the summer season, as local sources dry up and water has to be fetched from alternative and more distant places. In 2004, before the Narmada scheme had reached many areas in the state, women in the 'no water source' villages of Chodungri, Marvada and Gonguvada in North Gujarat sometimes had to walk more than 1 km to fetch water to fulfil domestic needs, an endeavour that occupied 3 to 4 hours every day (Upadhyay, 2004).

For girls, school attendance rates are highly sensitive to water availability and distance to water sources. With water available closer to every household and at an increasing number of schools, girls and boys face fewer impediments to attending school. In 1999–2000, the drop-out rate in elementary school (from I to V standard) in Gujarat stood at 20.83% for girls, 23.77% for boys and 22.3% in total. A decade later, census figures showed a considerable improvement in the completion of primary education. In 2010–11, the dropout rate was 2.11% for girls and 2.08% for boys. In 2001, 79.66% of males and 57.8% of females were literate, and the overall rate was recorded as 69.97%. Ten years later, the aggregate effect of macroeconomic growth in the state and the improvement of local conditions in its many villages has already had an encouraging impact on education and in narrowing the gender gap in school attendance and academic attainment. In 2011, 85.38% of men and 66.77% of women were literate, and total literacy reached 79.31% (Directorate of Economics and Statistics, 2012, 2013).

However, even with encouraging progress in educational attainment, women's participation in community activities is still limited by cultural barriers, traditionally lower literacy rates and the workload they are responsible for in both remunerated activities and domestic chores. Any constraints to their participation in community-based water management systems will compromise real representation, equity, effectiveness and affordability. Local bodies for water resources management have made targeted efforts to institutionalize the active involvement of women in decision-making and administrative activities. As of May 2013, more than 72,000 women have become pani samiti members, and they head these local bodies in 879 villages (WASMO, 2013).

The blue policy paths ahead

Water has come to mean one thing to Gujarat: a path to prosperity. It has become very important in maintaining and further enhancing the state's transformation. Its absence, on the other hand, has been equated with struggle, poverty, hardship, distress, and delays in socio-economic development. For decades, economic and industrial development in certain areas in Gujarat was severely constrained by insufficient water resources (Vyas & Gupta, 2001). Following a significant change in public policy, the state has now begun to capitalize on the large water-related investments that have been made in poorly endowed regions. It has also began to build upon the more generalized progress in poverty alleviation that has followed the surge of wide-spread availability of drinking water in the state.

In the past, notwithstanding the severity and frequency of water quantity and quality issues affecting Gujarat, policy measures remained mostly ad hoc, remedial, and oriented towards crisis management. Not even when naval vessels had to be ordered to ship 8 million litres of drinking water from Mumbai to Gujarat in 2000 were longer-term policies envisioned. At times of drought, local sources went dry, water extraction intensified, and tankers, trains and ships were dispatched to distribute water until the situation improved. As people migrated, quarrelled and struggled to protect their livelihoods, many communities dispersed and disintegrated. At the same time, deterioration of groundwater sources became a growing concern, but it was awarded little priority. Water security received negligible resources and attention and remained a side issue in the political agenda (Hirway, 2005; Hirway & Mahadevia, 2004)

In 2002, the government started to move away from the previous piecemeal and ad hoc policies and began to shape a resilient, durable and comprehensive approach to water management. Since then, large investment commitments in physical, social and managerial infrastructure have been poured into extending the network of the State-Wide Water Supply Grid, implementing the Sujalam Suphalam Project and supporting 450 regional schemes. These initiatives have now reached almost all water-stressed and water-quality-compromised habitations in both rural and urban areas. As sufficient and higher-quality drinking water is been made available throughout the year, especially in the critical summer months, health and hygiene conditions continue to improve, lagging regions catch up in terms of socio-economic development, and communities are brought together under, *pani samitis* to actively manage their water assets and requirements.

To realize the potential development spill-overs and externalities this project can bring to the state and its people, water authorities will have to strengthen their efforts beyond infrastructure creation and augmentation. The challenge ahead is to mobilize the physical, financial, human and social capital required to keep the grid's vast infrastructural network running efficiently. Beyond operation and maintenance needs, keeping Gujarat's water secure also calls for renewing and expanding partnerships with stakeholders that can support the government's efforts to continuously improve the water sector, strengthen data-collection systems, and take the necessary legislative steps to protect the existing structures from damage and unlawful use of the water they carry.

With time, the implementation of a sector-wide strategy will, make momentous strides to ward water security, improve the quantity and quality of water-supply services, extend water provision to uncovered habitations, strengthen and recharge local resources, and eventually deliver water-supply services 24/7. The construction of the State-Wide Water Supply Grid, however, represents a decisive step towards ensuring "sustainable water supply and sanitation services in the rural and urban areas to accomplish basic health and reach the hygiene levels leading to socio-economic development, peace and happiness in the society" (GWSSB inaugurated technical support unit, 2013).

Acknowledgements

The author gratefully acknowledges the organizational and personal support of Dr Rajiv K. Gupta, Principal Secretary and Chairman of Gujarat Water Supply & Sewerage Board, in the preparation of this paper.

References

Banerjee, R. (2007). Review of water governance in the Narmada River basin. Water Governance Project, Background Papers. New Delhi.

Bunsha, D. (2006). Heights of intolerance. 23/11 Frontline 108.

Commissioner of Health, Medical Services and Medical Education. (2013). Registration of births and deaths act. Government of Gujarat (GoG). Retrieved from http://www.gujhealth.gov.in/vs-publications.htm

Dass, A. (2006). *Building upon the adaptive capacity to livelihood resilience in arid, semi arid and flood prone regions*. New Delhi: Winrock International India.

Debroy, B. (2013, August 6). Gujarat's data on social indicators shows positive impact of policies. Retrieved from http://blogs.economictimes.indiatimes.com/policypuzzles/entry/gujarat-s-data-on-social-indicators-shows-positive-impact-of-policies

Directorate of Economics and Statistics. (2012). Socio-economic review 2011–2012. Government of Gujarat, Gandhinagar.

Directorate of Economics and Statistics. (2013). Directorate of economics and statistics. Socio-economic Review 2012–2013. Government of Gujarat, Gandhinagar.

Gujarat Water Supply & Sewerage Board. (2003). Sardar Sarovar Canal Based Drinking Water Supply Master Plan. Water Supply Department, Government of Gujarat, Gandhinagar.

Gujarat Water Supply and Sewerage Board. (2013a). GWSSB, Government of Gujarat, Gandhinagar.

Gujarat Water Supply and Sewerage Board. (2013b). Background note for plan discussion, annual plan 2013–2014. Water Supply Department, Government of Gujarat, Gandhinagar.

Gupta, R. K. (2001). Human rights dimension of regional water transfer: Experience of the Sardar Sarovar project. *International Journal of Water Resources Development, 17*, 125–147.

Gupta, R. K. (2004). Water governance in Gujarat state, India. *International Journal of Water Resources Development, 20*, 131–147.

Gurajat Jalseva Training Institute (GJTI). (2013). Gujarat Water Supply & Sewerage Board, Government of Gujarat, Gandhingar.

Hirway, I. (2005). Ensuring drinking water to all: A study in Gujarat. *4th IWMI-TATA annual partners research meeting*. Anand: Institute of Rural Management.

Hirway, I., & Mahadevia, D. (2004). *Gujarat human development report*. Ahmedabad: Mahatma Gandhi Labour Institute.

Jain, D. (1996). Valuing work: Time as a measure. *Economic and Political Weekly, 31*, 46–57.

James, A. J. (2011). *India: Lessons for rural water supply; assessing progress towards sustainable service delivery*. The Hague: IRC International Water and Sanitation Centre and Delhi.

Jhabvala, R., & Bali, N. (1991). *My family my work - a sociological study of SEWA's urban members*. Ahmedabad: SEWA Academy.

Joshi, M. B. (2009). Water for "GDP" or "HDI"?. The golden dilemma for Gujarat. Columbia Water Centre (CWC). Seminar on Water for Future - Issues & options.

Kumar, A. S. (1991). UNDP's human development index: A computation for Indian states. *Economic and Political Weekly, 26*, 2343–2345.

Kumar, D. M., & Singh, O. P. (2001). Market instruments for demand management in the face of scarcity and overuse of water in Gujarat, Western India. *Water Policy, 3*, 387–403.

Kumar, D. M., Jagadeesan, S., & Sivamohan, M. V. K. (2014). Positive externalities of irrigation from Sardar Sarovar project on farming enterprise and domestic water supplies. *International Journal of Water Resources Development, 30*, 91–109, doi: 10.1080/07900627.2014.880228.

Ministry of Finance. (2011–12). Economic survey. *Union Budget & Economic Survey*. Government of India (GoI). Retrieved from http://indiabudget.nic.in/survey.asp

Narmada, Water Resources, Water Supply and Kalpasar Department (2013). Unpublished documents. Gandhinagar: Government of Gujarat.

Parul, C. (2006). Drought risk assessment using remote sensing and GIS: A case study of Gujarat (ME thesis). Indian Institute of Remote Sensing, Dehradun & International Institute for Geo-information & Earth Observation, The Netherlands.

Patel, P. P. (1997). *Ecoregions of Gujarat*. Vadodara: Gujarat Ecology Commission.

Planning Commission. (1990). 9th five year plan. Government of Gujarat, Gandhinagar.

Planning Commission. (2001). *National human development report, India*. Government of India.

Planning Commission. (2011). *National human development report, India*. Government of India.

Sandesh (2013, February 17). GWSSB inaugurated technical support unit to address summer water scarcity problems. Gujarat: Rajkot City.

Sardar Sarovar Narmada Nigam Ltd. (2012). The Sardar Sarovar project. Retrieved from http://www.sardarsarovardam.org/Client/ContentPage.aspx

Sardar Sarovar Narmada Nigam Ltd. (2013a). Components of the projects: Features of Narmada. *Main Canal*. Retrieved from http://www.sardarsarovardam.org/Client/ContentPage.aspx

Sardar Sarovar Narmada Nigam Ltd. (2013b). Narmada - the lifeline of Gujarat, project at a glance. Retrieved from http://www.sardarsarovardam.org/Client/Index.aspx

Sharma, S., Dixit, S., Jain, P., Shah, K. W., & Vishwakarma, R. (2008). Statistical evaluation of hydrobiological parameters of Narmada River water at Hoshangabad city, India. *Environmental Monitoring and Assessment, 143*, 195–202.

Sharma, S., Dixit, S., Jain, P., Shah, K. W., & Vishwakarma, R. (2011). Evaluation of water quality of Narmada river with reference to physico-chemical parameters at Hoshangabad city, MP, India. *Evaluation, 1*, 40–48.

Sim, J. M., & Leong, K. M. (2011). Feasibility study on fluoride removal in drinking water in Mehsana, India. *International NGO Journal, 6*, 224–228.

Singh, M. (2013). Statewide drinking Water Supply Grid: An efficient water management. Water Supply Department Government of Gujarat. Gujarat Water Supply & Sewerage Board. Presentation for India's Water Week, 2013, Delhi.

United Nations Development Programme (UNDP). (2006). *Human development report: Beyond scarcity: Power, poverty and the global water crisis*. New York, NY: UNDP.

Upadhyay, B. (2004). *Gender roles and multiple uses of water in North Gujarat* Working paper 70. Colombo: International Water Management Institute.

Vyas, J. N., & Gupta, R. K. (2001). Editorial. *International Journal of Water Resources Development, 17*, 5–8.

World Health Organisation, United Nations Children's Fund. (2010). *Progress on sanitation and drinking-water, 2010 update*. Geneva: World Health Organization.

Positive externalities of irrigation from the Sardar Sarovar Project for farm production and domestic water supply

M. Dinesh Kumar[a], S. Jagadeesan[b] and M.V.K. Sivamohan[a]

[a]Institute for Resource Analysis and Policy, Hyderabad, India; [b]Sardar Sarovar Narmada Nigam Ltd, Gujarat, India

A detailed study was conducted in six districts of Gujarat, India, in gravity- and lift-irrigated commands of the Sardar Sarovar Project to assess the direct and indirect benefits of canal irrigation. Benefits such as savings in the cost of energy used to pump groundwater for irrigation, reduction in well failures, and increased income of well irrigators from farming (crops and dairy) were remarkable. Groundwater augmented by recharge from gravity irrigation resulted in large economic returns to the well irrigators in the command areas and reduced the cost of domestic water supply in villages and towns (through improved yield of agro-wells and drinking-water wells, respectively). Canal irrigation also raised wages for workers, through enhanced agricultural labour demand along with appreciation of land markets.

Introduction

Large irrigation projects are targets of increased criticism worldwide for the negative social and environmental impacts they are likely to cause. As noted by Biswas and Tortajada (2001), Shah and Kumar (2008) and Verghese (2001), critiques argue that the costs outweigh the intended benefits. However, it is also argued that developing countries have no choice but to build large storages (Biswas, 1994; Biswas & Tortajada, 2001; Kumar, Shah, Mukherjee, & Mudgerikar, 2008). The issue is how best to improve their overall effectiveness for human welfare, poverty eradication and preservation of the environment and how to make beneficiaries of those who pay the costs of the construction of such large structures. The Sardar Sarovar Project (SSP), constructed on the Narmada River, is one of the most controversial water development projects in independent India (Shah & Kumar, 2008; Verghese, 2001) and no stranger to these critiques.

The SSP is expected to irrigate nearly 1.8 million ha of agricultural land in the state of Gujarat through a network of canals comprising a main canal, branch canals, distributaries, minors and watercourses, with a total length of 75,000 km. The entire canal system is designed for gravity irrigation and is already irrigating nearly 0.62 million ha of land (Alagh, 2010). The state-wide water grid, with the Sardar Sarovar Canal–based Drinking Water Supply Project as its core, is expected to bring developmental benefits to around 47 million people in the state once it is completed (Biswas-Tortajada, 2014).

Till recently, the available analyses of the performance of the SSP (Parasuraman, Upadhyaya, & Balasubramanian, 2010; Shah, Gulati, Hemant, Shreedhar, & Jain, 2009; Talati & Shah, 2004) have been based on narrow objectives with ideological overtones and have not considered indirect benefits. For instance, gravity irrigation produces several positive externalities for local groundwater regimes (Chakravorty & Umetsu, 2003; Shah & Kumar, 2008; Watt, 2008) through changes in water availability in wells in the command area for irrigation, for the availability and quality of groundwater for drinking and domestic uses, and for water-table conditions. These changes are effected through groundwater recharge from irrigation return flows and canal seepage (Shah & Kumar, 2008; Watt, 2008). However, the 2012 analysis of the socio-economic impacts of the SSP carried out by the Institute for Resource Analysis and Policy (IRAP) did take into account these indirect benefits (IRAP, 2012).

Groundwater recharge can improve the yield of agro-wells and increase the area irrigated. At the same time, rising water tables can reduce energy consumption for groundwater pumping and reduce the incidence of well failures (IRAP, 2012; Ranade & Kumar, 2004; Shah & Kumar, 2008). These two effects have positive implications for the economics of irrigated agriculture. Return flows from canal-irrigated fields and canal seepage can sometimes generate greater economic value than would otherwise be generated if the water were used directly for irrigation (Chakravorty & Umetsu, 2003).

The recharge from canal seepage and irrigation return flows can often reduce salinity and the concentration of minerals like fluorides in native groundwater, which causes serious health hazards (Ranade & Kumar, 2004). Continuous recharge from canals and irrigated fields can ensure good yields of drinking-water sources, whose sustainability is threatened by aquifer depletion from over-pumping. Improvements in groundwater quality can have positive impacts on drinking water in areas where poor-quality groundwater is used to meet domestic water demand. Moreover, higher well yields can improve the drinking-water situation in areas that rely on hard-rock aquifers.

As a matter of fact, India depends heavily on groundwater to meet drinking-water demands: 50% of urban and 80% of rural water supply requirements are met from this resource. This includes areas with groundwater quality problems (Kumar, 2007). As a result, the indirect impacts can extend far beyond the agricultural sector.

While some of these externalities add to private benefits, some of them reduce public costs. For instance, reduced well failures and improved well yields bring down the production costs incurred by farmers, thereby raising the net private gain from irrigated crop production. Even when reduced energy consumption for groundwater pumping reduces, to an extent, overall economic costs, it does not necessarily affect the private costs for the farmers, because they do not incur the marginal cost of electricity for pumping groundwater under the present subsidy regime.

Similarly, in the case of drinking water, improved performance of water supply sources reduces the public cost of providing this service. In addition, irrigated agriculture produces its own positive externalities by increasing the demand for labour, thereby raising wages in the farm and non-farm sectors (Narayanamoorthy & Deshpande, 2003). Malik (2006), using a study of the Bhakra project in Punjab, showed that large water projects could generate significant indirect downstream effects, with a multiplier value of 1.9. These indirect benefits are systematically and empirically analyzed in this article through a study of the SSP command in Gujarat in western India. The study examined the externalities of canal irrigation in terms of: 1) savings in the cost of well deepening in the command area; 2) savings in the energy cost of groundwater irrigation; 3) incremental economic surplus of well irrigators from crop and dairy production; 4) increase in wages for agricultural labourers; 5) reduction in the cost of domestic water supplies in command-area villages and towns; and 6) increase in land prices. The findings help to characterize the positive externalities of canal irrigation for well irrigation and drinking-water supplies.

Study location, methods and data

This article presents the findings of a study carried out in six districts of Gujarat receiving surface irrigation from the SSP, either directly through gravity or through water-lifting from the irrigation canal. Ahmedabad and Mehsana receive water from the main system, and Bharuch, Narmada, Vadodara and Panchmahals receive water from gravity canals. The study was based on the collection of primary data from well irrigators in the command area of the gravity-irrigation system and well irrigators in the area receiving water from the main system through lifting. Data on the drinking-water situation were also collected from villagers in the command area and secondary data gathered on water-level fluctuations in observation wells in the command area for two time periods.

The collected primary data include information for before and after water supply from the Narmada Canal (also called the Sardar Sarovar Canal) regarding water levels, yields and well-deepening incidence in the command area, as well as water levels, yields and well failure incidence in villages under canal commands. They also include input and output data for farming enterprises (both crops and livestock), namely the area under different irrigated crops, livestock composition and size, and the quantum and cost of various crop and livestock inputs and outputs.

Social benefits from Narmada Canal irrigation

Changes in groundwater availability and water-level fluctuations in the region

Data from Sardar Sarovar Narmada Nigam Ltd (SSNNL) on static water levels and observation wells spread across the SSP command area for 1996–1998 (pre-Narmada) and 2004–2009 (post-Narmada) were analyzed. The results showed a marked improvement in groundwater levels in the command area after the introduction of Narmada Canal water. By and large, static water levels in all districts except Kheda not only showed an upwards trend but were higher than pre-Narmada levels. Unlike what is generally observed in surface-irrigation commands, in the SSP command area, the conjunctive use of surface and ground water extensively increased the ground water levels.

The rise in water levels has helped farmers in the command area with respect to energy required per unit of groundwater pumped and the cost of deepening wells, thereby resulting in increased irrigation potential (IRAP, 2012).

Positive externalities of Narmada irrigation

Energy-saving benefits for well irrigators in the command area

Surveyed sample wells in the command area show that, on average, after water from the Narmada project was supplied to those areas in 2002, there was a significant and consistent rise in water levels across seasons in all six districts (Figure 1. This change might have occurred due to 1) decreased groundwater draft, resulting from reduced dependence on wells, and 2) groundwater recharge from return flows of gravity irrigation using canal water. In addition, the high rainfall received in most of these areas between 2001 and 2006 might have influenced water-level trends, though the effect of rainfall would be much lower than that of imported surface water for gravity irrigation.

However, groundwater use in the tribal area of south Gujarat actually increased over time. More and more farmers belonging to the scheduled caste and scheduled tribes started investing in wells, under government schemes, in areas not receiving canal water from the Narmada. This might have influenced the groundwater table in the region, and is probably

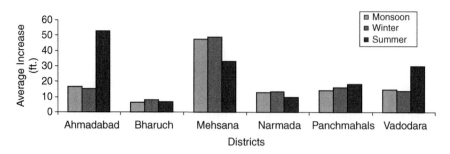

Figure 1.   Change in water levels after Narmada.

the reason for the weaker rise in water levels in command areas in the south Gujarat districts of Bharuch, Panchmahals and Narmada as compared to north Gujarat districts.

Every metre of reduction in pumping depth reduces the energy needed to pump one cubic metre of groundwater by nearly 0.055 kWh. Based on this conversion ratio, total energy savings can be estimated as:

$$E_{saved} = R_{\text{p-depth}} \times 0.055 V_{\text{groundwater}} \times A_{\text{well-irrigation}} \qquad (1)$$

Where $R_{\text{p-depth}}$ is the reduction in pumping depth, $V_{\text{groundwater}}$ is the average volume of irrigation water applied per hectare of well-irrigated area, and $A_{\text{well-irrigation}}$ is the net well-irrigated area in the Narmada Canal command (in ha). Estimates of the average volume of groundwater pumped by the farmers in each region and the energy saved per hectare of well-irrigated area are provided in Table 1.

As Table 1 indicates, Mehsana had the highest energy savings per unit volume of groundwater pumped. The reason is that the reduction in pumping depth was highest in Mehsana. The volume of groundwater used per hectare of land was also one of the highest, at 2542 m³/ha. Mehsana also had the highest total energy savings per hectare of well-irrigated area, at 1834 kWh/ha. The second-highest was in Vadodara (1170.7 kWh/ha). Vadodara also had the highest volume of groundwater use per hectare of well-irrigated area (3610 m³/ha), in spite of being less arid than Mehsana. It should be kept in mind that groundwater use is a function not only of climatic conditions (with arid climates demanding more water) but also of the cropping patterns selected by the farmers. While aridity would demand more water for agricultural produce in areas like Ahmedabad and Mehsana (also see Figure 2), the cropping pattern is such that the overall water

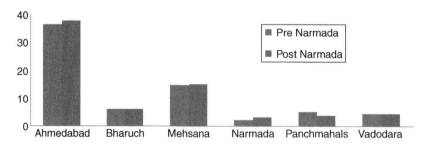

Figure 2.   Well command areas before and after Narmada.

Table 1. Average groundwater use for crop production in well command area and energy savings per hectare of irrigation.

District	Groundwater use after Narmada water (m³/ha/y)	Average reduction in pumping depth (m/y)	Groundwater-pumping energy savings per volume of water (kWh/m³/y)	Groundwater-pumping energy savings per irrigated area (kWh/ha/y)	Total economic benefit (INR/ha/y)
Ahmedabad	866.0	8.54	0.47	406.8	2034
Bharuch	1247.8	2.24	0.12	153.5	767.5
Mehsana	2542.6	13.12	0.72	1834.0	9170
Narmada	2665.1	3.76	0.21	551.4	2757
Panchmahals	1383.3	5.08	0.28	386.8	1934
Vadodara	3610.0	5.90	0.32	1170.7	5853.5

Source: Authors' analysis of primary data collected from sample farmers in the six districts ($N = 291$).

Table 2. Changes in incidence of well failures and well command area in the Narmada command area after the introduction of canal irrigation.

District	Well failures per year		Average well command area (ha)	
	Pre-Narmada	Post-Narmada	Pre-Narmada	Post-Narmada
Ahmedabad	3.00	1.2	36.6	37.8
Bharuch	4.75	5.2	6.1	6.05
Mehsana	0.00	1.2	14.7	15.1
Narmada	2.40	1.5	2.39	3.14
Panchmahals	0.00	4.00	5.10	3.90
Vadodara	9.50	0.00	4.40	4.50

Source: Authors' analysis of primary data collected from sample farmers in the six districts ($N = 291$).

requirement is much lower than in south Gujarat, where water-intensive crops such as wheat and paddy are grown.

The economic equivalent of this energy-saving benefit is equal to:

$$\text{ECOBEN}_{\text{save-energy}} = \propto \times A_{\text{well-irrigation}} \times \text{COST}_{\text{energy}} \tag{2}$$

Where $\propto$ is the energy saved (in kilowatt hours) per hectare per annum in well irrigation (Column 5 of Table 1); $\text{COST}_{\text{ENERGY}}$ includes the direct economic cost of producing and supplying electricity and the cost of reducing carbon emissions from power generation, which is equal to INR 0.47/kWh. The value of $\text{ECOBEN}_{\text{SAVE-ENERGY}}$ can be obtained by multiplying the value in the last column of Table 2 by the area irrigated by wells in the SSP command area in each district.

Reduction in failure of wells in the command area

After Narmada, the incidence of well failures was lower in four of the six districts surveyed. The change was remarkable in Vadodara District: from 9.5 per year to almost nil. In Ahmedabad and Narmada Districts, the reduction was less. And in contrast, in Panchmahals, there was an increase in well failures, from almost none to 4.0. On the other hand, after Narmada canal water, the area commanded by wells increased in four districts and remained the same in Bharuch (Table 2). The negative trends in Panchmahals vis-à-vis well failures and well command area could be due to the substantial increase in number of wells. This is perhaps disproportionately higher than the additional recharge available from the small canal-irrigated area, resulting in well interference. Except for Mehsana, it can also be seen that, wherever the incidence of well failures decreased, the command area of wells increased, as expected.

Increased income of well irrigators in the command area

Positive externalities of canal irrigation in increased income from well irrigation could be the result of: 1) increased area under well irrigation thanks to improved well yields; 2) shifts in cropping patterns towards water-intensive, high-value crops; 3) improved irrigation, leading to higher yields; or 4) reductions in costs of irrigation through reduced pumping depths and lower costs of well deepening. Another important source of income for well-owning farmers comes from higher water sales.

These findings reflect an assessment of whether there has been any change in cultivated area of various crops grown by the well-owning farmers who are the beneficiaries. The analysis of estimated average area under different crops of the sample well-owning farmers, covering all three seasons, before and after Narmada Canal water, showed reduced area for rain-fed crops (green gram, chick pea, maize and paddy). Area expanded for irrigated crops (such as cotton and castor), those sown in winter (such as wheat in some locations), and water-intensive sugar-cane in Bharuch.

Synthesizing the data presented in Table 2 and the outputs of analysis of changes in cropped area of well irrigators, one can see that the trend in cropped area of individual farmers is not in conformity with the trends in command area and water level, particularly for Ahmedabad and Mehsana. While water levels improved and well command area increased, gross cropped area fell slightly. This is perhaps because farmers do not own wells individually in such areas owing to the very high capital cost of well construction. In these areas, over a period of time, the number of shareholders of tube wells increased, while the area irrigated by individual farmers decreased. Smaller average land-holding size is another reason for smaller gross cropped area. Another possibility is that with greater reliability of groundwater resources, farmers replace rain-fed crops with irrigated ones, but grown in a smaller area. Whether this is the actual trend is examined in the later part of this section.

There was a significant increase in area of irrigated cotton and castor in Panchmahals, while the area under paddy cultivation, which is mostly rain-fed, fell. In Panchmahals, the formations underlying the command areas are consolidated rock (Gujarat Ecology Commission [GEC], 1997). In these consolidated formations, the aquifer storage potential is generally very poor, and therefore improvement in groundwater recharge through irrigation return flows from canals would bring about a marked difference in groundwater tables, making well irrigation more sustainable. Yet, this benefit of improved recharge is not reflected in the command area, perhaps because the farmers are irrigating their crops more intensively or because there has been an overall increase in the number of wells in the area. The second-highest increase in irrigated areas was observed in Vadodara, with increase in irrigated area of wheat (0.3 ha) and castor (0.12 ha).

Nevertheless, this change in cropping pattern is due to improved availability of water in the wells; the depth to water in wells has been reduced in these areas. Analysis of the yield of crops grown in different seasons in the well commands of the six locations shows mostly positive changes after the introduction of Narmada waters. Only winter maize (in one location) and green gram (in another location) showed some reduction in yield. The only two crops that did not show any changes in yields were groundnut and summer maize. For all other crops, positive changes were recorded in at least one district, and in some cases, in more than four crops. The percentage increase in yield was very high (32.8%) for castor in Bharuch. The increase in cotton yields was the lowest, at 27%, for Mehsana and the highest, at 60.9%, for the Narmada District. In the case of paddy, the highest yield increase, 90.9%, was found in Panchmahals. It is quite likely that the inputs which resulted in yield increases for canal irrigators might also have played a significant role for well irrigators. The collected empirical field data support this. For instance, the analysis shows that the intensity of groundwater use (m^3/ha of cropped land) in the well command areas increased after Narmada, clearly indicating that either farmers were applying more water to their irrigated winter crops or they were applying supplementary irrigation to crops otherwise grown under rainfed conditions (Figure 3). These suggestions could have an impact on yields.

To see how this has impacted the overall net returns from these crops, it is important to examine how the cost of inputs changed. The analysis shows that the cost of cultivation

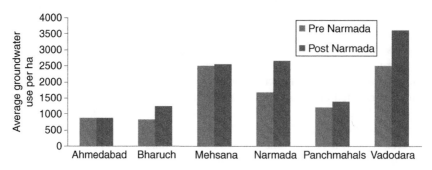

Figure 3.   Change in intensity of groundwater use (m³/ha).

has increased for all the crops except for tobacco in Narmada district, in which case the yield did not show any improvements. The cost of cultivation includes the cost of all inputs: ploughing, sowing, seed, fertilizer and pesticides.

Table 3 shows the changes in net income by crop. For most crops, farmers' net income from crop production has increased. The highest income increase was for cotton, with values ranging from INR 42,212/ha (USD 700/ha) in Bharuch to INR 71,030/ha (USD 1180/ha) in Vadodara. This is followed by castor, for which the highest increase was INR 102,755/ha (in the Bharuch district, famous for oil-seed production). In the case of green gram, a slight reduction was found. It is important to remember that this crop

Table 3.   Change in net income of well-owning farmers from crop production.

Season	Crop	District change in net income from crop production in well-irrigated commands (INR/ha)					
		Ahmedabad	Bharuch	Mehsana	Narmada	Panchmahals	Vadodara
Kharif	Paddy	23,467		−1,182	925	12,352	12,675
	Cotton		42,212	67,734	48,289	65,294	71,030
	Chick pea		1,7871		14,153	11,103	16,539
	Jowar		7,449				
	Green gram		15,188	−2,847			
	Castor		102,755	50,735		35,522	35,553
	Sugar-cane						
	Maize			21,900	11,658	5,311	12,600
	Bajra			14,085		10,087	
	Tomato			187,851			
	Tobacco						
	Banana					29,448	
Winter	Wheat			17,286			41,588
	Cumin	4,408	6,478	49,316	5,007	5,851	4,506
	Fennel			54,708			
	Tomato			806,391			
	Maize						
Summer	Jowar				6,728	11,169	52,131
	Bajra	−13,907					
	Maize						

Source: Authors' own analysis based on data collected through a primary survey.

generally grows under residual soil moisture and does not require many agronomic inputs; therefore, yields and returns would not change significantly as a result of improved well-water availability. In the case of summer *bajra* (millet), a major reduction in net income was identified because no yield improvements were recorded for this crop and average inputs costs went up.

An astonishingly high positive net income change of INR 806,391/ha was recorded for tomato in Mehsana. However, such values are unrealistic as farmers grow such crops in very small areas and a significant increase in its volatile market price can raise returns from a cultivated hectare. Nevertheless, the increase in net income is quite substantial for most crops, across districts.

Change in dairy production in well command areas

Dairy production is a very important activity in rural Gujarat. Intensive dairy farming is practiced in most districts currently covered by the SSP. Improved groundwater recharge, without a proportional increase in the number of wells, may result in an effective increase in well command area. This in turn can potentially influence the animal husbandry activities of the well owners as the availability of biomass in the farm (in the form of dry and green fodder and water from the wells for livestock drinking) increases. The analysis shows that holdings of indigenous cows (for milk) increased in Ahmedabad, Mehsana and Narmada, and marginally in Panchmahals and Vadodara; they decreased in Bharuch. As regards cross-bred cows, the holding size increased significantly in Vadodara and marginally (from nil) in Bharuch. A reduction (from 0.11 to 0.05) was seen in Ahmedabad. As regards buffalo, population size increased in Ahmedabad, Mehsana, Vadodara and Narmada, while it decreased in Bharuch and Panchmahals. Overall, the trend in livestock holdings appears to be positive in most locations, except Bharuch. This coincides with the general trend in cropped area: the gross cropped area under well command increased everywhere except Bharuch.

The absence of any change in composition of livestock held by farmers in Bharuch needs further explanation. In the case of Bharuch, the biggest change in cropping system is a shift from short-duration rainfed varieties of cotton and castor to long-duration irrigated varieties and supplementary irrigation of crops (*jowar* (sorghum), chick pea and green gram). Along with this, there has been a reduction in area of all these crops; so although yield has improved, overall output may not have increased. That said, the positive externality of canal water for well irrigation in an individual well command cannot be assessed, because the number of wells has increased over the years.

The average income of dairy farmers has also changed significantly for all livestock types in all locations, except for indigenous cows in Bharuch and Mehsana. The positive trend in buffaloes and cross-bred cows can be attributed to increased production of crops which yield dry or green leafy biomass, such as paddy, *jowar*, wheat, *bajra* and green gram, which are used as fodder,[1] and sometimes those which have by-products that can be used as feed for animals, such as green gram and groundnut. Another important factor that might have contributed to the increased yield of dairy animals is the better care they might be getting with a general improvement in the welfare of the farmers keeping these animals. On the other hand, the reduction in net income in the case of indigenous cows may be because of less interest shown by farmers in rearing low-yielding indigenous varieties, which are more hardy and preferred in situations of water and biomass shortages.

Positive externalities of canal irrigation for well irrigators

The economic value of positive externalities of canal irrigation for groundwater can be estimated as:

$$\text{WELL}_{\text{extern}} = A_{\text{well}} \times \varnothing_{\text{well}}^{1} + \Delta A_{\text{well}} \times \varnothing_{\text{well}} + N_{\text{well}} \times A_{\text{well}} \times \beta_{\text{well}}^{1} + \Delta N_{\text{well}}$$

$$\times A_{\text{well}} \times \beta_{\text{well}} \tag{3}$$

where A_{well} is the current gross groundwater-irrigated area in the command area of canals plus areas receiving irrigation through canal lift; $\varnothing_{\text{well}}^{1}$ is the average increase in net income from well irrigation per unit of gross well-irrigated area; ΔA_{well} is the increase in groundwater-irrigated area after canal-water introduction; $\varnothing_{\text{well}}$ is the net return from groundwater irrigation before canal-water introduction; N_{well} is the current average livestock population per ha of gross well-irrigated area; β_{well}^{1} is the increase in average net income from livestock production of well irrigators per unit of livestock (for all types of livestock owned by the well owners); and ΔN_{well} is the average increase in livestock population per hectare of gross well-irrigated area.

The same for a unit of gross well-irrigated area can be expressed as:

$$\text{WELL}_{\text{extern-unit}} = \varnothing_{\text{well}}^{1} + \{\Delta A_{\text{well}}/A_{\text{well}}\} \times \varnothing_{\text{well}} + N_{\text{well}} \times \beta_{\text{well}}^{1} + \Delta N_{\text{well}} \times \beta_{\text{well}} \tag{4}$$

The values of the different variables required to estimate the indirect impact of canal irrigation on well irrigation per hectare of gross well-irrigated area ($\text{WELL}_{\text{extern-unit}}$) are provided in Table 4. The estimates do not include Surendranagar, because the region's groundwater is totally saline; irrigation from Narmada is not expected to have any positive impact on the region's saline aquifers in the medium term.

Table 4 shows that while average area under well irrigation declined in four of the six cases, average net income from crop production substantially increased, with average incremental income often exceeding the average net income prior to Narmada waters. Here it must be mentioned that the average net income is the weighted average of the net income from various crops, estimated on the basis of the area under each one of the crops. Therefore, the shift in cropping pattern towards high-valued, irrigated crops has definitely influenced the overall net income per unit area under crops. On the other hand, dairying can also influence farm surplus. After Narmada water introduction, a marginal increase in the number of livestock is noticed, along with a substantial increase in average net income from dairy production per unit of livestock kept by the well irrigators.

It is theoretically incorrect to translate improved groundwater balance into increased irrigation potential of wells and actual well-irrigated area in the canal command, when it is merely because of reduced draft, and not because of increased recharge from return flows. This is because the utilizable groundwater resources do not get enhanced there. Therefore, the reduction in well-irrigated area found in this survey is quite natural, in at least some of the locations.

Increased income of labourers owing to higher wages

Empirical studies in the past have shown that increase in irrigated area per unit of agricultural labour force raises agricultural wages in rural areas by raising labour demand (Narayanamoorthy & Deshpande, 2003). Canal irrigation raised the labour demand in the areas directly receiving irrigation water either through gravity or through canal lift, as

Table 4. Changes in farm surplus of well irrigators in canal command areas.

	Ahmedabad	Bharuch	Mehsana	Narmada	Panchmahals	Vadodara
Sample size	61	21	63	57	29	60
Current average gross irrigated area (ha/farmer)	0.17	4.47	3.80	0.87	3.50	3.05
Pre-Narmada average gross irrigated area (ha/farmer)	0.17	5.67	4.28	1.01	3.32	2.95
Average increase in gross irrigated area (ha/farmer)	−0.01	−1.20	−0.48	−0.14	0.18	0.10
Current average net well-irrigated area (ha/farmer)						
Kharif	0.08	4.02	2.41	0.79	2.34	2.14
Winter	0.08	0.45	1.36	0.08	0.73	0.76
Summer	0.00	0.00	0.03	0.00	0.43	0.15
Current gross well-irrigated area in SSP command area						
Average net income from well-irrigated crops, pre-Narmada (INR/ha)	11,320.3	10,923.2	24,151.4	5,852.2	9,451.8	17,966.4
Average increase in net income from well-irrigated crops (INR/ha)	9,814.1	34,836.7	45,249.5	28,703	18,212.3	36,228
Average livestock holdings, present (head per ha gross well-irrigated area)	8.82	0.09	0.23	2.03	0.55	0.77
Average net income for livestock, pre-Narmada (INR/head)	12,071.3	3,179.3	14,910	8,484.9	5,018.4	6,478
Increase in average net income for livestock (INR/head)	11,088.4	7,664.5	8,292.2	5,157.4	8,118	8,809.8
Average increase in livestock (head per ha gross well-irrigated area)	0.55	−0.04	0.17	1.29	0.31	0.59
Positive externality of canal irrigation for well irrigation (INR per ha gross well-irrigated area)	**113,587.1**	**32,466.9**	**46,640.7**	**49,176.3**	**24,719.0**	**47,422.6**

Source: Authors' own estimates based on primary data analysis.

reflected in the number of days of employment per year received by wage labourers (IRAP, 2012).

Increased demand for labour would ideally raise wages for casual labour in both the farming and the non-farming sectors, particularly in areas where there is already a demand for temporary workers (Narayanamoorthy & Deshpande, 2003). In all the surveyed districts which are adjacent to urban centres (Baroda, Ahmedabad, Mehsana and Bharuch), the demand for un-skilled labour in the non-farming sector is high. Further, agriculture is generally prosperous in these regions. The only exception is the Panchmahals District, where agriculture is still not very well developed and irrigation from the Narmada Canal is still low. Analysis shows the current wages and the increase in wages (after Narmada water was supplied) in the six districts. In these areas, Bharuch recorded the highest growth in wages in the agricultural sector. The increase is even higher than in Ahmedabad's command areas, which are quite close to the metropolitan area. The disproportionately high wages in areas like Bharuch and Narmada may be attributed to the intensive irrigated agriculture being practiced in these areas, thanks to Narmada canals.

It is important to remember that rural wages for casual labour increased all over the state of Gujarat in the past few years (Hirway & Shah, 2011) because of inflation and also the effect of the National Rural Employment Guarantee Scheme, which offers 100 days of labour in every village in a year. For instance, wages for casual male labour rose from INR 43.9 to INR 68.5 per day between 1999–2000 and 2007–2008, a period of 8 years in the state. Wages for casual female workers rose from INR 34.4 to INR 58.9 per day during the same period. This is an annual growth rate of 5.7% for male workers and 7% for female workers (Hirway & Shah, 2011).

Therefore, it is necessary to factor out these effects while estimating the part of the increase in wages in the farm sector due to irrigation from the Narmada. It is assumed here that the conditions are quite unfavourable for wages to rise in Panchmahals as a result of Narmada irrigation, for the reasons explained above, and therefore any increase in wages in that area could be considered the effect of inflation and the National Rural Employment Guarantee Scheme, in conformation with the overall trends in wages in Gujarat. Thus, the effect of irrigation expansion owing to the Narmada was estimated by subtracting the wage increase observed in Panchmahals over the period considered in this analysis from the increase prevailing in the locations concerned.

An alternate method to understand the effect of irrigated-area expansion on wages in Narmada commands is to compare wages in these areas against the average in Gujarat. The average wage in rural Gujarat for casual work (adjusted to a rate of inflation of 7%) in 2011 is around INR 83.3 per day for male workers and INR 72.3 per day for female workers (estimates based on Hirway & Shah, 2011). On the other hand, the average wage for casual workers across the four districts of Narmada, Bharuch, Ahmedabad and Mehsana is INR 88.1 per day for male workers and INR 85.9 for female workers: much higher than the average. These are conservative estimates, and the actual difference in wages between Narmada command and non-command areas is probably larger. This is because the estimates of average wages in Gujarat mentioned above might have included some command-area districts. Female workers have the bigger benefit, with an average wage increase of INR 13.3; for male workers, the average gain is INR 4.8.

Furthermore, large water infrastructure projects have multiplier effects on the economy of the region they serve, through a variety of indirect benefits they produce. Though many of the indirect benefits have been quantified here, the aggregate figures of some of these benefits could not be estimated in the absence of data on parameters such as the number of wells benefited by recharge in the canal-irrigated area and the number of labourers who received higher wages due to increased demand for agricultural labour. Hence, a 'multiplier' has been used, equal to the lowest in the range (of 1.4 to 2.0) available from published literature for large water projects on the average farm surplus from canal irrigation, to obtain the total effect on the economy. The total effect of canal irrigation on the region's economy was estimated to be INR 68.208 billion (81,200 × 1.4 × 0.6 × 10^6). This is based on: (1) an estimated farm surplus of INR 81,200 per hectare of gross irrigated area; (2) a gross area of 0.60 million ha irrigated by the Narmada Canal system; and (3) an assumed multiplier coefficient of 1.4. This means there was an indirect economic benefit (multiplier effect) of INR 32,480 (81,200 × (1.4 − 1.0)) per ha of irrigation, producing a direct economic benefit of INR 81,200.

Reduction in cost of domestic water supplies in command-area villages and towns

The pipeline network based on the Sardar Sarovar Narmada Canal and the Mahi Canal is expected to serve nearly 54% of the villages in Gujarat, as well as all 125 towns (GWSSB, 2012). All of Saurashtra and Kachchh and most parts of north and central Gujarat are to be covered under this scheme. But there are thousands of villages in south and east Gujarat which are not to be covered by this pipeline network. These areas are generally considered the well-endowed region of the state in terms of water resources.

But even within south Gujarat, there are two distinct geohydrological environments. The first is the alluvial belt covering parts of Vadodara, Narmada, Surat and Bharuch. This area does not face problems of physical shortage of water during any part of the year, thanks to the rich alluvial aquifers in the area, which get sufficient replenishment from rainfall, and plenty of surface water in ponds – though there are problems of water quality. The other is the hard-rock region, with consolidated rocks of Deccan Traps basalt. Parts of Vadodara, Narmada and Bharuch, which fall inside the Narmada command, are in the Deccan Traps area. Now, Panchmahals in east Gujarat is fully underlain by crystalline hard-rock formations. In spite of moderate-to-high rainfall, this hard-rock region has poor groundwater potential (GEC, 1997). Wells dry up in summer months, causing drinking-water shortages.

Like irrigation wells, the drinking-water supply sources in the command area that tap local aquifers are likely to be benefited by canal irrigation through return flows from irrigated fields and seepage from canals. These benefits include: (1) rise in water levels in the wells, which can reduce the cost of pumping groundwater, thereby reducing the operational costs of the village panchayats[4] running these schemes; (2) reduced incidence of well failures and therefore reduced investment for well deepening, etc.; (3) rejuvenation and improved yield of wells, resulting in increased supply of water, especially during summer months; and (4) dilution of the minerals present in the groundwater, thereby improving the quality of the drinking water supplied by the local well-based schemes. While benefits (1) and (2) can be put in monetary terms, evaluating (3) and (4) requires estimation of water demand functions, and this method is attempted here.

The economic benefit from improved yield of drinking-water wells and sustainable drinking-water supply can be taken as equal to the cost of transporting water from distant sources to meet water supply needs during the summer. Further, the economic benefits from improved chemical quality of water in drinking-water wells can be taken as equal to the cost of treating poor-quality water in processes like desalination or defluoridation, depending on the case. While the first three types of impacts of canal-water introduction would be more visible in hard-rock regions, because of the unique nature of aquifers in those regions, the fourth type of impact (dilution of minerals present in groundwater) is more likely to be seen in the alluvial areas of north Gujarat. But, unfortunately, all the villages surveyed for canal lift in Ahmedabad and Mehsana are covered by the Narmada Canal–based pipeline scheme, and therefore the issue becomes non-existent in these areas. Therefore, the social benefits of canal irrigation in the form of improved sustainability of groundwater-based drinking-water schemes would be effected in the south and east Gujarat parts of the Narmada command.

The economic benefit from this externality can be computed as:

$$\text{BENEFIT} = P_{\text{well}} \, (R_{\text{p-depth}} \times 0.055 V_{\text{drink-water}} \times \text{COST}_{\text{elect}} + V_{\text{drink-summer}}$$

$$\times \text{PRICE}_{\text{tanker}} \quad\quad\quad (5)$$

where P_{well} is the total size of the population dependent on groundwater-based schemes for domestic water supply in the region; $R_{\text{p-depth}}$ is as defined earlier for Equation (2); $V_{\text{drink-water}}$ is the per capita volume of water used for drinking in a year (in m^3); $\text{COST}_{\text{elect}}$ is the average cost of generating and supplying one kilowatt of electricity; $V_{\text{drink-summer}}$ is the per capita volume of water used for drinking and domestic uses in summer; and $\text{PRICE}_{\text{tanker}}$ is the market price of a cubic metre of tanker-supplied water.

The reduction in pumping depth is estimated to be 12.5 feet (3.75 m), based on Table 1. The cost of generating and supplying energy for groundwater pumping is taken as INR 5/ kWh. The volume of water required for domestic water needs is estimated to be $36.5 \, m^3$ per capita per year (100 L per capita per day). While this demand has to be met from wells during most parts of the year, during summer months, only part of it will be met from wells, and water will have to be supplied though tankers, at the rate of 40 L per person per day, in the absence of surface irrigation from Narmada canals. For tanker water, the market price was taken to be INR $50/m^3$. Water delivery through Narmada canals would augment the water supplies from wells so as to avoid the dependence on tankers. The population depending on groundwater-based drinking-water supply sources in the scarcity-hit region is about 5 million. Thus, the total economic benefit is estimated to be INR 1069.65 million per annum ($213.93 \times 5 \times 10^6 = 1069.65$ million). The detailed calculations are presented in Table 5.

In addition to the benefits from reduction in pumping depths and improvement in water supply quantity, benefits also accrued in improvement in quality of water, through dilution of groundwater. Research carried out in one of the villages in Vadodara District which receives canal water for irrigation shows significant improvement in the quality of groundwater used for domestic purposes. The village is in an area with underlying basalt formations. The community in the village is dependent on bore wells drilled on the banks of the Orson River for domestic water supply. There has been a notable reduction in the number of families reporting problems of water quality in the sources, and the families attribute the quality improvement to dilution of minerals present in groundwater across the seasons. As Figure 4 shows, after the introduction of Narmada Canal water in the village, no household reported high total dissolved solids (TDS) in the water used for drinking and cooking from their public water sources, which included the hand pumps in the locality. Before Narmada water was introduced, at least five households encountered problems with their drinking water source (i.e., the distant bore well located on the river bank). The water quality is improved because the bore well which is tapped for drinking water gets replenished continuously by river water, which is free of salts.

Table 5. Indirect benefit of canal irrigation through improved water supplies.

Type of water supply source	Water supply requirement met from the source (litres per person per day)	Reduction in pumping head due to canal recharge (m)	Energy savings per m^3 of pumping due to reduction in pumping head by 1 m (KWhr)	Volume of water used (m^3/y)	Cost saving per m^3 of water (INR)	Economic benefit per capita (INR)
Bore well/open well	100 in monsoon and winter; 60 in summer	3.75	0.055	32.90	1.03	33.93
Tanker supply	40 in summer	n/a	n/a	3.60	50.0	180.00
Total cost savings for a population of five million people depending on water supplies						1069.4 m

Source: Authors' analysis based on primary and secondary data.

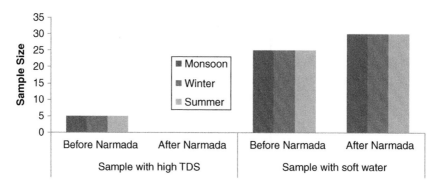

Figure 4.   Impact of canal on quality of groundwater for drinking and cooking.

But the village households use water from local bore wells and hand pumps for domestic water supply and livestock drinking, which again is available through individual tap connections and stand posts. As Figure 5 shows, 25 out of the 30 families surveyed reported problems with their domestic water sources in winter and summer prior to the introduction of Narmada canal water in the village (no families complained about water quality during the rainy season). But after Narmada canal water was introduced, no families reported problems of salinity. This is quite possible because the wells get recharged during the monsoon, with the fresh water remaining at the top of the water table. This water gets used up during the rainy season, with the saline water remaining in the lower strata of the consolidated formations; and this water gets used during winter and summer. Since the introduction of the Narmada Canal, the wells are recharged continuously by return flows from canal irrigation.

Impacts of Narmada Canal on land markets

During the field survey, an attempt was made to capture the changes in agricultural land value resulting from the availability of canal water for irrigation. The questions about land transactions included the price at which land was sold and the caste to which the people buying and selling land in the area belonged. But, aside from one or two isolated cases, the farmers and other respondents did not report any recent land sales. However, in the Banaskantha District, in north Gujarat, people have reported some land transactions in the

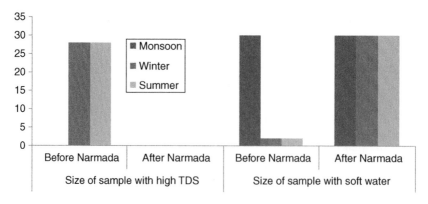

Figure 5.   Impact of canal water on quality of groundwater for domestic uses.

designated canal command areas. Most of these transactions happened 7 to 8 years ago, before the Narmada Main Canal reached the district. The farmers, belonging to the Patel community, bought land in the Wav and Tharad *talukas*[5] from landowners belonging to the Darbar (Thakur) and Koli communities[2] on hearing about SSNNL's plans to start the construction of main canals up to the north-western parts of the district. The price of land ranged from INR 100,000 to INR 300,000 per *vigha*[3] (approximately INR 400,000 to INR 1.2 million per ha). But once canal construction started, the farmers stopped selling their land, expecting that the parched lands in their area would receive canal water.

Findings and conclusions

The supply of surface water from the Narmada Canal for irrigation has resulted in changes in groundwater levels over time. This has been marked by relatively higher annual water levels in the observation wells in the command area, except in the Kheda district. Similarly, there has been a marked reduction in the salinity of groundwater over time. Irrigation wells in the command area of the Narmada Canal have benefited from seepage. This is manifested by consistent rise in groundwater levels across seasons, resulting in reduced depth of pumping. The highest average rise in well-water level during monsoon (47 feet) and winter (49 feet) was found in wells in Mehsana, and during summer (53 feet) in Ahmedabad. There has been a notable reduction in incidence of well failures in the canal command area, and an increase in command areas of wells, since Narmada.

The reduction in well failure has been very remarkable in Vadodara District, from 9.5 per year to almost nil today. But the same trend was not visible in Panchmahals District. A likely reason is the substantial increase in the number of wells tapping the hard-rock aquifers of the district over the past few years, which perhaps is disproportionately higher than the additional recharge available from the small canal-irrigated area, resulting in well interference.

Since the canal systems of the SSP started delivering water in the command area, the cropping pattern of well irrigators in the command has changed; there have been substantial increases in yield and income returns per unit of land (INR/ha) for well irrigators. While there were incidences of major reduction in area of the 'normally' rainfed crops of the *kharif* (rainy) season, the area under irrigated crops such as cotton, castor and wheat increased in some locations, and the same result is visible for water-intensive crops such as sugar-cane in Bharuch. Almost every crop grown in the well command areas of the six districts showed positive yield changes after the introduction of Narmada waters. The percentage increase in yield was as high as 328% (for castor in Bharuch). The highest income increase was found in the case of cotton. The increase in yield and income from crops in the well commands could be explained by the greater dosage of irrigation given to these crops, which is reflected in the increase in average volume of groundwater applied by the farmers per hectare of land since Narmada. There was a marginal increase in livestock holdings among well irrigators with Narmada water. Overall, the trend in terms of livestock holdings appears to be positive in most locations, except Bharuch.

Increased demand for farm labour resulted in substantial increases in wages in the selected locations after the Narmada water introduction – disproportionately higher than the historical increase in wages in other areas of Gujarat that are not so much benefited by Narmada canals. Bharuch recorded the highest growth in wages in the agriculture sector, with an aggregate net increase of INR 34 per day in the case of male workers and INR 37 per day in the case of female workers. The exceptionally high wages in areas like Bharuch and Narmada are attributable to the presence of gravity irrigation through canals, which permits intensive irrigated agriculture in these areas.

The indirect benefit from canal irrigation in the form of reduced economic cost of energy used for pumping groundwater for irrigation was estimated to be huge. For every hectare of well-irrigated area in the SSP command, the calculated economic benefit to society through energy savings in groundwater pumping ranges from INR 768 in Bharuch to INR 9170 in Mehsana. The indirect economic impact of canal irrigation in the form of improved sustainability of groundwater-based drinking-water supply schemes in the south and east Gujarat parts of the Narmada command, for a population of 5 million, is estimated to be INR 1069.65 million per annum. The primary survey conducted in Vadodara District showed improvement in the quality of groundwater used for domestic water supply. The total of direct and indirect economic benefits from canal irrigation was estimated to be INR 68.25 billion, considering a total net farm surplus of INR 85,200 from every hectare of irrigation, an economic multiplier of 1.4 for large surface-irrigation projects on the region's economy, and a gross irrigated area of 0.60 million ha. It is important to note that the reduction in energy use for groundwater pumping for irrigation does not translate into private benefits for well-owning farmers, because of the flat-rate pricing of power supplied to the farm sector, which makes the marginal cost of pumping nearly zero. However, it adds to the overall economic benefits, as the public expenditure for power subsidies is reduced.

In the past, many large and medium-sized water resources projects in India have been critiqued for their poor performance in terms of irrigated area. However, too little attention has been paid to the impact such projects have on other sectors of the economy. The present analysis of the SSP shows that the project could change Gujarat's well-irrigation economy by increasing the net returns of groundwater irrigators in the command area, as well as by lowering electricity costs for groundwater pumping and public expenditure on the provision of fresh-water supplies, including alternate sources tapped during lean seasons. The incremental economic outputs from sustainable well irrigation thanks to augmented recharge from gravity irrigation are too large to be ignored.

Notes

1. Paddy, wheat and *bajra* provide dry fodder; *jowar* provides green fodder.
2. Patel, Darbar and Koli are names of local castes belonging to the Hindu religion.
3. The *vigha* is a local measure of land area. Nearly 4.5 *vighas* make one hectare.
4. *Panchayat* is a local self-government institution at the village or small town level in India and has a Sarpanch as its elected head.
5. A *tehsil* consists of an area of land with a city or town that serves as its headquarters, with possible additional towns, and usually a number of villages. As an entity of local government, the *tehsil* office (*Panchayat samiti*) exercises certain fiscal and administrative power over the villages and municipalities within its jurisdiction. It is the ultimate executive agency for land records and related administrative matters. Its chief official is called the *tehsildar* or less officially the *talukdar* or *taluka muktiarkar*. In some instances, *tehsils* are called "blocks" (*Panchayat* union blocks).

References

Alagh, Yoginder K. (2010). A sardar sarovar riddle. *Financial Express*. April 19, 2010.
Biswas, A. K. (1994). Sustainable water resources development: Some personal thoughts. *International Journal of Water Resources Development, 10*, 109–116.
Biswas, A. K., & Tortajada, C. (2001). Development and large dams: A global perspective. *International Journal of Water Resources Development, 17*, 9–21.

Biswas-Tortajada, A. (2014). The Gujarat state-wide water supply grid: A step towards water security. *International Journal of Water Resources Development, 30*, 78–90. doi: 10.1080/07900627.2013.871971.

Chakravorty, U., & Umetsu, C. (2003). Basinwide water management: A spatial model. *Journal of Environmental Economics and Management, 45*(1), 1–23.

Gujarat Ecology Commission (GEC). (1997). *Eco regions of Gujarat.* Vadodara: Gujarat Ecology Commission.

Gujarat Water Supply and Sewerage Board (GWSSB). (2012). *State wide water supply grid in Gujarat.* Gandhinagar, Gujarat: Gandhinagar Gujarat Water Supply and Sewerage Board.

Hirway, I., & Shah, N. (2011). Labour and employment under globalisation: The case of Gujarat. *Economic & Political Weekly, 46*, 57–65.

Institute for Resource Analysis and Policy (IRAP). (2012). *Realistic Vs Mechanistic: Analyzing the real economic and social benefits of Sardar Sarovar Narmada project* (Report submitted to SSNNL, Gandhinagar). Hyderabad: Institute for Resource Analysis and Policy.

Kumar, M. D. (2007). *Groundwater management in India: Physical, institutional and policy alternatives.* New Delhi: Sage Publications.

Kumar, M. D., Shah, Z., Mukherjee, S., & Mudgerikar, A. (2008, April). *Water, human development and economic growth: Some international perspectives.* Paper presented at the IWMI-Tata water policy research program's seventh annual partners' meet, ICRISAT, Hyderabad.

Malik, R. P. S. (2006, December). *Do dams help reduce poverty?* Paper presented at the International Conference on Statistics and Informatics in Agricultural Research, New Delhi, India.

Narayanamoorthy, A., & Deshpande, R. S. (2003). Irrigation development and agricultural wages: An analysis across states. *Economic and Political Weekly, 38*, 3716–3722.

Parasuraman, S., Upadhyaya, H., & Balasubramanian, G. (2010). Sardar Sarovar project: The war of attrition. *Economic & Political Weekly, 45*, 39–48.

Ranade, R., & Kumar, M. D. (2004). Narmada water for groundwater recharge in North Gujarat: Conjunctive management in large irrigation projects. *Economic and Political Weekly, 39*, 3510–3513.

Shah, T., Gulati, A., Henant, P., Shreedhar, G., & Jain, R. C. (2009). Secret of Gujarat's agrarian miracle after 2000. *Economic and Political Weekly, 44*, 45–55.

Shah, Z., & Kumar, M. D. (2008). In the midst of the large dam controversy: Objectives, criteria for assessing large water storages in the developing world. *Water Resources Management, 22*(12), 1799–1824.

Talati, J., & Shah, T. (2004). Institutional vacuum in Sardar Sarovar project: Framing 'rules-of-the-game'. *Economic and Political Weekly, 39*, 3504–3509.

Verghese, B. G. (2001). Sardar Sarovar Project revalidated by Supreme Court. *International Journal of Water Resources Development, 17*(1), 79–88.

Watt, J. (2008). *The effect of irrigation on surface-ground water interactions: Quantifying time dependent spatial dynamics in irrigation systems.* (Unpublished doctoral thesis). School of Environmental Sciences, Faculty of Sciences, Charles Sturt University, Sydney NSW, Australia.

OPINION

Environmental over enthusiasm

Chetan Pandit

Consultant, and Visiting Faculty, MBA Programme in Infrastructure Management at Symbiosis Centre for Management and Human Resource Development, Pune, India

India needs large dams for water storage, hydropower and flood control. It also needs long-distance inter-basin water transfers. However, India has a complex and strict environmental regulatory system which ignores a developing economy's needs and peoples' aspirations and is often impractical. This is used by activists to thwart infrastructure building, and, when faced with development slowdown, the government tries to thwart the laws they themselves have made. India's food, water and energy security, economic, and poverty-alleviation plans are in jeopardy unless environmental regulators realize that the regulations are being misused and that environmental over-enthusiasm is benefiting neither development nor the environment.

Introduction

India is a large country, approximately 3214 km from north to south and 2933 km from east to west, which makes for considerable variation in rainfall across the country. Mean annual rainfall varies from less than 150 mm in the western state of Rajasthan to more than 2500 mm in the north-east and along the western coast; rainfall is moderate in central India. The Ganga, Brahmaputra and Meghana basins and the west-flowing rivers of the western coast account for only 36% of the land area but carry 71% of the water resources, while the other 64% of land area has to make do with the remaining 29% of the water resources. Therefore, long-distance water transfers, including inter-basin transfers, are necessary, from areas that are relatively water rich to areas that are water stressed. More than 80% of the annual rainfall takes place during the four months of the monsoon. Therefore, water has to be collected during these four months and stored for use during the rest of the year.

There exists a misconception, assiduously promoted by those opposed to water infrastructure, that rainwater harvesting in small check dams and artificial recharge of groundwater, referred to as 'traditional technology', is the appropriate paradigm for India to manage her water resources. This argument acts as a red herring in any discussion in favour of infrastructure. Therefore, it is necessary to examine how valid it is.

This so-called traditional technology was the default paradigm in practice till about the 1950s. Historically, and till 1950, the groundwater level was at its highest, because extraction was done only through shallow dug wells and by animal power. There were no chemical fertilizers or pesticides; to say nothing of genetically modified crops, there were not even hybrid seeds; there were no cash crops. The depletion of forests had yet to start.

And, last but not least, there were no large dams. In short, the landscape and the agricultural practices were exactly what the conservationists dream of. And the population to be fed was a fraction of what it is today.

Yet, India has always been a land of severe food shortages and has suffered some of the world's worst famines. An estimated 23 million people died in 7 major famines in the 175-year period from 1769 to 1943. At the time of independence in 1947, India, with a population of just 330 million, was unable to grow sufficient food for her people and had to depend on food imports.

A major expansion of irrigation facilities was taken up immediately after independence. Only in the late 1970s did India become self-sufficient in food-grain production. The storage capacity in reservoirs of all sizes at the time of independence was only $15.6\,km^3$; this now stands at $225\,km^3$. India still experiences periodic droughts, but now droughts do not mean famines. The traditional technologies could not produce enough food for a population of less than 300 million then, and there is no question of their producing enough food for 1600 millions, or more, now.

Electricity

In any case, the traditional-technology argument completely ignores electricity generation and livelihood opportunities for a very large population. Groundwater is expected to supply about 40% of India's water use, and agricultural pumping is a major consumer of electricity. An increasing population and fixed land resources have reduced the average land holding size to very small units that are financially not viable. Every year a large population has to shift from agriculture to industry-based livelihoods, and electricity is a key input for any kind of industry.

The annual per capita electricity use in India is 749 kWh, which is not only far below that of developed nations but is lowest even amongst the BRICS nations (Brazil, Russia, India, China and South Africa), the next-lowest being Brazil, at 2369 kWh.

Of an estimated hydropower potential of 150,000 MW, only 39,384 MW has been harnessed. The share of hydropower which is peaking power is only 18% against a recommended 40%, resulting in peak power deficits and load shedding.

The variability of monsoon rainfall is expected to increase with global climate change, and increasing the surface storage capacity is a key response to adapt to the increased system variability and uncertainty.

Thus, from all considerations – surface storage for assured supplies of water year round in a monsoon-driven tropical climate; transfer of water from relatively water-rich areas to water-scarce areas; climate change-induced increased variability and uncertainty in rainfall; generation of hydroelectricity; and flood control too – for all of these reasons, India needs large dams, irrigation, inter-basin water transfers, and hydropower projects.

Infrastructure building in India

In the years immediately after independence in 1947, many large reservoir, irrigation and hydropower projects were taken up, which included some very large dams like the Bhakra-Nangal system, Hirakud, Nagarjun Sagar and Koyna. Together with the use of agrochemicals and high-yielding varieties of seeds, by the late 1970s the nation was finally self-sufficient in food production.

All this was before the evolution of concerns with regard to the environmental and social impacts of infrastructure building. Also, a society experiencing acute food shortages, black markets of food items, and the humiliation of food imports would not have taken kindly to environmental concerns obstructing the march towards self-sufficiency in food production.

Environmental concerns entered the national agenda in the mid-1970s, when Article 48A was added to the Constitution, stating that the state shall endeavour to protect and improve the environment and to safeguard the forests and wildlife of the country (Constitution of India, 1950). A Department of Environment was created in the central government in 1980 and was upgraded to the Ministry of Environment and Forests in 1985.

Environmental concerns like submergence of forests, abstraction from rivers and impacts on flora and fauna, are different from social concerns like submergence of monuments of archaeological importance, displacement of people, and so on. Possible adverse social impacts evoke a stronger sympathy than possible adverse environmental impacts, but presenting them as environmental concerns enables application of environmental regulations, which are very powerful. Perhaps for this reason, activists have dragged many social issues into the environmental arena, and now the distinction between the two has become quite blurred. Therefore, in the rest of this paper, which is about roadblocks in the path of infrastructure, the word 'environmental' is used to convey both environmental and social concerns, while taking note that the two are different.

Over the years, the government has enacted various acts and legislation for protection of the environment and forests. Prominent among these are:

- The Environment (Protection) Act, 1986 (Ministry of Environment and Forests, 1986), which gives the government wide powers for protecting the environment
- The Forest Conservation Act of 1980 (Ministry of Environment and Forests, 1980)
- The Environmental Impact Assessment Notification Act of 1994 (Ministry of Environment and Forests, 1994), amended in 1997
- The Panchayats (Extension to the Scheduled Areas) Act of 1996 (Ministry of Panchayati Raj, 1996) – a *panchayat* is a village-level self-governance agency
- The National Green Tribunals Act (Ministry of Environment and Forests, 2010)
- The Right to Fair Compensation and Transparency in Land Acquisition, Rehabilitation and Resettlement Act of 2013 (Ministry of Law and Justice, 2013).

An environmental clearance is now mandatory for all new projects and for expansion or modernization of existing projects covering 29 disciplines, which include hydro-power, major irrigation and flood-control projects. Since 1997, it is mandatory to hold a public hearing before granting environmental clearance (Center of Excellence in Environmental Economics, 2003). The Panchayats Act empowers panchayats to safeguard and preserve the traditions and customs of the people, their cultural identity, community resources and the customary mode of dispute resolution. It requires that the panchayat be consulted before the acquisition of land for development projects and for resettlement of persons affected by such projects in their areas. Their recommendations are mandatory for grant of license for the mining of minor minerals.

If the project intersects any forest land, then a separate forest clearance is required. Forest land means land which is classified as forest in the revenue records, irrespective of whether a forest actually stands on it at present.

Obtaining environmental clearance is itself very difficult. But the clearance is always accompanied by a set of terms and conditions that are difficult to comply with and even more difficult to demonstrate compliance with. This means that the clearance can be revoked at the slightest complaint of a violation of any of the terms and conditions of the clearance. Almost every project faces litigation for violating some law or other. Even if it eventually comes out that there was no violation of any law, several years of time will have been lost.

All this increases project costs, makes infrastructure projects vulnerable to manipulation by activists, and generally creates a climate hostile to infrastructure building. As a result, during the last 20 years or so building new infrastructure has become increasingly difficult. Many projects have thus suffered and are suffering. Given below are a few examples of how environmental regulation, meant to improve the design and performance of projects on environmental indicators, has actually resulted in creating roadblocks in the path of infrastructure. The state is having to work to find ways to extricate itself from a morass of its own creation.

Forest clearance for highways

India badly needs more and better highways. A major plan to construct new modern highways and improve the existing ones has been taken up by the National Highways Authority of India. Like any other project, the highways require environmental clearance, and if any part of the highway intersects a land classified as forest, then a forest clearance is also required. The regulation for environmental clearance is relatively lenient; for forest clearance, the rules are far more stringent.

For projects that intersect a forest area, the Ministry of Environment and Forests started the practice of bundling the two clearances. Even if the process for the environmental clearance was completed, the clearance was issued only after the forest clearance was also processed and assured. This practice did not affect the projects that are 2-dimensional (spread over an area), because even if the environmental clearance had been issued, they could not start any work till forest clearance was also issued. However, highways, power transmission lines, canals and railway lines are linear projects – with a great length, of which only a small portion might intersect forest land. In linear projects, it is possible to start the work in stretches that do not intersect forest land, even while processing the forest clearance for stretches where it is required, thus reducing overall project execution time. Therefore, it makes sense to delink environmental clearance from forest clearance for linear projects.

But the Ministry of Environment and Forests rejected all pleas to delink the two clearances in the case of highways, and so the work could not be taken up even in the stretches that did not pass through forest land. The matter came to a breaking point, and in January 2013 two private-sector partners pulled out of two major highway projects (the Kishangarh-Udaipur-Ahmedabad project and the Shivpuri-Dewas project) because of the client department's inability to obtain environmental clearance.

In January 2013, in an unprecedented move, the National Highways Authority sought judicial intervention in the matter, reportedly with backing from the highest levels in the government. That is, the government resorted to approaching a court to undo a rule of its own creation. Things moved swiftly thereafter, and within a few days, even before the case came up for hearing, the environment ministry issued orders delinking environmental clearance and forest clearance for highways.

The Western Ghat Ecology Expert Panel

The Western Ghats refers to mountain ranges that run parallel to the west coast for 1500 km, from a little north of the city of Mumbai to the southernmost tip of India. The Western Ghats have 11% of India's water resources, but only 4% of the population.

Abundant rainfall on the steep slopes creates a hydropower potential of 9430 MW. The area is also rich in mineral resources. With a 1500 km coastline and lush green forests, the entire Western Ghats area has a huge tourism potential.

The Western Ghats are also considered a biodiversity hot spot; they are habitat to many rare species of birds, mammals, reptiles and plants. In March 2010, with a view to protect the ecology of the Ghats, the Ministry of Environment and Forests formed the Western Ghats Ecology Expert Panel (WGEEP), chaired by an environmental scientist of considerable repute, to study the ecology of the Ghats and make recommendations for conservation and rejuvenation of the environment in the Ghats area.

The panel produced a report that completely disregarded economic objectives and development imperatives, giving a set of recommendations that either banned various development and infrastructure activities outright or recommended impossibly stringent conditions (WGEEP, 2011). Not only future activities but even existing projects would be shut down. Three examples should suffice.

- "Zero pollution" is prescribed for all thermal power projects, new or existing. Pollution can reduced up to a certain limit, but zero pollution is an impossible condition for a fuel-burning plant. If accepted, this recommendation would mean no more thermal electricity generation in the entire Western Ghats.
- Diversion of streams for power generation would be banned, not only for new projects but also for existing projects. If accepted, this recommendation would mean no more hydroelectric generation in the Western Ghats as water would not be diverted in head race tunnel or channel, penstocks and to the turbines.
- Use of all agro-chemicals, i.e. fertilizers, pesticides, weedicides, etc., would be banned across the entire Western Ghats region. If accepted, this recommendation would mean a return to subsistence agriculture for all farmers in the Western Ghats.

Similar crippling recommendations were slapped across all other sectors. In addition to being impractical, many of the recommendations pertain to matters that are in the jurisdiction of state government, and beyond the powers of the central government to impose any blanket direction. Many recommendations are also contrary to government policy.

Various activist groups have already approached the courts seeking implementation of the report. Technically, the government is not obliged to accept the recommendations of a committee, and the default condition is that unless explicitly accepted, the recommendations are a nullity. But lack of clarity about what the government might accept has created an atmosphere of uncertainty, resulting in project promoters' putting infrastructure projects on hold or even withdrawing – a classic example of chess master Aron Nimzowitsch's dictum, "A threat is stronger than the execution" (Winter, n.d.).

The report has put the central environment ministry in a tight spot. The government knew the report could not be accepted, but was not able to bring itself to say so up front. Seeking a way out, the ministry appointed another committee, the High Level Working Group on Western Ghats, to examine the report of the earlier committee, with additional terms of reference to examine the imperatives of equitable economic and social growth in the region; the rights, needs and development aspirations of local and indigenous people; and centre-state relations. Also, the new committee was more multidisciplinary and did not consist entirely of conservationists. The committee wrote a new report from scratch (Ministry of Environment and Forests, 2013a, 2013b) which is much more practical. As of October 2013, the matter has not been concluded. The ministry now has two different reports, making two different sets of recommendations, and the difficult prospect of having to reject the set that is outwardly more pro-environment and pro-conservation.

The point to note in all this is that all this embarrassment could have been avoided if the references to development and economy had been included in the mandate of the first committee and if its composition had been more multi-disciplinary and balanced.

The Sardar Sarovar project

The Sardar Sarovar case is a milestone in the history of environmental awakening and activism. It has many important lessons for law-makers and policy-makers, as well as for infrastructure builders. The Sardar Sarovar project on the Narmada River is one of the largest multipurpose projects in India, comprising a concrete gravity dam that creates a live storage capacity of $5.86 \, km^3$ and hydropower capacity of 1450 MW and will provide irrigation to 1.905 Mha of land in some of the most water-stressed areas of the country. The reservoir displaced 46,721 families. The resettlement package for the displaced persons of Sardar Sarovar project has been hailed as one of the best so far. It includes, amongst other things, 2 ha of irrigated agricultural land for each family, and counting every major son (age 21 years or more) as an independent claimant entitled to a full package.

The construction work was started in the mid-1980s. In March 1994, a group of social activists filed a petition against the project with the Supreme Court of India. The petition contended, *inter alia*, that the project was not in the public interest; that it was being implemented in violation of various environmental-protection acts; that its benefits had been over-estimated; and that the forced displacement of people from the submergence area violated their fundamental rights.

Work on the dam remained suspended for six years, from 1994 to 2000, while the case was argued in the Supreme Court. In October 2000, the court dismissed all the contentions and cleared the project. The court also issued certain directions for further construction, amongst these being that for each contour level, resettlement of all project-affected persons up to that contour must be completed before the dam may be raised to that level.

This principle – first resettle, then displace – is unexceptionable. However, the real impact of the decision has not been speedy resettlement for the displaced but an indefinite delay in both resettlement and construction. Every time a decision is taken to increase the height, the activists challenge it in court and seek stop-work orders. When such a complaint is made, the onus is on the project promoters to prove that resettlement has been completed. There is no onus on the complainant to prove that it has not been completed, and there is no penalty on the complainant if eventually it is found that his complaint was not based on facts. There is no penalty for frivolous complaints, which makes it a zero-cost game for the activists.

For project promoters, this means they have to be extra-careful, not only to complete the resettlement as stipulated, but also to be able to prove before a court that there was no wilful disobedience of the first-resettle-then-displace principle. This has resulted in the designing of an extraordinarily complex procedure to verify the resettlement work and create the necessary record. So complex is this procedure that the last increase in the height of the dam was completed in 2006. There has been no further work since then. As of January 2012, resettlement had been completed for 46,457 out of 46,721 project-affected families. Only 264 of these 46,721 families have yet to be resettled.

Further, the dam body has been completed up to the spillway crest level; now only the gates have to be installed. Resettlement of all persons up to the spillway crest level has already been completed. Installing the gates but keeping them in the open position would keep the submergence level fixed at the spillway crest level. Thus, installing the gates and keeping the gates in the open position till resettlement of any remaining families is completed would not violate the principle of first resettle then displace. Yet, the government is unwilling to do that, and the fourth-tallest dam in India has been functioning as an un-gated weir for the last six years.

The land acquisition bill

A new law has been passed recently, ostensibly to simplify land acquisition and ensure fair compensation to the displaced; but it will actually make land acquisition even more difficult, and often impossible. The Right to Fair Compensation and Transparency in Land Acquisition, Rehabilitation and Resettlement Act of 2013 will affect not only river-valley projects but all infrastructure activity. Here are some of its provisions and their implications and likely consequences.

- Land acquisition for a public purpose to be implemented by a private company can take place only if at least 80% of the project-affected families give their consent for the acquisition. Thus, if 21% of the affected families do not agree (or are persuaded to not agree), then the land acquisition cannot take place.
- Project-affected families include not only land owners but also right holders under the Forest Rights Act of 2006 (Ministry of Tribal Affairs, 2006); livelihood losers (families whose livelihood over the past three years has been primarily dependent on the land being acquired, *viz.* landless agriculture workers, tenants or sharecroppers); and people who are dependent on the forests or water bodies to be acquired (*viz.* forest gatherers, hunters, fisher folk and boatmen). Thus a very large number of people must be given resettlement benefits at project cost. This can make many projects economically unviable.
- Multi-crop irrigated land may not be acquired except as a demonstrably last resort, and in any case not more than 5% of the multi-crop irrigated area in a district can be acquired. Thus, since canals, of course, pass through agricultural land where more than one crop is the norm and there is invariably some kind of irrigation, at the very least from a dug well or village pond, this makes it "multi-crop irrigated land" which cannot be acquired. Even if it is accepted that acquisition for an irrigation canal is necessary "as a demonstrably last resort", the clause limiting such acquisition to not more than 5% in a district still remains applicable. This means that a canal, railway line or highway must terminate at the border of the first district it encounters where 5% or more of the multi-crop irrigated area has already been acquired.

The bill was passed only this year (2013), so its impacts are not yet visible, but industry analysts are almost unanimous in the view that it has delivered a mortal blow to infrastructure. An analysis in the Financial Express of 5 September 2013 says that with the new law in operation "the commerce and industry minister has lost his battle and can just as well officially abandon the new manufacturing policy with its objective of increasing the manufacturing sector's share in GDP to 18%. LARR [the new law] will stop in its track the ambitious DMIC [Delhi-Mumbai Industrial Corridor] project and bring to a standstill the process of planned urbanisation in the country" (Kumar & Kumar, 2013, p. 1).[1] The same holds true for infrastructure.

Reports of corruption

Where subjective decisions are involved, and where the decision has major financial implications for the private sector, there is scope for corruption. The environmental regulatory process most certainly involves subjective decisions. And not only the denial of clearance but even a delay in granting environmental clearance, or prescribing conditions that impose a huge cost on the project, can make or break a project. The following three incidents have been reported in the press and indicate that the possibility of corruption in the enforcement of environmental regulations cannot be denied.

- A report in the Times of India dated 22 September 2011 alleged corruption at the highest level in handing out forest clearances. The report said that an inspector general of forests was transferred out of the Forest Advisory Committee and a vigilance inquiry was instituted against him and two other forest officials for allegedly fudging documents to clear a hydroelectric project in Himachal Pradesh (Sethi, 2011, p. 1).
- Iron ore mining and export is a major component of the economy of the state of Goa. On 6 September 2012, the Indian Express published a report ("Goa CM Calls Ministry," 2012) wherein the chief minister of Goa was quoted as making very serious charges of corruption in granting environmental clearances. No investigation has so far been conducted, and nothing has yet been proved. But charges made by the chief minister of a state cannot be dismissed lightly.
- On 17 January 2013, the Indian Express reported that an officer of the Ministry of Environment and Forests was arrested for allegedly accepting a bribe for procuring environmental clearance for a power and steel company (Tripathi, 2013). A consultant (which is often a euphemism for broker) was also arrested. In the wake of these arrests, the ministry put on hold all projects associated with the implicated consultant (Vishnoi, 2013).

Corruption in the processing of environmental clearances can act in two ways: giving clearance where it is not warranted, and withholding clearance where it is warranted. The former is damaging for the environment. The latter creates a climate that puts off sincere operators and nurtures unscrupulous ones. Particularly worrisome is the withdrawal of a clearance granted earlier, because once a clearance is given, the project promoter starts operations and incurs expenses. Subsequent withdrawal of a clearance can inflict huge financial losses on the project promoter and thus makes him vulnerable to demands. Only time will tell whether the cases that have come to notice are just aberrations or the proverbial tip of the iceberg.

The hypothesis of 'environmental over-enthusiasm'

Why does the government make laws and rules that will be used against the government's activities? This cannot be a case of mere populism, the political class chasing electoral prospects. In each of the four case studies presented above, the government itself has made efforts to undo the impact of stifling regulation. In the case of the land-acquisition bill, while one ministry pushed it, other ministries voiced their concerns. In the case of highways, one government department took the unprecedented step of approaching a court of law to undo an order issued by another government department. In the case of the Western Ghat recommendations, the government appointed a committee to undo the impossible recommendations made by a committee it had appointed earlier. Since the government itself tried to undo the damage, it cannot be a case of chasing votes. In any case, there are no votes to be earned by stopping infrastructure and economic development. On the contrary, votes have been lost for failing to provide infrastructure.

In the opinion of the present author, the government and the so-called intellectuals in the society are possessed by an overwhelming desire to project a self-image of being environmentally and socially correct, even at the cost of blocking infrastructure and development. This is a case of environmental over-enthusiasm and of vanity. This environmental posturing results in the enactment of laws and rules that are often impractical and not commensurate with national goals of development. Then, in due course, the government realizes its folly and tries to undo the damage.

A vicious cycle has set in. First, the administration creates crippling regulation. Next, it is used by the activists to create roadblocks in the path of infrastructure building. Then the administration wakes up and toils to find ways to rescue the projects obstructed by the regulations which were its own creation. But by then it is often too late.

What next?

Some infrastructure watchers, the present author included, believe that this romance with the environment can not last too long. For 45 years, from 1947 to 1992, India's experiment with the socialist model of economy kept the nation poor and the majority of Indians had no first-hand experience of good infrastructure and national prosperity. But in 1992 India took the path of economic liberalization, and in the years that followed, things changed rapidly. While the life of an average Indian is still far from being as comfortable as life in developed countries, there has been a marked improvement. The people have now tasted what good infrastructure and national wealth mean and are in no mood to meekly accept daily load shedding, six hours' driving time for the 200 km distance from Delhi to Agra, or 3% annual growth.

A reduced growth rate has hugely different implications in a developed country and in a developing country. In a developed country it may mean a marginal reduction in the level of comfort, or perhaps not even that. In a developing economy it means job losses and poverty. And no politician can afford to inflict upon the people the economic consequences of idealistic environmental concerns. Therefore, the romance with environment cannot last too long. Some recent developments suggest that a reversal has already set in, slowly but surely.

In February 2013, the Ministry of Environment and Forests stripped the gram sabhas, local bodies at the village level, of their power to approve or reject proposals for the use of forest lands for building roads, transmission lines, canals or other linear projects. The very idea that a village-level body, often comprising people who are at best semi-literate, would have the necessary perspective to make trade-off decisions of a certain quantum of forest area vis-à-vis an infrastructure, was questionable. Worse, it was easy for professional activists to sway the villagers' opinions against infrastructure with baseless and malicious propaganda and emotional appeals, making the gram sabha a front end for the activists. With this amendment, the activists have lost a proxy veto power.

In January 2013, responding to complaints of delays in environmental clearances, the government formed a Cabinet Committee on Investment to review the procedure followed by the ministries in granting or refusing clearances for infrastructure and manufacturing-sector projects, and to expedite projects by setting timelines for the concerned ministries. The committee is headed by the prime minister. This is interpreted as a move to check the environmental regulatory process without actually dismantling it, and is a tacit acceptance of having over-reached in formulating the environmental regulatory process.

Conclusions

The environment is important. The world is not free of unscrupulous operators who have no care for the environment, and therefore regulations are necessary. But unscrupulous operators also exist in the domain of activism, and they can and do use regulations as a weapon to kill infrastructure.

The Saradar Sarovar case held important lessons for all. The activists were quick to learn that there is no need to question a project on its merits. The objective of holding up the project almost indefinitely, perhaps even scrapping it, can be achieved much more easily by questioning every step in the process that must be followed as per the law. But the administration did not learn the corresponding lesson: that a project cannot sail through on its merits alone. Excessively stringent environmental regulations, ostensibly meant to protect the environment, benefit neither development nor the environment.

It would be easy to write in this Conclusions section recommendations such as that environmental regulation needs to be made more pragmatic and reasonable; that the possibility of its misuse should be anticipated and factored in while formulating the regulation; and so on. The problem with all such recommendations is that they cannot be made to appear in a pop-up window and get attention when the regulation is being drafted. They remain dormant, and environmental over-enthusiasm prevails over any moderating voices. A few suggestions that could help bring about a change are given below, though it is difficult to say who should take the initiative to act on them.

- For too long, people have deceived themselves that there is no conflict between development and conservation. There is a conflict. Construction of a dam does submerge large areas and displace people; abstraction of water from a river for irrigation does significantly reduce the flow in the river, affecting river ecology; and so on.
- There are some beneficial impacts, too. Hydropower is the cleanest source of renewable energy. And in any case, infrastructure projects are necessary for livelihood security and poverty alleviation. But that does not alter the fact that there are some adverse environmental impacts. Accepting this would help in evolving solutions to minimize adverse impacts and maximize positive ones, and also in evolving a regime of trade-offs between environmental objectives vis-à-vis development objectives.
- While the anti-infrastructure components of civil society are in a state of overdrive, the pro-infrastructure community is in a coma. The first principle that needs to be established is this: the environment is too serious a matter to be left to environmentalists. Instances of environmental over-enthusiasm and consequent harm to the public interest need to be brought to the discussion table, perhaps through public interest litigation. There is no law that says that litigation can only be filed against infrastructure. It can as well be for infrastructure, or against impractical regulation. The National Highways Authority has demonstrated that the mere filing of a case in a court can be sufficient.

But the main hope lies in the democratic pressures exerted by the common people, demanding jobs, income, and food security. The people at large broadly care for the environment, and that is a good thing. But in the 20 years since the economic liberation that started in 1992, peoples' aspirations have changed. The political class cannot ignore these aspirations, and hopefully these pressures will compel society as a whole to grow out of its infatuation and into a more mature relationship vis-a-vis the environment.

Note

1. The Delhi-Mumbai Industrial Corridor is a USD 90 billion project to establish a 1483 km industrial corridor between Delhi and Mumbai.

References

Center of Excellence in Environmental Economics (2003). Amendment in 1997 for introduction of public hearing. Retrieved from http://coe.mse.ac.in/Legalprovisions.asp

Constitution of India (1950, January 26). Part IV, article 48A. Retrieved from http://lawmin.nic.in/olwing/coi/coi-english/Const.Pock%202Pg.Rom8Fsss%287%29.pdf

Goa CM Calls Ministry of Environment and Forests 'Corrupt' (2012, September 6). The Indian express. Retrieved from http://www.indianexpress.com/news/goa-cm-calls-ministry-of-environment-and-forests-corrupt/998885/

Kumar, R., & Kumar, P. (2013, September 5). Land bill a mortal blow to India's modernisation. *The Financial Express*. Retrieved from http://www.financialexpress.com/news/land-bill-a-mortal-blow-to-india-s-modernisation/1164699

Ministry of Environment and Forests (1980). *Forest (conservation) Act, 1980*. New Delhi: Government of India. Retrieved from http://www.envfor.nic.in/legis/fc.htm

Ministry of Environment and Forests (1986). *The environment (protection) Act, 1986* Department of Environment, Forest and Wildlife. New Delhi: Government of India. Retrieved from http://envfor.nic.in/sites/default/files/eprotect_act_1986.pdf

Ministry of Environment and Forests (1994). *Environmental impact assessment notification of 1994 amended in 1997*. New Delhi: Government of India. Retrieved from http://envfor.nic.in/legis/env_clr.htm

Ministry of Environment and Forests (2010). *National green tribunal Act, 2010*. New Delhi: Government of India. Retrieved from http://envfor.nic.in/rules-regulations/national-green-tribunal-ngt

Ministry of Environment and Forests (2013a). *Report of the high level working group on Western Ghats volume I*. New Delhi: Government of India. Retrieved from http://envfor.nic.in/sites/default/files/HLWG-Report-Part-1_0.pdf

Ministry of Environment and Forests (2013b). *Report of the high level working group on Western Ghats volume II*. New Delhi: Government of India. Retrieved from http://envfor.nic.in/sites/default/files/HLWG-Report-Part-2.pdf

Ministry of Law and Justice (2013). *Right to fair compensation and transparency in land acquisition, rehabilitation and resettlement Act, 2013*. New Delhi: Government of India. Retrieved from http://dolr.nic.in/dolr/actandrule.asp

Ministry of Panchayati Raj (1996). *PESA Act 1996*. New Delhi: Government of India. Retrieved from http://www.panchayat.gov.in/pesa

Ministry of Tribal Affairs (2006). *Forests rights Act 2006*. New Delhi: Government of India. Retrieved from http://tribal.nic.in/Content/ForestRightActOtherLinks.aspx

Sethi, N. (2011, September 22). MoEF crackdown on corrupt babus for green nods. *The Times of India*. Retrieved from http://articles.timesofindia.indiatimes.com/2011-09-22/developmental-issues/30189197_1_forest-advisory-committee-forest-clearances-forest-officials

Tripathi, R. (2013, January 17). MoEF deputy director held for taking bribe, Rs 1 cr seized. *The Indian Express*. Retrieved from http://www.indianexpress.com/news/moef-deputy-director-held-for-taking-bribe-rs-1-cr-seized/1060898

Vishnoi, A. (2013, February 20). CBI raid fallout: MoEF puts on hold select mining projects. *The Indian Express*. Retrieved from http://www.indianexpress.com/news/cbi-raid-fallout-moef-puts-on-hold-select-mining-projects/1076623/

WGEEP (Western Ghats Ecology Expert Panel) (2011). *Report of the Western Ghats Ecology Expert Panel part I*. (Submitted to Ministry of Environment and Forests, Government of India). Retrieved from http://moef.nic.in/downloads/public-information/wg-23052012.pdf

Winter, E. (n.d.). *A Nimzowitsch story*. Retrieved from http://www.chesshistory.com/winter/extra/nimzowitsch.html

The changing role of hydropower: from cheap local energy supply to strategic regional resource

Jacob Snell, Daniel Prowse and Ken Adams

Manitoba Hydro, Winnipeg, Canada

The role of hydropower has evolved from being a local, low-cost energy source to being a flexible resource offering a variety of ancillary services including regional frequency control and energy storage for large interconnected power systems. This paper explores this development as it relates to a North American midcontinent electrical power region. It reviews traditional benefits from hydropower in a thermal-power-dominated region and traditional efforts to quantity those benefits. With the challenges of integrating increasing quantities of variable generation such as wind and solar power, new benefits from hydropower have been identified and new methods to quantify those benefits have been developed. Recent results of a major study of the sub-hourly behaviour of a hydropower system in a Midwestern United States electrical market are reviewed.

In the past, there have been many drivers for integrating Canadian hydropower systems with thermal systems in the United States. They included the sale of surplus hydraulic energy, leveraging the load diversity between warmer and cooler climates, short-term energy arbitrage, system reliability improvements, and fuel diversification and emission reduction.

More recently, increased penetration levels of variable renewable generation, such as wind and solar power, are increasing the uncertainty and variability in the electric load–supply balance. This poses challenges to the operation of regional electrical systems. The flexibility and energy-storage characteristics of hydropower can assist electrical utilities and system operators in managing the variability through load balancing and shifting energy production to more opportune times. Many hydro facilities already provide similar balancing services for load, while others may not be able to because of operational restrictions.

Traditional benefit analyses may not adequately capture all the economic benefits attributable to flexible hydro generation, thus leaving something on the table when justifying new developments. With the growth in variable renewable resources, there is an increased need for more comprehensive benefit calculations. Several major studies in the US have attempted to fully quantify the benefits hydropower brings to the electrical system using hourly market simulations (GE Energy, 2010; *Quantifying*, 2012a). A key conclusion of these studies is that to fully capture the benefits arising from the synergy of hydropower and variable renewable generation, sub-hourly modelling and analysis are required.

The Manitoba Hydro Wind Synergy Study (MHWSS), completed by the Midcontinent Independent System Operator (MISO) and Manitoba Hydro (MH), is one of the first power-market modelling studies aimed at quantifying the benefits of hydropower at sub-hourly timeframes. The study explicitly models the variability in wind power and the energy-storage capabilities of major hydropower facilities in Manitoba, in addition to the typical characteristics of day-ahead and real-time energy and ancillary-services markets. The benefits are quantified in terms of system operating-cost reductions. Other benefits, including reductions in wind curtailments, and a description of the synergy between wind and hydro are presented.

This article is broken into several sections. The first section presents the history of electric power growth in Manitoba and the traditional benefits associated with hydro–thermal integration. The second section describes the role of hydropower in the integration of variable generation technologies and the previous efforts to quantify the benefits from hydropower. The final section presents a recent study in the US Midwest and conclusions from that work.

History of electric power in Manitoba, interconnecting to neighbouring markets, and traditional hydro–thermal integration benefits

Hydropower resources are not distributed uniformly around the globe. Some regions are hydro-rich; others have few existing or potential hydro-generation sites. Regions rich in hydropower resources have traditionally developed hydro-dominated generation fleets and benefited from low-cost energy, while in regions with fewer hydropower resources, hydropower, where available, has played a relatively minor role.

Three common electrical power sources in North America are steam-thermal (e.g. coal and nuclear), combustion turbine (gas) and hydropower. Steam-thermal stations are relatively difficult to start and stop and to ramp up or down. As a result, they are typically used for continuous, base-loaded operations. Combustion turbines and hydropower are much more flexible and are typically used to respond to peak energy demand.

Hydro stations have much lower operating costs than steam-thermal or combustion turbines, primarily thanks to zero fuel costs. However, hydro does have its own set of drawbacks. Hydropower depends on streamflow volumes, and its energy output is often limited by current hydro-climatic conditions. Additionally, the water resource is typically shared with other users and hydropower operation can be restricted in consideration of these other uses.

In Canada, hydropower plays a major role: for more than a century, hydropower has represented more than 60% of Canada's electrical generation. Three of its provinces (Quebec in the east, British Columbia in the west and Manitoba in the heart of the country) get more than 90% of their electricity from water (Rosano, 2013). This paper is written from the perspective of Manitoba Hydro.

Commercial use of electricity began in Manitoba in 1882, with the first year-round hydropower plant being developed in 1906. That first plant, Pinawa, produced electricity that fueled the dramatic growth of the province for 45 years, until it was shut down to allow another plant, Seven Sisters, to use the water more efficiently (IEEE Canada, 2008). The Seven Sisters generating station continues in operation over 80 years past its first production – an outstanding example of low-cost, reliable, renewable energy (IEEE Canada, 2000).

As Manitoba was developing its almost exclusively hydropower generating fleet, neighbouring provinces and states were generally developing thermal-powered generation or a mixture of coal-, nuclear-, gas- and hydro-fueled generation, as appropriate.

Manitoba built its first extra-provincial interconnection, a 115 kV connection from Seven Sisters to north-western Ontario, in 1956. A 138 kV interconnection to Saskatchewan was built in 1960. The completion of several hydroelectric stations in the early 1960s and into the late 1970s provided Manitoba with a surplus of generating capacity and energy, leading to the construction of nine additional interconnections between 1970 and 1980. Seasonal diversity exchanges – agreements that leverage the load diversity between colder and warmer climates – were the key economic driver for the largest of these interconnections, a 500 kV line between Manitoba and Minnesota. The 12th and most recent interconnection was built in 2002, a 230 kV line connecting western Manitoba to North Dakota (Bateman, 2005; Manitoba Hydro, n.d.)

In the 1990s, the US deregulated energy markets to increase competition and thus to reduce residential and commercial power rates and encourage innovation. Today, access to the transmission system is open to all. This has led to the development of electrical-energy markets with increased transparency and reduced market dominance from utilities, providing customers with economic benefits through reduced electrical-energy costs.

Manitoba Hydro's hydropower system lies within the Churchill–Nelson river basin (Figure 1), which has a drainage area of approximately 1.2 million km2. Manitoba Hydro currently has 17 generating stations (15 hydropower and 2 thermal), with a total rated capacity of 5700ºMW (Figure 2). Over 70% of Manitoba Hydro's installed capacity is from three hydro stations located downstream of the Stephens Lake Reservoir in northern Manitoba: Kettle, Long Spruce and Limestone. This allows a large portion of Manitoba Hydro's power generation to utilize the short-term storage available in Stephens Lake.

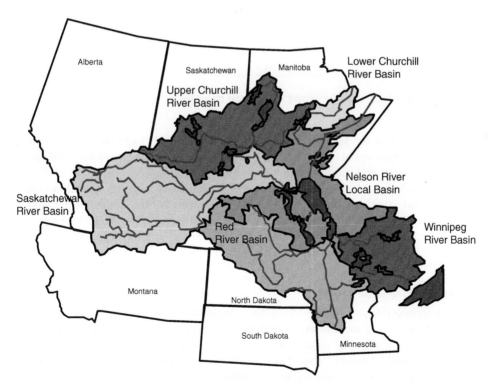

Figure 1.   The Churchill-Nelson drainage with its six sub-basins. All but the Lower Churchill River basin feed water to Manitoba Hydro's hydroelectric generating stations.

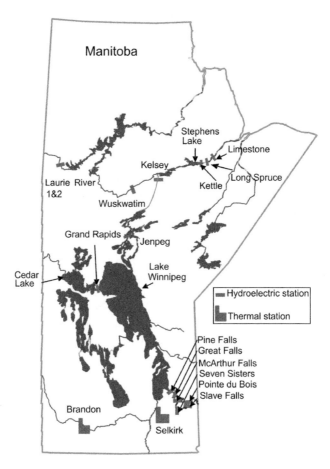

Figure 2.   Manitoba Hydro's generating stations and major lakes.

Another key station for Manitoba Hydro is the Grand Rapids hydroelectric generating station located at the outlet of Cedar Lake. Grand Rapids has a capacity of 480ºMW and is used for both long- and short-term storage operations.

The majority of Manitoba Hydro's energy exchange is with the market operated by MISO and counterparties within the MISO market. MISO is the second-largest energy market in the US by capacity. It is 86% thermal-based (48% coal, 32% oil and gas, and 6% nuclear) (MISO, 2013); the remaining 14% comes from hydro, wind and other sources.

Traditional integration benefits

The interconnections between Manitoba's hydro-dominated system and thermal-dominated systems in the US were developed based on mutually beneficial economics arising from integrating the characteristics of the two systems. These include hydraulic surplus, seasonal diversity, short-term arbitrage, fuel diversification and emission reduction, and electrical system reliability support.

Hydraulic surplus is a resulting characteristic of hydropower systems as streamflow in rivers varies from year to year based on hydroclimatic conditions. Streamflow variability is a major concern for hydroelectric utilities because it causes significant changes in annual generation. For example, in fiscal year 2003–2004 (a lower-streamflow year), Manitoba Hydro generated 19.3ºTWh. In fiscal year 2004–2005 (a higher-streamflow year), Manitoba Hydro generated 31.5ºTWh (Manitoba Hydro, 2005). This represents a change in generation of 62% between two consecutive fiscal years. Hydro-dominant utilities typically plan to have enough energy supply to serve their load requirements during periods of low flow. During periods of average or greater flow, there is an excess of energy that can be sold to neighbouring utilities or markets. Thermal-based utilities are ideal customers for surplus hydro energy because they have the ability to offset more expensive thermal power to serve their load with lower-cost hydro generation.

Seasonal diversity is a geographical characteristic that describes the difference in energy demand between two areas. The Midwestern US is a summer-peaking area; Manitoba is winter-peaking. This seasonal difference in the peak demand between areas provides an opportunity to leverage the capacity across systems to reduce individual capacity requirements and exchange energy. This greater resource utilization provides benefits for both parties.

Short-term arbitrage is the concept of taking advantage of the difference in energy prices over a short period of time, typically on a daily or weekly scale, by purchasing energy in a low-priced period and reselling when prices are higher. Reservoir and pumped-storage hydro, in addition to other energy-storage technologies, are capable of shaping their generation output to coincide with the diurnal and weekly patterns of energy prices. Pumped-storage hydro arbitrage is generally well understood (Ekman & Jensen, 2010; Ibrahim, Ilinca, & Perron, 2008; Lu, Chow, & Desrochers, 2004). Stations pump water to refill their upper reservoirs during low-priced hours and generate power during high-priced hours. Similarly, conventional reservoir-storage hydro plants can operate in a peaking mode, generating high output during high-demand hours, drawing the reservoir down, and then lowering output during low-demand hours and allowing natural streamflow to refill their reservoirs.

Fuel-diversification and emission-reduction benefits stem from offsetting fossil fuel resources with hydropower resources. Thermal utilities are able to offset their exposure to fossil fuel prices by purchasing additional energy from hydropower stations. Assessments of hydro facilities using life-cycle analyses find that hydro stations have the lowest greenhouse gas, sulphur dioxide and nitrogen oxide emissions (Gagnon, Bélanger, & Uchiyama, 2002). Therefore, by including purchased hydroelectric energy in their energy portfolio, thermal-dominated utilities are further able to hedge their exposure to the risk of carbon taxes or other emission policies.

Reliability support is a characteristic of integrating larger pools of generating stations. Electric-system operators typically plan to have enough backup resources in case of failures of major components of the electric system. Larger pools of stations provide additional resources from which to obtain these backup reserves. This reduces the total operating reserve requirements, providing economic benefits.

Role of hydropower in variable renewable power integration

It is fundamental to reliable power-system operation that supply and demand be balanced at all times. Variability of supply and demand is an ongoing operational issue for electric-system operators, who need to balance the electric load in real time. Typically, system operators can use flexible generation sources to manage the uncertainty and variability in the load balance.

The electric system uses a variety of operating reserves, also referred to as ancillary services, to regulate fluctuations and changes in demand, as well as to cover larger contingency events such as generator outages. These operating reserves help to maintain the integrity and reliability of the power system.

There is an abundant wind resource in the Midwestern US, which is being developed. In MISO, there is currently over 12,000ºMW of installed wind capacity; and in its planning scenarios, MISO includes an additional 13,000ºMW to 42,000ºMW of renewable (mostly wind) generation (Bakke, Zhou, Gu, & Mudgal, 2013).

Wind generation is inherently variable, creating a challenge for electric-system operators. Wind output can change rapidly and is difficult to predict accurately, especially the farther out in time the forecast is from the operating hour. Additionally, in the Midwest, the diurnal wind patterns have lower output during the day, when energy demand is the highest (EnerNex Corporation & Wind Logics, Inc., 2004).

Utilities and system operators could use existing technology and methods for renewable integration. This approach is likely to require additional reserves (Ela, Milligan, & Kirby, 2011; Milligan et al., 2010) and increased cycling of thermal resources (Lew et al., 2012), both of which have additional costs.

The North American Electric Reliability Corporation identified several methods for the electrical industry to research and evaluate for assisting with the integration of variable renewable energy (NERC, 2009). These include:

1. improving forecasting techniques
2. enhancing the transmission system
3. diversification of variable generation technologies
4. the use of flexible, large-scale energy-storage technologies
5. increased access to larger pools of available generation and demand

Many other research and industry groups have identified several of these items as well (Acker, 2011; National Hydropower Association, 2012; Zafirakis, Chalvatzis, Baiocchi, & Daskalakis, 2013).

Integrating hydro into a thermal-dominated market can help with wind-generation challenges in three of these ways.

1. Hydropower typically requires the development of long-distance transmission, which can be more efficiently used in combination with wind resources.
2. Reservoir and pumped-storage hydropower are additional, flexible, large-scale energy-storage technologies.
3. Development and integration of hydropower increases the pool and diversity of resources.

Quantification of hydropower benefits

Despite the aforementioned suitability of hydro to meet the challenges of variable renewable generation, developers of hydropower struggle to justify and license new projects. While this is partly due to the lack of suitable sites and increased restrictions on hydropower development (e.g. environmental constraints), another reason is a shift in the development of hydroelectric projects from governments to private developers, where financial efficiency is of even greater importance (Oud, 2002). This further emphasizes the need to quantify all the benefits. The CEATI (Center for Energy Advancement through Technological Innovation) report on the hydroelectric industry's role in integrating wind energy (Acker, 2011) contains a large review of existing literature related to wind integration and hydro's interaction with it, including many attempts to quantify the costs of wind integration and the benefit of hydropower.

More recent studies by major research groups in the US have addressed evaluating hydropower benefits in large markets with increasing levels of variable renewable power generation. Typically, these studies include a more comprehensive evaluation of hydropower benefits. However, much of the current research acknowledges that not all potential hydropower benefits are accounted for in their analyses. For example, the National Renewable Energy Laboratory's (NREL) Western Wind and Solar Integration Study only evaluated the energy-arbitrage component of pumped-storage hydro, ignoring the ancillary-services benefits (GE Energy, 2010).

A major study in the Western US by the Electric Power Research Institute (EPRI) found that the value of hydropower can be increased in three key areas: operational improvements, new hydro technologies and electricity market improvements (*Quantifying*, 2012a). One of the key electricity market improvements was the settling of energy markets on a sub-hourly basis to improve arbitrage opportunities that energy-storage technologies can take advantage of. The EPRI report recommended additional research into sub-hourly modelling of the electrical system to better capture the benefits hydropower can bring to variable renewable power integration. Subsequent US Department of Energy projects plan on looking into some of these items (*Quantifying*, 2012b).

An NREL study focusing on wind and solar integration in the Western US (Acker & Pete, 2012) quantified the benefits of hydropower in terms of system operating costs and generator revenues. It found that the flexibility of hydropower reduces the total system operating cost in the Western Electricity Coordinating Council region by USD 860 million per year (2.9%) when 35% variable renewable resources are integrated, compared to using hydro as a run-of-river resource. Part of the NREL's Western Wind and Solar Integration Study used analyses at sub-hourly timeframes. However, this was limited to select days to illustrate aspects of system performance in a broader context (GE Energy, 2010).

Review of the Manitoba Hydro Wind Synergy Study

Overview & modeling approach

The MHWSS aimed to evaluate the benefits the Manitoba Hydro hydroelectric system brings to the MISO market, recognizing that MISO has a significant wind resource and that hydro has the potential to alleviate some of the challenges with larger penetration levels of variable generation technologies. Models were developed that simulate both the hourly, day-ahead (DA) and the 5-minute, real-time (RT) energy and ancillary-services markets over a one-year study period.

The study used PLEXOS market-modelling software. PLEXOS utilizes a production-cost model that schedules the deployment of resources to minimize the total cost of electrical energy production while balancing electrical energy supply and demand as well as other system constraints. The model simulates the DA and RT energy and ancillary-services markets, including a unit commitment and economic dispatch process. 'Unit commitment' refers to the prior scheduling of a minimum level of generation that must be operating to protect for a contingency, which is more an issue for less flexible generation such as steam-thermal generation. 'Economic dispatch' refers to the market clearing and dispatch of generation to minimize the overall cost of meeting demand, given all the cost-based offers of supply to the market. The DA market is represented at an hourly timescale and completes a unit commitment and economic dispatch. The RT market is represented at a 5-minute timescale and completes an economic dispatch where units have already been committed in advance.

A new process, called Interleave, was developed specifically for use in the MHWSS. The Interleave process closely mimics market participation by hydroelectric resources and the real-life interaction between the DA and RT markets by allowing information to flow between the DA market simulation and the RT market simulation. This allowed the current energy storage position of the major reservoirs in Manitoba to be passed between the models in a chronological sequence to make informed market decisions in the next DA model calculation. Figure 3 gives an overview of the modelling process.

The footprint for the MHWSS included the entire Eastern Interconnect except Florida, ISO New England and eastern Canada. The models were based on the same information used in MISO's transmission expansion planning (MTEP) process for 2011 and 2012, which includes many assumptions about the characteristics of the bulk electric system, including generator characteristics, transmission system characteristics, system expansion cases and others (MISO, 2012).

Both uncertainty and variability of wind and load were represented in the model. Typical MISO modelling uses hourly wind and load profiles. These profiles were used in the DA market simulation. To capture the uncertainly and 5-minute variability, the hourly profiles were augmented to generate 5-minute profiles using the statistical variances between the DA and RT markets.

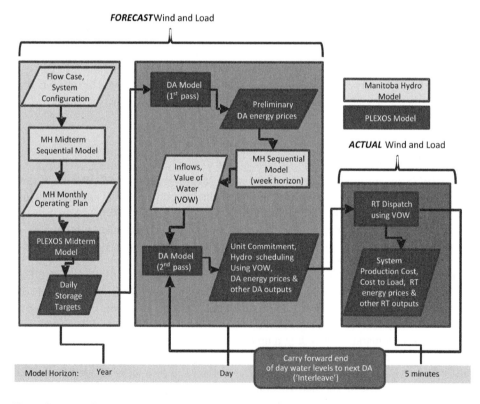

Figure 3. Model sequencing and information flow for the Wind Synergy Study. Manitoba Hydro provided information from its own hydro model to the PLEXOS model, which ran the DA-RT Interleave process.

The operating characteristics and energy storage capabilities of two major short-term storage reservoirs in the Manitoba Hydro system, Cedar Lake and Stephens Lake, were represented in the model. Inputs for reservoir size, inflow, operational limits, station characteristics (turbine efficiencies and ramp rates; spill capacity) and storage value curves were provided by Manitoba Hydro.

Storage value curves represent the future value of the hydro resource. The storage value curve is derived by using an energy-price forecast for the simulation period in an analysis that determines the value of water for various points in time at different reservoir levels. Typical storage value curves demonstrate more value near the bottom of a reservoir's operating range, because there is less reserve available to meet future energy requirements, and the hydro market participant is willing to pay more to replenish storage or will only offer additional generation (or use of this storage) at a relatively high price. As the reservoir level approaches the top of the operating range, the value of water approaches zero because additional water must be passed over a spillway and cannot be used to generate electricity. Figure 4 is an example of a typical storage value curve.

The hydro dispatch process uses the storage value curve to balance the long-term value of water with the short-term need to meet energy demand. The DA model uses the value of water from the storage value curve to determine the opportunity cost of water for the day. This opportunity cost is then used as the variable operating cost of hydro in the DA optimization, which produces the dispatch schedule for all generators for the day. From the dispatch, the planned ending storage level is compared against the storage value curve to determine the opportunity cost of water for use in the subsequent RT simulation. The RT simulation then runs at a 5-minute time step with actual wind and load profiles. The RT hydro generation profile is simulated to determine the ending storage position for the day, which is passed to the next DA market simulation to determine the updated value of water and continue with the process, day by day throughout the entire one-year study period. Figure 5 illustrates the process graphically.

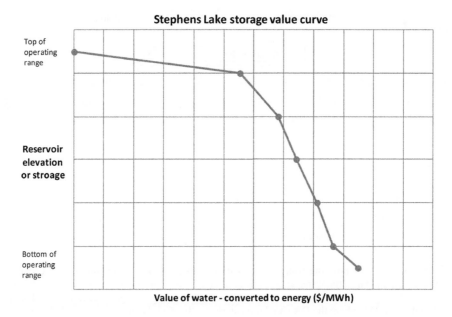

Figure 4.   Example of a storage value curve.

The method allows for the RT dispatch to differ from the DA dispatch, which enables the flexibility of the hydro generators to assist in the RT electric load balance. Tiered price/MW offers and bids are created using offsets from the value of water in storage price and the generation quantity from the DA dispatch. Multiple increments are created upwards and downwards from the current operating point to the full range of the generator capability. This prevents all-or-nothing behaviour in the generating units by requiring a certain price threshold to be met before incremental hydro energy is dispatched or stored.

Metrics used to evaluate market benefits include production cost savings, reserve cost savings, wind generation changes, and thermal cycling reductions. All values are determined by using a delta analysis, where a base scenario is compared to a changed scenario. The differences between the two model results are attributed to the power-system differences represented in the two models.

The system-wide production cost is computed as the sum over all generators in the system of the product of the production cost and the energy generated. Production cost savings represent the difference in system-wide operating costs between scenarios.

Reserve cost savings reflect the changed cost of providing energy reserves in the MISO ancillary-services market. While some benefits were observed in the analysis, generally the values were several orders of magnitude smaller than production cost savings.

Thermal cycling reductions refer to reducing the wear and tear on thermal power sources caused by ramping the unit up and down. A modest reduction in thermal cycling was observed; however, the value of the reduction was small compared to production cost savings.

The increased cycling of hydro stations may result in added costs through the added wear and tear or stress on the hydro units or on Manitoba Hydro's high-voltage direct-current transmission system. These costs have not been evaluated in this study.

Ultimately, the synergy between hydro and wind results in production savings, because more wind energy is delivered to the market (reduced wind curtailments) and is stored to be delivered at periods of higher demand (energy storage economics). Results

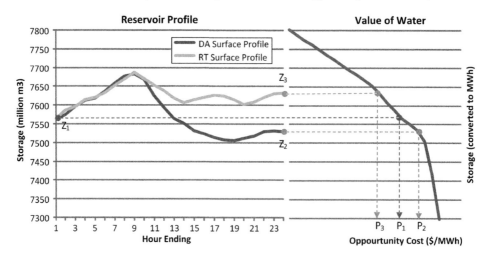

Figure 5. Example of how the water value is used in the Interleave method. The DA starts at storage level Z_1 and takes the water value to be at price P_1. After solving, the ending storage level Z_2 is used to look up price P_2 for use in the RT simulation. The ending storage level from the RT, Z_3, is passed to the next DA where the DA simulation starts for the next day again at price P_3. The process is repeated for the entire simulation period.

were analyzed to better quantify the synergy between wind and hydro resources. The correlation between wind generation in northern MISO and interchange along the Manitoba Hydro MISO interface was evaluated to measure how the production profiles of the two resources were related.

Expanded system: examining new hydro and transmission

The MHWSS utilized a scenario with an expanded hydroelectric system in Manitoba and a new transmission interconnection between Manitoba and MISO. A base-case scenario set in fiscal year 2027 was generated using the business-as-usual economic scenario from MTEP (MISO, 2012) and a median-inflow condition for the Manitoba Hydro system. This scenario was compared to a system with an additional, large hydro development rated at 695ºMW and a new 500ºkV MH transmission interconnection to MISO to determine the expansion benefits using the metrics described above. The comparisons were completed with an analysis that considered the DA market only, and with one which considered both the DA and RT markets by using the Interleave method.

Three different transmission routes were evaluated, denoted as East, West and Central corresponding to the geographical routings from Manitoba into the MISO market. The characteristics of the transmission options were comparable but terminated at different stations, resulting in power being pushed and pulled from different locations in the MISO footprint. The exact routings and additional details of the transmission options can be found in the study report (Bakke et al., 2013).

Table 1 shows the production cost savings for each method. The use of the Interleave method increased the calculated production cost savings by between 0.3% and 20.1% of the total savings, depending on the transmission route.

Pearson correlation coefficients between hydro and wind and hydro and load were evaluated to examine the wind–hydro synergy. Table 2 below shows the range of correlations observed in the three cases presented. The MH-to-MISO interface is used to approximate the power flowing from Manitoba Hydro's hydro system into MISO. The negative correlation between the MH-to-MISO interface flow and MISO wind generation indicates that hydro generation in Manitoba backs off as MISO wind generation picks up – a positive synergistic effect. The positive correlation between the MH–MISO interface flow and MISO load indicates that hydropower flows to MISO when it is needed most. The near-zero correlation between MISO wind generation and MISO load indicates that wind power and MISO load vary independently of each other, thus the challenge in using wind to supply MISO's peak loads.

Further review of the hydro–wind synergy can be seen on Figure 6, where the MH-to-MISO interface flow is compared with the MISO wind power generation. It is evident that hydro power in the simulation compensates for diurnal wind patterns as well as for shorter-term variability in wind output.

Table 1. Production cost savings comparing DA hourly-only modelling to the Interleave DA hourly and RT sub-hourly modelling for the 2027 analysis year.

Transmission route	DA-only production cost savings (USD millions)	Interleave production cost savings (USD millions)	Difference (USD millions)
East	79.02	94.88	15.86
West	82.99	86.70	3.71
Central	101.37	101.70	0.33

Table 2. Correlations depicting synergy between hydro operations and wind generation and between hydro operations and MISO load, and conversely, the independence of wind generation and MISO load.

Variables	Correlation
Manitoba Hydro–MISO interface vs. MISO wind	-0.40 to -0.44
Manitoba Hydro–MISO interface vs. MISO load	0.38
MISO wind vs. MISO load	-0.005 to -0.007

Existing system: examining market rule changes

The MHWSS evaluated the benefits of a change in the MISO market rules for the existing system. A model of the electrical system based on fiscal year 2012 similar to the one developed for the expanded system analysis was used.

MISO market rules allow Manitoba Hydro price-sensitive participation in the RT market using a certain market product, an External Asynchronous Resource (EAR). One of the restrictions on the EAR product is that Manitoba Hydro can only deliver energy to the MISO market; MISO cannot push energy to Manitoba Hydro using it. Manitoba Hydro can also participate in the RT energy market outside of the EAR market product by delivering a fixed quantity which is not sensitive to RT market price changes. The analysis evaluated a scenario where the MISO market rules are changed to expand the EAR market product by allowing Manitoba Hydro to both deliver and receive energy in response to market signals in the RT energy market.

The model idealized the representation of Manitoba Hydro's participation in the RT energy market by combining EAR and non-EAR energy products into a single market activity. The increased flexibility associated with the bi-direction EAR was captured by reducing the price hurdle in the RT tiered price/MW bids for reduced energy output from Manitoba Hydro's dispatchable generators.

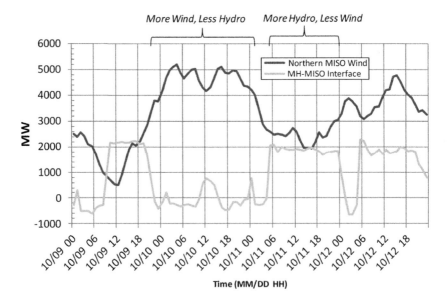

Figure 6. Comparing power flow from Manitoba Hydro to MISO as a proxy for hydro generation in Manitoba to wind generation in northern MISO. It is evident that Manitoba's hydro power decreases when wind increases, both on shorter and longer time frames.

By relaxing the market rules and allowing Manitoba Hydro's energy transfers with MISO to be more responsive to RT market signals, MISO production cost savings of USD 8.74 million for the 2012 planning year were observed, as well as a 21ºGWh reduction in wind generation curtailment. This illustrates how expanding the flexibility of hydro in the MISO thermal-dominated system results in measureable production cost benefits, in addition to traditional benefits and wind power integration enhancements.

Conclusions

This paper reviewed the history of hydroelectric development in Manitoba and the major economic drivers for integrating Manitoba's hydro system with the Midwestern US's thermal-dominated electric system. It then looked at challenges the electric-power industry is facing with the increased expansion of variable renewable power technologies and how hydropower can assist with this integration. In a world which demands increasing financial efficiency, the future development of new hydro projects may depend on more sophisticated modelling which can quantify the substantial benefits of hydropower in modern energy markets, including its contribution to the integration of variable renewable power technologies.

The results of a major study using advanced energy-market and hydropower modelling techniques were reviewed. DA hourly modelling was directly compared to a new, combined DA hourly and RT sub-hourly modelling method. System-wide predicted production cost savings in MISO increased by up to 20% using the new method, but were not typical of all scenarios. The study also demonstrated that additional hydropower flexibility benefits can be evaluated using these new study methods that may not have been captured by less detailed methods.

It is evident that sub-hourly modelling of hydropower in thermal-dominated energy markets can help in creating a more comprehensive analysis of the benefits of hydropower. Further research is recommended to evaluate and characterize additional factors that impact the benefits arising from sub-hourly representation of hydro.

Acknowledgements

The authors would like to thank Jordan Bakke, Zheng Zhou and Dale Osborn from MISO, Kevin Gawne and Karl Reznichek from MH and Tao Guo from Energy Exemplar for their collaboration on the MHWSS.

References

Acker, T. L. (2011). *The Hydroelectric Industry's Role in Integrating Wind Energy*. (CEATI Report No. T102700-0371). CEATI International. Retrieved from http://www.ceati.com/freepubl ications/0371_Web.pdf

Acker, T., & Pete, C. (2012). *Western Wind and Solar Integration Study: Hydropower Analysis*. doi:10.2172/1037937

Bakke, J., Zhou, Z., Gu, Y., & Mudgal, S. (2013). *Manitoba Hydro Wind Synergy Study Final Report*. MISO. Retrieved from https://www.misoenergy.org/_layouts/MISO/ECM/Download. aspx?ID=160821

Bateman, L. A. (2005). A History of Electric Power Development in Manitoba. *IEEE Canada Review(Winter)*, 22–25. Retrieved from http://www.ieee.ca/canrev/cr49/pages22-25.pdf

Ekman, C. K., & Jensen, S. H. (2010). Prospects for large scale electricity storage in Denmark. *Energy Conversion and Management, 51*, 1140–1147. doi:10.1016/j.enconman.2009.12.023

Ela, E., Milligan, M., & Kirby, B. (2011). *Operating Reserves and Variable Generation*. doi:10. 2172/1023095

EnerNex Corporation & Wind Logics, Inc. (2004). *Characterization of the Wind Resource in the Upper Midwest*. UVIG. Retrieved from http://variablegen.org/wp-content/uploads/2013/01/ XcelMNDOCwindcharacterization.pdf

Gagnon, L., Bélanger, C., & Uchiyama, Y. (2002). Life-cycle assessment of electricity generation options: The status of research in year 2001. *Energy Policy, 30*, 1267–1278. doi:10.1016/S0301-4215(02)00088-5

GE Energy. (2010). *Western Wind and Solar Integration Study.* (NREL/SR-550-47434). NREL. Retrieved from http://www.nrel.gov/docs/fy10osti/47434.pdf

Ibrahim, H., Ilinca, A., & Perron, J. (2008). Energy storage systems—Characteristics and comparisons. *Renewable and Sustainable Energy Reviews, 12*, 1221–1250. doi:10.1016/j.rser.2007.01.023

IEEE Canada. (2000). Seven Sisters Generating Station. IEEE Canada Showcase of Canadian Engineering Achievement. Retrieved August 15, 2013, from http://www.ieee.ca/millennium/seven_sisters/seven_about.html

IEEE Canada. Historic Pinawa Generating Station recognized as engineering milestone. IEEE Milestones in Canada. Retrieved June 11, 2008, from http://www.ieee.ca/history/milestones/pinawa.html

Lew, D., Brinkman, G., Kumar, N., Besuner, P., Agan, D., & Lefton, S. (2012, August). *Impacts of Wind and Solar on Fossil-Fueled Generators: Preprint.* Presented at IEEE Power and Energy Society General Meeting, 22–26 July 2012, San Diego, California. Retrieved from http://www.nrel.gov/docs/fy12osti/53504.pdf

Lu, N., Chow, J. H., & Desrochers, A. A. (2004, May). Pumped-Storage Hydro-Turbine Bidding Strategies in a Competitive Electricity Market. *IEEE Transactions on Power Systems, 19*, 834–841. doi:10.1109/TPWRS.2004.825911

Manitoba Hydro. (2005). *Manitoba Hydro-Electric Board 54th Annual Report.* Winnipeg, Manitoba: Manitoba Hydro.

Manitoba Hydro. (n.d.). History of Regional Interconnections. Manitoba Water Power. Retrieved from http://www.manitobawaterpower.com/electricity_trade/history.html

Milligan, M., Donohoo, P., Lew, D., Ela, E., Kirby, B., Holttinen, H., & Kamwa, I. (2010, October). *Operating Reserves and Wind Power Integration: An International Comparison.* 9th Annual International Workshop on Large-Scale Integration of Wind Power into Power Systems as well as on Transmission Networks for Offshore Wind Power Plants Conference. Quebec City, Canada. Retrieved from http://www.nrel.gov/docs/fy11osti/49019.pdf

MISO. (2012). *MTEP 12 Economic Models Assumptions Document.* MISO. Retrieved from https://www.misoenergy.org/Library/Repository/Meeting%20Material/Stakeholder/Planning%20Materials/Economic%20Study%20Models%20User%20Group/20120809/20120809%20ESMUG%20MTEP12%20Economic%20Model%20Assumptions%20with%20LRZ%20Info.pdf

MISO. (2013). MISO Corporate Information [fact sheet]. Retrieved from: https://www.misoenergy.org/Library/Repository/Communication%20Material/Corporate/Corporate%20Fact%20Sheet.pdf

National Hydropower Association. (2012). *Challenges and Opportunities For New Pumped Storage Development.* Retrieved from: http://www.hydro.org/wp-content/uploads/2012/07/NHA_PumpedStorage_071212b1.pdf

NERC. (2009). *Accommodating High Levels of Variable Generation.* Retrieved from: www.nerc.com/files/ivgtf_report_041609.pdf

Oud, E. (2002). The evolving context for hydropower development. *Energy Policy, 30*, 1215–1223. doi:10.1016/S0301-4215(02)00082-4

Quantifying the Value of Hydropower in the Electric Grid: Final Report. (2012a). 1023144. EPRI, Palo Alto. CA. doi:10.2172/1057586

Quantifying the Value of Hydropower in the Electric Grid: Modeling Results for Future Scenarios. (2012b). 1023141. EPRI, Palo Alto, CA.

Rosano, M. (2013, June). Energy in Canada. *Canadian Geographic.* Retrieved from: http://www.canadiangeographic.ca/magazine/jun13/energy_in_canada.asp

Zafirakis, D., Chalvatzis, K. J., Baiocchi, G., & Daskalakis, G. (2013, May). Modeling of financial incentives for investments in energy storage systems that promote the large-scale integration of wind energy. *Applied Energy, 105*, 138–154. doi:10.1016/j.apenergy.2012.11.073

Interbasin water transfers at the US–Mexico border city of Nogales, Sonora: implications for aquifers and water security

Andrea Harrop Prichard[a] and Christopher A. Scott[a,b]

[a]School of Geography and Development, University of Arizona, Tucson, USA; [b]Udall Center for Studies in Public Policy, University of Arizona, Tucson, USA

Nogales, Sonora, on the US–Mexico border, employs interbasin water and wastewater transfers to address water scarcity in the context of a rising population, a warming climate, and cross-border institutional asymmetries. A unique feature of its geography and border context is Nogales's export of wastewater both north to the US and, starting with the August 2012 commissioning of a strategically positioned wastewater treatment plant, south to the Alisos basin, which is its principal drinking-water source. Thus, when the new plant is fully operational, it will result in indirect potable reuse of effluent via recharge of the source-water aquifer. This paper finds that such strategies contribute to increased water scarcity in Nogales, and to detrimental health, livelihood and environmental impacts in the source basin, thus raising questions about interbasin transfers as a principal water management strategy.

Introduction

With global trends of population growth, urbanization and climate change, water is becoming increasingly difficult to procure in sufficient supply and quality to meet urban demand, which in many contexts is the highest water-policy priority (Molle, 2007). Particularly in arid and semi-arid regions, municipal water providers face an ever-growing challenge to locate sufficient water resources. The "hard path" approach to providing water is one that employs major infrastructure projects to pump, store and convey water to the sites of greatest demand (Gleick, 2003) and greatest political power. This approach can be limited to those who have the funds to construct and maintain such costly operations, so these projects tend to be authorized by central governments and serve major cities (Scott & Pineda Pablos, 2011). The hard path is consistent with a supply-driven approach to meeting water needs, in contrast to the "soft path", which seeks to increase water efficiency and manage demand. Smaller cities find it difficult to mobilize the resources necessary to pursue hard path approaches, but Nogales has done so – perhaps without adequate attention to a broader set of water management options.

Interbasin transfers are often detrimental to rural communities in the source areas where the transferred water is extracted. When surface-water diversions or pumping of deep wells results in overdraft of the water source, the hydrological imbalance can displace the livelihood activities of local residents or, in extreme cases, the people themselves. In many areas of Mexico, water is a limited resource, either due to a semi-arid climate, such as in Nogales, or an exceedingly large demand, such as the case of Mexico

City. The Metropolitan Area of the Valley of Mexico receives 31.5% of its water from external sources such as the Cutzamala River and Lerma-Balsas River basins and 66.4% of its water from local wells (Tortajada, 2006). The over-exploitation of the aquifer has caused widespread subsidence locally and adverse impacts elsewhere in the State of Mexico. For this reason, the government of the State of Mexico sued the government of Mexico City for USD2.2 billion for damages caused by the overdraft of the aquifers, though charges were later dropped with a change in government (Tortajada, 2006). The interbasin transfers, too, have caused social conflict and degradation of the soil in the Lerma Valley, largely ignored by the government, whose primary concern was to supply water to Mexico City (Tortajada, 2006; Tortajada & Castelán, 2003). Analogous to the case of Mexico City although at a far smaller scale, Nogales, Sonora, has pursued interbasin transfers primarily as a strategy to supply water and manage wastewater within its service area. Little attention has been paid to the environmental and social impacts in the source basin of Nogales's interbasin transfer, which forms the majority of the city's water supply.

Situated at the US–Mexico border, Nogales, Sonora (Figure 1), population 220,000 (INEGI, 2010), has for decades supplemented its drinking water supply with external aquifers and sent its wastewater downhill towards Rio Rico, Arizona, for treatment in the Nogales International Wastewater Treatment Plant (NIWTP). Starting 31 August 2012, however, Nogales began pumping a portion of its wastewater uphill to the south, in a second interbasin transfer, in an effort to conserve its effluent resource (Milman & Scott, 2010) within Mexico and to reduce the fees paid to the United States for wastewater treatment at the NIWTP (Sonora SI, 2011).

In the form of interbasin transfers, Nogales, Sonora has enlarged its hydrologic sphere to encompass the Los Alisos basin. While interbasin transfers are enabling improved water service to Nogales city residents, some populations within the Los Alisos basin are marginalized in the process, because this previously self-contained community is now exporting its clean water and receiving Nogales's wastewater in return.

The double interbasin transfer makes the Nogales case unique in that the new destination of the city's pumped wastewater is the same location as Nogales's principal source of freshwater, the town of Cíbuta, Sonora, in the Los Alisos basin. This creates a double interbasin transfer of water, in opposing directions, and results in indirect potable use of wastewater (via effluent recharge of the source water). In this manner, Nogales has created an artificial upstream–downstream relationship with Cíbuta, since Nogales may now use its 'upstream' position to take the majority of the freshwater and release contaminated water 'downstream' to Cíbuta, despite the natural elevation divide which had previously prevented this type of relationship.

This paper focuses on interbasin water transfers and their impacts on the water security of both the major border city of Nogales, Sonora, and the source basin community of Cíbuta. We use the definition of water security offered by Norman et al. (2010): "sustainable access, on a watershed basis, to adequate quantities of water of acceptable quality to ensure human and ecosystem health". Both human and ecosystem health are considered in this study, for both of the basins involved in Nogales–Los Alisos water transfers. Although interbasin transfers are common around the world (Alagh, Pangare & Gujja, 2007; Carvalho & Magrini, 2006; Gupta & Van der Zaag, 2008; Howe & Goemans, 2003; Saurí & Del Moral Ituarte, 2001), little attention is given in the planning process and in subsequent studies to their effects in the source basin (the hydrological basin from which the water originates). This unique case of the inversion of the upstream–downstream relationship, as artificially constructed by the hard path approach to water resources management, has permitted us to

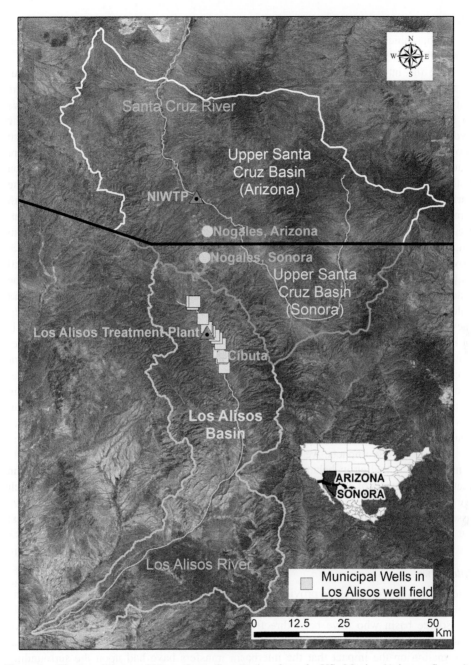

Figure 1. The Los Alisos and Upper Santa Cruz Basins along the US–Mexico (Arizona–Sonora) border. The Upper Santa Cruz basin is transboundary, as is the Santa Cruz River, which crosses the international border twice. Map by Andrea Prichard, University of Arizona Basin boundaries from INEGI and Arizona NEMO Coordinate System: GCS-GRS 1980 September 22, 2012.

frame and address in this paper the following research question: To what extent do the interbasin transfers between Cíbuta and Nogales resolve water scarcity concerns, and with what social, hydrological and ecological impacts on the source basin?

Methods and results

As a geographical analysis encompassing human and environmental interactions through time, this case study has required different methods to address each component. To evaluate the interbasin water transfers' impact on water security in both basins, our methods included the following, with brief mention here of the objectives: (a) interviews with key informants to determine present water availability; (b) remote sensing analysis to link past ecological trends (especially of riparian vegetation) with changes in the hydrological regime resulting from water transfers; and (c) a basic estimation and projection of the hydraulic balance for both source and demand basins to assess future water security scenarios. Interviews with ranchers in the source basin provided insight on both social and hydrological impacts of interbasin transfers via accounts of decreasing surface and well water. Interviews with water managers provided perspective on both strategic infrastructure plans and the supply and demand trends of the municipal water. Remote sensing vegetation change indices were evaluated to determine the ecological impacts of transfers of groundwater that is linked, via shallow groundwater, to surface flows in the riparian corridor. Satellite scenes enabled glimpses into the past which served as proxies for historical water records. Last, hydraulic balance projections clarified the extent of present and future water displacement resulting from interbasin transfers, as calculated using varying scenarios of aquifer recharge and population growth. Together, these techniques form a more complete view of the interbasin transfer challenge, which is of increasing global importance. Internationally, cities are growing and per capita water use is rising, so the urban demand is greater even as in many cases the supply dwindles or becomes contaminated. To meet this demand, the supply must come from farther – either deeper, in the case of some groundwater sources, or farther afield, such as surrounding basins. When these costly transfers occur, they inherently disrupt natural flows and can have significant impacts on communities and ecosystems dependent on those water sources.

To assess these impacts, we have used mixed methods including interviews, remote sensing, and a hydraulic balance analysis of the basins involved. We report here the methods and results of each component of the study, beginning with the interviews, which we then relate to remote sensing–based assessment of ecological condition. Finally, we assess the hydraulic balance resulting from the interbasin transfers with their implications for human and ecological communities in the source basin.

Interviews

Interviews were conducted to provide background, context, and subjective accounts of the water supply, both from an urban water manager's perspective and from that of ranchers in the source basin who have been directly affected by the transfers. In the absence of hydrological data such as river and well levels in the area, interviews provided crucial information on the impact that the interbasin transfers have had upon the surrounding areas. Preliminary interviews, in which ranchers reported the deaths of hundreds of fruit trees in response to aquifer drawdown around a municipal well, prompted the choice of a remote sensing study to assess vegetation change along the Los Alisos riverbed to see whether this phenomenon occurred throughout the Los Alisos well field. Other preliminary interviews revealed the unsustainability of the groundwater extraction via accounts of dried-up wells and the disappearance of the Los Alisos River since municipal pumping began in the summer of 1996; this information provided the impetus for the hydraulic balance study to evaluate the degree to which the outflow exceeds the inflow.[1]

Ten residents of Cíbuta and Nogales were interviewed, including ranchers, common-pool landholders, and urban residents. A further 10 water service professionals in Nogales, Sonora, were interviewed, ranging from site managers of the new Los Alisos wastewater treatment plant to managers, technicians and planners at the municipal water service provider of Nogales (Organismo Operador Municipal de Agua Potable, Alcantarillado y Saneamiento, or OOMAPAS). All interviews were conducted in Spanish and recorded for accuracy. Water professionals were selected for interview based on their specialized knowledge and were interviewed individually, while residential participants were often interviewed as families and were selected based on the snowball method, in which interviewees suggested other participants who might be able to contribute to the study.

When asked about the interbasin water transfer in the Los Alisos basin, residents' opinions varied, depending on their relationship with OOMAPAS. Those on communally owned (*ejido*) land had agreed to allow the drilling of two municipal wells on their property in exchange for free access to piped domestic water, which, they say, has never failed them. The majority of Cíbuta residents, however, have no such agreement with OOMAPAS – indeed, some wells were drilled on private property without legal permits. Town residents must not only pay for the municipal water, but they have had to abandon their private wells, which have, in large part, run dry since high-powered municipal wells in the area have lowered the water table.

Two families of ranchers expressed fears of losing their land holdings because their wells and reservoirs are drying and they cannot afford gasoline to pump water for irrigation. They may consequently lose their cattle, unless rain refills their reservoirs, which had been fed by surface springs before the drop in the water table. One family said that within six months of the installation of a nearby municipal well, their well level dropped by six metres, requiring them to pay to operate the pump in their deepest well in order to have enough water for their cattle. They stated that despite numerous droughts, never before had the water dropped so severely in their 74 years of ranching. They feel they have not been compensated for this infraction on their property and water rights. This type of interaction has been seen throughout Sonora, where urban water management choices have jeopardized traditional agricultural and livestock livelihoods (Díaz-Caravantes & Sánchez-Flores, 2011). Despite water-management centralization in Mexico (Scott & Banister, 2008), some city governments have attempted to play a proactive role in the implementation of interbasin transfers. For example, in north-eastern Mexico, farmers downstream of the city of Monterrey's diversion of the Río San Juan were compensated both financially for unirrigable land and hydrologically in the form of effluent allocations to use for irrigation (Scott, Flores-López & Gastélum, 2007). In Cíbuta, one vocal family of ranchers had made public complaints in the newspaper and over the radio about their loss of livelihood from the municipal groundwater extraction, but they did not receive or expect any compensation from the municipal water company.

Nogales water managers at OOMAPAS, on the receiving end of the transfer, did not feel that Cíbuta was affected and were instead concerned about the welfare of the city of Nogales. They felt that their infrastructure was out of date and could not keep up with the rise in demand. Figure 2 shows Nogales's stark rise in population, which is due in large part to urban migration, or the movement of workers from rural areas to urban areas, generally in transition from the agricultural sector to the industrial or commercial sector. The water demand has risen not only because of population growth but also for extensive industrial use, such as in the 95 active factories (as of 2006) in Nogales (Wilder, Scott, Pineda-Pablos, Varady & Garfin, 2012).

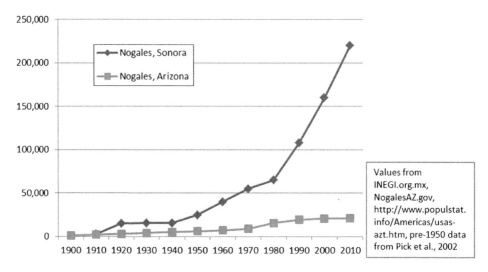

Figure 2. Populations of Nogales, Sonora, and Nogales, Arizona, 1900–2010. Values from http://www.inegi.org.mx, http://www.nogalesaz.gov, and http://www.populstat.info/Americas/usas-azt.htm; pre-1950 data from Pick et al., 2002.

The result of this city-ward migration is that there are too many water users for the limited supply. Only 39% of Nogales residents benefit from a 24-hour water connection in their homes (Cervera & Rubio, 2003). Although water managers say they do not have a long-term sustainable supply plan, they are hopeful that repairs of leaky pipes and initiatives to promote water conservation will prove effective in increasing efficiency of water use. For instance, OOMAPAS implemented metering of domestic water in many parts of Nogales in 2010, and in one year's time they saw dramatic reductions in consumption as a result.

Part of the income generated by the water metering goes toward the construction and operation of the new wastewater treatment plant in Los Alisos. The purpose of this plant, according to managers, is to treat a portion of the city's wastewater and thus relieve the burden on the NIWTP, which on average has been treating an excess volume of Mexican wastewater: 126% over the volume authorized by binational accords between Mexico and the United States (434 litres per second, or lps) (IBWC, 1988; NADB, 2012). Other benefits of this plant, they say, include providing first-time sewerage to over ten thousand citizens, as well as supplying recharge to the over-exploited aquifer using effluent from the treatment plant, which is just upstream of the majority of the wells in the Los Alisos municipal well field (La Prensa Sonora-Arizona, 2012). When asked for details, however, project managers had no clear answers on the amount of recharge that would take place. There was no plan to construct infiltration basins to maximize recharge; the plan, they said, is for the effluent to flow downstream in the Los Alisos River bed.

Residents of Cíbuta are hopeful that the return flow of the effluent will bring life back to the river that once flowed through the town, but they have misgivings about the water's quality. In 2010, several children were reported by local residents to have serious illnesses that were traced to the river, which flows ephemerally after rainstorms. The illnesses, including hepatitis, were attributed to contamination from a jail located a few kilometres upstream, whose sewage flowed into the riverbed, sickening or killing animals that drank from it. Another upstream source of contamination is the new housing development, Fraccionamiento La Mesa, a government low-income housing area of about 5000 homes constructed in the Los Alisos basin to accommodate the growing population of Nogales. The wastewater treatment plant for this community is inadequate because according to water managers, it was only designed to treat about half of the 30 lps of wastewater produced. Residents fear that the Los Alisos wastewater treatment plant, which receives about 10 times the volume of wastewater that is produced in Fraccionamiento La Mesa, would have serious negative impacts on the health of all downstream, including wildlife, if it should let untreated water flow downstream in the same way that Fraccionamiento La Mesa does.

In summary, the exploitation of the Los Alisos aquifer by OOMAPAS has lowered the water table in Cíbuta, as evidenced by the disappearance of the Los Alisos River and the drying of personal wells throughout the town of Cibuta since the onset of large-scale pumping in the Los Alisos well field. The drop in the water table has harmed the livelihoods of several residents, especially ranchers, who depended on their wells to irrigate their pastures and give water to their cattle, and they feel uncompensated for this loss. The southward expansion of the city of Nogales has caused the contamination of the Los Alisos River upstream of Cíbuta due to the introduction of untreated wastewater from Fraccionamiento La Mesa and other sources, provoking illness in Cíbuta. While the Los Alisos treatment plant may prove beneficial by raising the water table, it also presents a potential hazard to water quality if there are flaws, accidents or excess volumes of wastewater pumped to the treatment plant – which could then have impacts reaching Nogales, since the municipal well field is in the same stretch of the riverbed as the treatment plant.

Remote sensing: riparian vegetation change in the interbasin transfer source basin of Los Alisos

Residents of Cíbuta have reported major negative impacts on the ecosystem since municipal pumping began about 15 years ago. In response to the eyewitness accounts of the drying river, wells and trees, we sought records of historic well levels in the area to verify and quantify the drop in the water table. Unfortunately, those records were unavailable, so in this study we have used riparian vegetation health along the banks of the Los Alisos River as a proxy for groundwater level around the well field (Elmore, Mustard, Manning & Lobell, 2000), since the health and abundance of the riparian vegetation in periods of little or no precipitation is associated with the height of the water table (Johnson, Dixon, Simons, Jenson & Larson, 1995). We performed a remote-sensing analysis of the riparian vegetation change along Cíbuta's well field since 1996 to see whether the drawdown of groundwater showed significant impact on local vegetation and represented an unsustainable decline within the basin of the now-ephemeral Los Alisos River.

Methods include Normalized Difference Vegetation Index (NDVI) and image differencing to analyze the riparian vegetation changes in Landsat images from 4 May 1996 to 28 April 2011. If the NDVI image showed a decline in riparian vegetation after the extensive groundwater extraction from the well field along the river, this analysis would corroborate the claims of the interviewed residents of Cíbuta, who stated that the municipal pumping had negative ecological impacts in the area. According to OOMAPAS-Nogales, the pumping in Los Alisos began in 1996, and the most recent well began pumping in July 2010. The choice of this time span was made to capture any

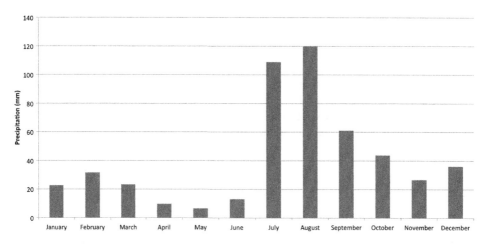

Figure 3. Average monthly precipitation for Nogales, Sonora, based on data for 1971–2000. The summer monsoon period is the most significant contributor of precipitation. *Source:* Servicio Meteorológico Nacional (http://smn.cna.gob.mx/climatologia/normales/estacion/son/NORMAL26187.TXT).

changes in vegetation that might be a result of municipal pumping of the groundwater in the Los Alisos basin. The subset of the Landsat 5 image is based on the location of the Los Alisos well field, which includes the town of Cíbuta and the Los Alisos River. Anniversary dates for the images are in late April/early May, which precede the summer monsoon season and follow a long period without rain (Figure 3). Therefore, vegetation health at this time of year reflects the supply of groundwater rather than the amount of precipitation. The targeted riparian species are those that are not desert adapted. Drought-sensitive riparian vegetation is a more sensitive indicator of water loss than mesquite trees, for example, which can survive under drier conditions (Stromberg, Tiller & Richter, 1996). The selected years, 1996 and 2011, had similar precipitation, patterns showing little spring rainfall. The greatest amount of vegetation change took place along the Los Alisos River, although the type of change varied. Around the town of Cíbuta, there was an increase in vegetation (which residents say, may be attributed to intentional planting), but downstream, there was a decrease in the natural riparian vegetation along the riverbed.

Overall, the image difference of this NDVI subset does not show significant change along the riparian corridor for this time period. Additional change detections of different time frames corroborate the reports of dead or dying oak trees in the hills, but riparian vegetation has a similar amount of greening and dieback. It is known, however, that the wells have been pumped steadily and that the water table is dropping. Since reduction of riparian vegetation is an expected outcome of groundwater decline (Jin, Schaepman, Clevers, Su & Hu, 2011), our hypothesis was that the resultant image from the NDVI change detection of the 1996 and 2011 riparian area downstream of the well fields would demonstrate this decrease in riparian health and vegetation productivity; but since there was little change, it appears that either the riparian vegetation is drought resistant, or the water table is still within reach of the vegetation's roots. The remote-sensing vegetation analysis showed great ecological impact resulting from the decade of drought in the study period, but did not reveal a strong decline in vegetation due to interbasin transfer in the riparian area downstream of the Los Alisos well field.

Hydraulic balance of source and destination basins

To quantitatively estimate the impacts of Nogales's interbasin transfers, we conducted simple hydraulic balance studies on both the Sonoran Upper Santa Cruz basin and the Los Alisos basin for three time periods. The objective was to estimate how the inflow compares (and will compare) to the outflow, and thus to gauge the stability of the aquifer and the city's freshwater supply. In 2009, Mexico's National Water Commission conducted in-depth studies of aquifer water balances, including precipitation, infiltration, storm water and sub-surface flows (CONAGUA, 2011), so our methodology focuses on the current and projected hydraulic balances of the two basins. Also, the CONAGUA report shows an 11 million m^3 surplus of water for the Los Alisos basin in 2009, which contradicts observations from water professionals that the water table has been consistently dropping, as seen in the Los Alisos well field (personal communication, OOMAPAS, November 2011). The reported surplus of water in CONAGUA's water balance is probably related to the omission of significant extractions by wells without permits. Several of the high-productivity municipal wells in Los Alisos well field are currently untitled (personal communication, OOMAPAS, November 2011).

The city of Nogales overlies the Nogales Wash aquifer and the transboundary Santa Cruz aquifer, both of which lie in the Upper Santa Cruz basin (Figure 1). Water for municipal purposes comes mostly from three sources: the Mascareñas well field along the Sonoran Santa Cruz River to the east; multiple small wells throughout the city centre; and the Los Alisos well field. Of the three sources, only Los Alisos must be pumped over an elevation divide to supply the city. For this reason, we have only included the water transfer from Los Alisos in the calculation, since water originating in the Sonoran Santa Cruz basin either remains in that basin (for outdoor use) or goes down the drain and enters the sewage system, which currently is included in the measured volume of water moving across the border toward the NIWTP in Rio Rico, Arizona. In this study of interbasin transfers, we have only included quantities of water that terminated in basins other than where they originated.

The Sonoran Santa Cruz sub-basin has a net loss of about 8.8 million cubic metres (mcm) of water per year. This number is based on the 2011 water transfers, which included an average 270 lps inflow from the Los Alisos basin and a 548 lps outflow to the NIWTP (Table 1) (personal communication, OOMAPAS, June 13, 2011). This annual loss of water due to transfers to the United States is not indicative of sustainable water management practice. According to a study by Morehouse et al. (2000), Mexican water officials have stated that by 2015, Nogales would require an additional 11,750 acre-feet of water per year (14.5 mcm/y) to sustain its population, a quantity equal to 63.5% of the annual volume of municipal water used (Diaz & Morehouse, 2003).

This water deficit in Nogales, Sonora, will go from bad to worse in coming years. Six neighbourhoods in the south of Nogales, with a combined estimated population of 34,560, will soon be connected to the wastewater collection system for the first time (EPA, 2008), which means improved sanitation conditions, but less return flow to the Sonoran Santa Cruz basin. The wastewater generated in this area, which has historically remained in the basin in the form of cesspools and septic systems (EPA, 2008), will be sent over the nearby elevation divide to be treated and released as effluent in the Los Alisos basin. Once this is implemented, probably in early 2013 (personal communication, OOMAPAS engineering supervisor, 13 June 2011), there will be about a 22% increase in the wastewater leaving the Sonoran Santa Cruz basin.[2] The hydraulic balance calculations presented here are based

Table 1. Projected hydraulic balance of the Sonoran Santa Cruz basin, 2011, 2015 and 2020 (flow rates in litres per second). Inflow is dependent on the productivity of the Los Alisos well field. The net loss of water from this sub-basin begins at 278 lps in 2011 to a maximum potential loss of 601 lps in 2020. Despite an effort to increase well productivity in the Los Alisos basin, which depends on the recharge capacity of the effluent from the Los Alisos treatment plant, the Sonoran Santa Cruz basin has a growing net loss of water due to its export of wastewater to the United States and to the Los Alisos basin.

| | 2011 | | 2015 | | | 2020 | | |
	Inflow	Outflow	Inflow (zero recharge)	Inflow (100% recharge)	Outflow	Inflow (zero recharge)	Inflow (100% recharge)	Outflow
From Los Alisos	270		247	418		202	418	
To Rio Rico, AZ		548*			434**			503
To Los Alisos					271			300***
Net		**278**			**287–458**			**385–601**

* The permissible limit is 434 lps of wastewater to send to Rio Rico, so in 2011, OOMAPAS paid high rates for treatment of the additional 114 lps (average) of wastewater sent to the NIWTP.

** OOMAPAS plans to continue sending 434 lps to the NIWTP (Rio Rico) and send the overage to Los Alisos.

*** The Los Alisos plant's maximum capacity is 330 lps, and it receives 30 lps from Fraccionamiento La Mesa. It is unknown whether the excess 69 lps will be sent to Rio Rico or Los Alisos.

on the assumption that this project will be implemented in full on the timeline stated by the interviewed engineer.

We can project for 2015 a 705 lps wastewater discharge from the city of Nogales, to be distributed between the two wastewater treatment plants leaving the Sonoran Santa Cruz sub-basin (Table 1), based on a 22% increase in wastewater produced from the six neighbourhoods on top of an additional 30,480 people living in the area. This increased population is extrapolated from the 13.8% population rise between the 2005 interim census and the 2010 National Census (INEGI, 2005, 2010). As for inflow, the actual amount of water that will be pumped from the Los Alisos well field is unknown since it is dependent on climatic factors, unknown amounts of recharge from the new effluent resource, and potential new decisions on municipal pumping. One OOMAPAS water manager stated that the current plan is not to drill additional wells but to improve efficiency in the system by repairing leaks and increasing water metering to encourage conservation. Assuming there will be no additional wells, we can infer that the productivity of the Los Alisos well field will continue its downward trend. An OOMAPAS engineer with 13 years of experience working on the Los Alisos well field stated that the production of the wells has declined by about 30% since their original installation.

Residents in the Los Alisos basin have also witnessed drops in the water table. Many municipal wells are on private property, and landowners reported that technicians have come to deepen the wells since initial installation. The residents and engineers estimated that the municipal wells were 80–100 metres deep. In view of the 20-metre depth of the private wells that previously served the ranchers, the fact that it was necessary to deepen an 80-metre well on the same property indicates a severe drop in the water table.

In order to calculate the hydraulic balance using the 30% decline estimated by OOMAPAS from 1996 to 2011 (a 15-year period), we can infer a 9 lps drop in production each year. Since the average production of the well field between 2008 and 2011 has been 315 lps (personal communication, OOMAPAS, 13 June 2011), that would suggest that the original production was 450 lps before the 30% drop: $(450 \times 0.3) / 15 = 9$ lps for every year since 1996. It should be stressed that this represents a historical average over 15 years; any future changes would be subject to a range of processes including recharge influenced by surface flow events, climatic change and other uncertain factors. With no additional input, this yields a total estimated outflow of 279 lps from Los Alisos in 2015 and 234 lps in 2020. Of this outflow, however, 32 lbs will go to Fraccionamiento La Mesa, so Nogales would receive 247 lps of water in 2015 and 202 lps in 2020 from Los Alisos (Tables 1 & 2).

For wastewater projections, we must look into population projections. Using the same 13.8% rise in population that occurred between 2005 and 2010 (INEGI, 2010), we can project a 2015 population of 250,772 and a 2020 population of 285,468 residents in Nogales, Sonora. The corresponding rise in exported wastewater can be estimated as follows.

The six neighbourhoods represent 16% of the 2010 census population, and once they receive sewerage, the Nogales population served will rise from 70% to 86%. If 86% of the 2015 population (215,664) produces 705 lps of wastewater, then 86% of the 2020 population estimate will produce about 803 lps of wastewater.

Potential effluent recharge of the groundwater beneath the Los Alisos well field

The water supply coming from Los Alisos is likely to continue to decline as the water table continues to drop, though there is the hope that the return flow generated by the effluent from the Los Alisos treatment plant will recharge the aquifer to some extent, depending on (1) the amount of water which is treated there (to a maximum rate of 330 lps, the maximum

Table 2. Projected hydraulic balance of the Los Alisos basin, 2011, 2015 and 2020 (flow rates in litres per second). Outflow is dependent upon the effluent recharge of the well field. The net water loss from this basin begins at 270 lps in 2011 to a potential gain of 98 lps in 2020 (with zero effluent recharge) or a potential loss of 118 lps with 100% effluent recharge. The greater the recharge of the well field, the more water will be pumped to the Sonoran Santa Cruz basin. If there is minimal recharge, the cones of depression will continue to deepen and the volume of water pumped from Los Alisos will decrease.

	2011		2015			2020		
	Inflow	Outflow	Inflow	Outflow (zero recharge)	Outflow (100% recharge)	Inflow	Outflow (zero recharge)	Outflow (100% recharge)
From Nogales	271	270	271	247	418	300*	202	418
To Nogales		270						
Net	24		24		147	98		118

* The maximum inflow for the Los Alisos treatment plant is 330 lps, of which 30 lps comes from Fraccionamiento La Mesa. La Mesa values come from personal interviews with OOMAPAS employees and do not include future projections.

capacity of the plant), and (2) the amount of effluent that percolates through the ground to the level of the aquifer.

The plan is to release 434 lps (the limit specified in the binational agreement) of municipal wastewater to the NIWTP in Arizona and the rest of the wastewater to the Los Alisos plant, which, in turn, will discharge all of its effluent into the Los Alisos River channel. This will allow the effluent to flow south through the neighbouring towns beyond the Los Alisos well field, which spans about 10 kilometres directly downstream of the treatment plant. We estimate that about 3% of the effluent will evaporate (based on pan evaporation data from Nogales, Arizona) and that another portion will flow further downstream rather than recharging the groundwater of the well field. Since the hydraulic gradient of the water table in general follows the slope of the surface, the water that percolates to recharge the aquifer south of the well field will be out of reach of the Los Alisos well field. We can, however, make well production estimates for the best-case (100% percolation of effluent just downstream of the plant) and worst-case (zero percolation) scenarios, knowing that the actual recharge will lie between these values. If there is 100% recharge of the additional effluent inflow, we can then increase the estimated well production, up to a maximum of 450 lps, or the estimated initial flow rate before the water table was lowered from over-extraction. This uncertainty in aquifer recharge leads to the range of well productivity values found in Tables 1 and 2.

Discussion

The Los Alisos basin, from which about half of the city of Nogales's municipal water originates, has shown severe signs of groundwater decline. The municipal well field is situated along the ephemeral Los Alisos stream in Cíbuta, a town of 630 residents (Foro-Mexico, 2011). The majority of the water from the Los Alisos well field goes to Nogales, but about 32 lps goes to a major housing development, Fraccionamiento La Mesa (personal communication, OOMAPAS, 13 June 2011). Since La Mesa is in the Los Alisos basin, north (upstream) of Cíbuta, this water is not considered an export from the Los Alisos basin. In 2011, the hydraulic balance of the Los Alisos basin shows a deficit of 270 lps, which has been felt by the local community, particularly the ranchers, who can no longer afford the pumping costs to provide water for their livestock, water which had hitherto flowed naturally from springs.

When the Los Alisos plant began treating wastewater from Nogales in 2012, it generated substantial return flow for the Los Alisos basin, which for over a decade had only been exporting water. A major factor in the Sonoran government's decision to operate a treatment plant on Mexican soil was to avoid paying high rates for wastewater treatment at the NIWTP in Arizona in excess of the 434 lps permitted by US–Mexico official agreement.[3] In addition to the quantity in excess of 434 lps, an estimated 113 lps of inflow to Los Alisos will come from the installation of wastewater services for the six neighbourhoods mentioned above, which will have sewage connections for the first time once the project is completed around 2013. The hydraulic balance estimates for 2015 include this additional inflow, and are shown in Table 2, where there is a column for the 100%-recharge scenario and another for the zero-recharge scenario. We can assume that the actual values will lie in between, but percolation will not be optimized because there are no plans for an infiltration basin to facilitate the recharge of the effluent near the well fields. Also, there is a risk of reduced infiltration due to biological factors. Experience on the Arizona side of the Santa Cruz basin, where effluent has long been released to natural channels, indicates that nitrogen and phosphorus may contribute to the formation of an algal mat that lines the stream channel and impedes infiltration over a distance of several miles downstream of the effluent release point. This biological factor could represent another impediment to infiltration and subsequent recharge.

For the 2020 estimate, the outflow of the Los Alisos well field under the zero-recharge scenario is again reduced according to the 9 lps/y estimated decline in well productivity (based on historical averages, as indicated above), and the maximum outflow is set at the initial pumping rate before over-extraction occurred, or 450 lps minus 32 lps for La Mesa. The wastewater produced by Nogales and La Mesa will at that point have exceeded the maximum capacity of the Los Alisos plant (330 lps), so in Table 1 the additional volume of wastewater is added to the side of the NIWTP in Arizona, for a total of 503 lps, which exceeds the 434 lps limit and is very near the average rate of flow to the NIWTP before the inauguration of the Los Alisos treatment plant. In other words, it will take an estimated eight years of operation before the additional capacity of the plant is utilized as a result of the city's growth. Based on the projections in Table 2, the increased production of sewage will necessitate the construction and completion of the second stage of the plant (from its present 220 lps capacity to its maximum 330 lps capacity), possibly sooner than engineers anticipated. This estimate indicates that it will be necessary to complete the second stage of the treatment plant construction before the year 2015, since 2015 shows 301 lps to be treated in Los Alisos (271 lps from Nogales + 30 lps from La Mesa).

For a period of about eight years, the municipal water company will be able to avoid paying additional fees at the Nogales International Wastewater Treatment Plant on the US side of the border by staying within the 434 lps average permitted rate. In approximately eight years, at current growth rates, total wastewater will have surpassed the combined limits of both treatment plants. At that point, it is uncertain what will be done with the excess wastewater, and its implications for contamination and public health are unknown. If treatment capacity is not increased, then the choice must be made whether to overload and contaminate the US side, resulting in higher costs for OOMAPAS, or to overload the Los Alisos treatment plant, which would raise contamination on the Mexican side of the border. OOMAPAS will then decide whether to exercise its natural upstream relationship with Arizona or to exert its engineered upstream relationship with the rural peri-urban community of Cíbuta by pumping excess wastewater to an overloaded treatment plant in the Los Alisos basin.

Conclusion

The objectives of this study were to evaluate the implications of the two-way interbasin transfer (water supply and the reverse flow of wastewater) between Nogales and Los Alisos in terms of the long-term water security of inhabitants of both basins, and to extract lessons of broader relevance. Interviews with water managers reveal that they are, indeed, concerned about Nogales's future but do not have a long-term plan to ensure supply. With limited funds, managers are relying on both water transfers and efficiency measures within existing infrastructure to try to meet the demands of the residents and the industries they support. Ranchers of Cíbuta have been negatively impacted by the interbasin transfer because the cones of depression surrounding the municipal wells have reduced or dried out altogether the personal wells for their homes, the spring-fed reservoirs for their cattle, and the Los Alisos River, which, according to residents, changed from perennial to ephemeral shortly after major pumping began. Additionally, Cíbuta residents have shown concern about the new wastewater treatment plant just upstream of them, which was commissioned on 31 August 2012. Though they are hopeful that the river may return, they fear contamination, which has been a problem in the past as a result of other wastewater flows from urban development on the Alisos side of the elevation divide.

Most interviewees of Cíbuta spoke of reduced vegetation in the area over the last decade – some reduction due to deforestation, some due to drought, and some due to fire. We ran vegetation change analyses using NDVI of 'before' and 'after' satellite images of the Los Alisos riparian area, but the changes in the image were not drastic and vegetation health appeared to vary in different areas of the river. We concluded, upon a follow-up interview, that the reported tree deaths were non-native fruit trees, and thus more vulnerable to water shortage, but that the desert-adapted mesquite, alder, and near-riparian oak trees had not suffered significantly up to that point.

Hydraulic balance considerations show that while both the Los Alisos and the Sonoran Santa Cruz basins had a net water loss in 2011, the addition of large volumes of effluent to the Los Alisos basin may bring the water balance to equilibrium, and could partly restore ranching livelihoods and ecological habitats that were harmed by extensive pumping. It has yet to be determined to what extent the influx of effluent will augment the potable water available to Nogales via the Los Alisos well field, since much of the effluent is likely to pass downstream along the river channel rather than percolating to the water table beneath the wells. The Sonoran part of the Upper Santa Cruz basin, however, will not have any additional return flow. In fact, higher volumes of water will be leaving the basin in the form of wastewater due to the increases in population and in sewerage service to existing residents, exacerbating the current water security problems.

This study has provided case evidence of urban growth in water-scarce conditions and the associated trade-offs in water management options. Economic factors worldwide are driving urban migration, but urbanization trends are at odds with sustainable natural resources management, because resource extraction and waste disposal are moving farther away from urban centres to accommodate demands for goods and services. Interbasin water transfers occur in cities with the financial and technological means to carry them out, with or without consultation or permission from residents of the source basin, whose health and safety can be affected. Particularly in northern Sonora, where a decade of drought is being followed by increased temperatures, (Christensen et al., 2007; Scott, Megdal, Oroz, Callegary, & Vandervoet, 2012), a long-term plan must be devised that will not only conserve the water resource but also share it in an equitable fashion with human and environmental needs.

Acknowledgements

The research presented in this paper was supported in part by the U.S.-Mexico Transboundary Aquifer Assessment Program, the National Science Foundation (NSF, Grant DEB-1010495), the Inter-American Institute for Global Change Research (Grant SGP-CRA #005, which is supported by NSF Grant GEO-1138881), and the National Oceanic and Atmospheric Administration's Climate-Society Interactions Program. The authors would like to thank, in particular, OOMAPAS (Organismo Operador Municipal de Agua Potable, Alcantarillado y Saneamiento)-Nogales, residents of Cíbuta, and the Instituto Municipal de Investigación y Planeación-Nogales for their assistance in the field.

Notes

1. Mexico's National Water Commission reports an 11.26 mcm net gain in the water balance of the Los Alisos basin (CONAGUA, 2011), but some municipal extractions are unaccounted for in this balance, as described in a subsequent section of the paper.

2. The 22% increase is based on the following estimates: 70% of the 2010 population of 220,292 has sewerage, generating 504 lps of wastewater (EPA, 2008; INEGI, 2010; personal communication, OOMAPAS, 2011). If that seventy percent (154,204 people) creates on average 504 lps average of sewage, then 34,560 people (from the EPA estimate of the population of the six neighborhoods who will soon be connected to the sewage system) would produce 113 lps of wastewater, or a 22% increase in the 2010 number leaving the city.
3. Per minute 276 of the 1944 treaty as administered by the International Boundary and Water Commission, IBWC/CILA (IBWC, 1988).

References

Alagh, Y. K., Pangare, G., & Gujja, B. (2007). *Interlinking of rivers in India: Overview and Ken-Betwa link* (pp. 194). New Delhi: Academic Foundation.

Carvalho, R. C., & Magrini, A. (2006). Conflicts over water resource management in Brazil: A case study of inter-basin transfers. *Water Resources Management, 20*(2), 193–213.

Cervera, L. E. C., Gomez, & Rubio, R. Salas. (2003). Basic criteria for a sustainable water management at the US-Mexico border: The case of Ambos Nogales. *Estudios Fronterizos, Nueva Epoca, 4*(7). Retrieved from: http://www.uabc.mx/iis/ref/REFvol4num7/Ref7_2.pdf

Christensen, J. H., Hewitson, B., Busuioc, A., Chen, A., Gao, X., Held, I., Jones, R., Kolli, R. K., Kwon, W. -T., Laprise, R., Magaña Rueda, V., Mearns, L., Menéndez, C. G., Räisänen, J., Rinke, A., Sarr, A., & Whetton, P. (2007). Regional climate projections. *Climate Change*, The Physical Science Basis. Contribution of Working Group I to the Fourth Assessment Report of the Intergovernmental Panel on Climate Change [Solomon, S., D. Qin, M. Manning, Z. Chen, M. Marquis, K.B. Averyt, M. Tignor and H.L. Miller (eds.)] 2007. Cambridge, United Kingdom and New York, NY, USA: Cambridge University Press.

CONAGUA (2011). Determinación de la disponibilidad de agua en el acuífero 2613 Río Alisos, estado de Sonora. [Determination of the availability of water in the aquifer 2613 Alisos River, state of Sonora] Available at: http://www.conagua.gob.mx/Conagua07/Aguasubterranea/pdf/DR_2613.pdf (Accessed November 2011).

Díaz, H. F., & Morehouse, B. J. (Eds.). (2003). *Climate and water: Transboundary challenges in the Americas* Advances in Global Change Research Series. Dodrecht: Kluwer Academic Press.

Díaz-Caravantes, R. E., & Sánchez-Flores, E. (2011). Water transfer effects on peri-urban land use/land cover: A case study in a semi-arid region of Mexico. *Applied Geography, 31*(2), 413–425.

Elmore, A. J., Mustard, J. F., Manning, S. J., & Lobell, D. B. (2000). Quantifying vegetation change in semiarid environments: Precision and accuracy of spectral mixture analysis and the normalized difference vegetation index. *Remote Sensing of Environment, 73*(1), 87–102.

EPA (Environmental Protection Agency) (2008). Supplemental environmental assessment and finding of no significant impact for the Los Alisos wastewater treatment plant and conveyance system construction Nogales, Sonora, Mexico. Prepared by Tom Konner.

Foro-Mexico (2011). Información de Cíbuta (Nogales). [Information about Cíbuta (Nogales)]. Available at: http://www.foro-mexico.com/sonora/Cibuta/mensaje-270185.html (Accessed October 2011).

Gleick, P. H. (2003). Global freshwater resources: Soft-path solutions for the 21st century. *Science, 302*(5650), 1524–1528.

Gupta, J., & Van der Zaag, P. (2008). Interbasin water transfers and integrated water resources management: Where engineering, science and politics interlock. *Physics and Chemistry of the Earth, 33*, 28–40. doi: http://www.sciencedirect.com/science/article/pii/S1474706507000666

Howe, C. W., & Goemans, C. (2003). Water transfers and their impacts: Lessons from three Colorado water markets. *Journal of the American Water Resources Association*. (non-paginated).

INEGI (2005). Conteo de Población y Vivienda 2005. [Count of Population and Households 2005] Available at: http://www.inegi.org.mx/sistemas/TabuladosBasicos/Default.aspx?c=10398s=est (Accessed August 2012).

INEGI (2010). Censo de Población y Vivienda 2010. [Census of Population and Households 2010] Available at: http://www.inegi.org.mx/sistemas/mexicocifras/default.aspx (Accessed October 2011).

IBWC (1988). Conveyance, treatment and disposal of sewage from Nogales, Arizona and Nogales, Sonora exceeding the capacities allotted to the United States and Mexico at the Nogales International Sewage Treatment Plant Under Minute No. 227. Available at: http://www.ibwc. gov/Files/Minutes/Min276.pdf (Accessed August 2012).

Jin, X. M., Schaepman, M. E., Clevers, J. G. P. W., Su, Z. B., & Hu, G. C. (2011). Groundwater depth and vegetation in the Ejina area, China. *Arid Land Research and Management.*, *25*(2), 194–199.

Johnson, W. C., Dixon, M. D., Simons, R., Jenson, S., & Larson, K. (1995). Mapping the response of riparian vegetation to possible flow reductions in the Snake River, Idaho. *Geomorphology*, *13*(1-4), 159–173.

La Prensa Sonora-Arizona (2012). Inaugura Gobernador Padrés planta tratadora "Los Alisos" en Nogales. [Governor Padrés inaugurates "Los Alisos" treatment plant in Nogales]. (August 30, 2012). Available at: http://www.laprensasonora.com/vernoticias.php?artid=16142&categori a=1 (Accessed September 2012).

Milman, A., & Scott, C. A (2010). Beneath the surface: Intranational institutions and management of the United States – Mexico transboundary Santa Cruz aquifer. *Environment and Planning C: Government and Policy*, *28*(3), 528–551.

Molle, F. (2007). Scales and power in river basin management: the Chao Phraya River in Thailand. *The Geographical Journal*, *173*(4), 358–373.

Morehouse, B. J., Carter, R. H., & Sprouse, T. W. (2000). The implications of sustained drought for transboundary water management in Nogales, Arizona, and Nogales, Sonora. *Natural Resources Journal.*, *40*, 783–817.

NADB *North American Development Bank* (2012). Nogales, Sonora celebrates completion of the Los Alisos Wastewater Treatment Plant. August 30, 2012. Available at: http://www.nadb.org/ Reports1/Press_Releases/english/2012/083012.htm (Accessed August 2012).

Norman, E., Bakker, K., Cook, C., Dunn, G., Allen, D. Water Security: A Primer (2010). Policy Report. Developing a Canadian Water Security Framework as a Tool for Improved Water Governance for Watersheds (2008–2012).

Pick, J. B., Viswanathan, N., Tomita, K., & Keshavan, S. (2002). Border demographic impacts on the urban environment and sustainable development of Imperial County, California, and Mexicali Municipio, Mexico. Final report to California Urban Environmental and Research Center. Redlands, CA: University of the Redlands, p. 202.

Saurí, D., & Del Moral Ituarte, L. (2001). Recent developments in Spanish water policy. Alternatives and conflicts at the end of the hydraulic age. *Geoforum*, *32*(3), 351–362.

Scott, C. A., & Banister, J. M. (2008). The dilemma of water management 'regionalization' in Mexico under centralized resource allocation. *International Journal of Water Resources Development*, *24*(1), 61–74, DOI: 10.1080/07900620701723083.

Scott, Christopher A., Flores-López, F., & Gastélum, J. R. (2007). Appropriation of Río San Juan water by Monterrey City, Mexico: implications for agriculture and basin water sharing. *Paddy and Water Environment*, *5*(4), 253–262.

Scott, C. A., & Pineda Pablos, N. P. (2011). Innovating resource regimes: Water, wastewater, and the institutional dynamics of urban hydraulic reach in northwest Mexico. *Geoforum*, *42*(4), 439–450, doi:10.1016/j.geoforum.2011.02.003.

Scott, C. A., Megdal, S., Oroz, L. A., Callegary, J., & Vandervoet, P. (2012). Effects of climate change and population growth on the transboundary Santa Cruz aquifer. *Climate Research*, *51*(2), 159–170, doi: 10.3354/cr01061.

Sonora SI, Sonora Sistema Integral. Available at: http://sonorasi.mx/web/index.php?option=com _content&view=article&id=104&Itemid=224 (Accessed November 1, 2011).

Stromberg, J. C., Tiller, R., & Richter, B. (1996). Effects of groundwater decline on riparian vegetation of semiarid regions: The San Pedro, Arizona. *Ecological Applications*, *6*(1), 113–131.

Tortajada, C., & Castelán, E. (2003). Water management for a mega-city: Mexico City Metropolitan Area. *Ambio*, *32*(2), 124–129.

Tortajada, C. (2006). Who has access to water? Case study of Mexico City Metropolitan Area. Occasional paper for the 2006 UNDP Human Development Report.

Wilder, M., Scott, C. A., Pineda-Pablos, N., Varady, R. G. & Garfin, G. M. (Eds.). (2012). *Moving Forward from Vulnerability to Adaptation: Climate Change, Drought, and Water Demand in the Urbanizing Southwestern United States and Northern Mexico - Casebook.* Tucson: Udall Center for Studies in Public Policy, University of Arizona.

POLICY BRIEF

The 2012 Murray-Darling Basin Plan – issues to watch

James Horne

James Horne and Associates, Australia

The Murray-Darling Basin Plan is now in place, marking a further significant step in water policy development and water reform in Australia's Murray-Darling Basin (MDB). While it is an important planning and regulatory framework in its own right, and one that should further enhance the efficiency and effectiveness of water markets in the MDB, implementation and enforcement of the plan and continued action by governments, communities and stakeholders on key reform commitments are required to ensure much-needed improvement in economic, social and environmental sustainability. This article outlines seven watch points that will affect whether the desired outcomes are achieved.

Introduction

Six years ago, in January 2007, the Australian prime minister made a major statement on water policy, focusing on the Murray-Darling Basin (MDB) (Howard, 2007). Implementation of significant aspects of the statement has been undertaken, with considerable progress in some key areas. After the change of government in late 2007, the Labour government largely adopted the substance of the former government's *"National Plan for Water Security"* under its *"Water for the Future"* banner. This includes: institutional and regulatory reform, including through the Water Act of 2007 (Commonwealth of Australia, 2009), water market and charge rules, and the establishment of a new Murray-Darling Basin Authority (MDBA); massively improving the quality of water information (including establishment of the Bureau of Meteorology water function and a national water account); and making a large start on recovering water for the environment to bolster environmental outcomes (including through a cost-effective water buy-back programme and the establishment of a Commonwealth Environmental Water Holder). Overall, and over the medium term, the reforms implemented thus far should in time have a positive impact on the sustainability of the basin's environment, agriculture and communities (Horne, 2012a, 2012b).[1]

In late November 2012, a further element of the policy package was put in place with the passage of the Murray-Darling Basin Plan (hereafter the Basin Plan) by the Australian Parliament, with support of the Labour Party, Liberal Party and National Party but not the Australian Greens. The Basin Plan and the detailed Explanatory Memorandum prepared for parliamentary consideration can be found on the MDBA website (MDBA, 2012a; Minister for Sustainability, Environment, Water, Population & Communities, 2012).

The coming into force of the Basin Plan is clearly a further important step forward in Australian water policy.

- It articulates clearly its objectives and the desired outcomes, with the overall outcome being a healthy and working Murray-Darling Basin.
- It also articulates how these are to be achieved, including the planning and regulatory framework and roles to be played in monitoring and evaluation.
- It provides the basis for enforceable "sustainable diversion limits" (SDLs) for surface and groundwater, a step forward from the old "cap" arrangements.[2]
- It codifies the water trading rules (to be introduced from July 2014), strengthening water trading by removing many of the remaining restrictions on water trade and drawing attention to the value of water (though the full force of these rules may not be felt until the expiry of transitional and interim water resource plans).
- It strengthens the Australian government's role in water policy, and the national "whole of basin" perspective this brings with it, and is well resourced by the Australian government to achieve the stated outcomes.
- While not strongly supported by all state governments, it has a measure of state support.
- It builds on the Water Act (2007), the effective implementation of the Australian government's water buy-back programme, water market strengthening initiatives (such as the market and charge rules), and the Bureau of Meteorology's water information programme.
- It is based on a detailed and extensive community and government-to-government consultation process extending over more than three years.

As always, however, the devil is in the details of the Basin Plan itself and of its forthcoming implementation, and the application of remedies if any parties decide not to fully pursue implementation. It is, like the Water Act (2007) and countless intergovernmental agreements before it, a political document, with compromises, areas of work in progress, and areas that have not been fully nailed down.

This article examines a number of areas of the Basin Plan, and the development and implementation of the existing water recovery strategy and natural resource management programmes in the Murray-Darling Basin that go to the issue of the contribution the Basin Plan might make to achieving sustainable outcomes within the MDB. It is not intended to be an exhaustive list. These areas are structured as watch points to underscore that *the political success of finalizing the Basin Plan will only have substantial meaning if and when it is fully and faithfully implemented. Effective compliance and enforcement programmes will be critical.*

While much has been achieved over the past half-decade, and putting the Basin Plan in place is the most recent part of this, it will take the best part of the next decade before we can properly assess whether this set of measures is able to achieve in a measurable way what the Australian and state governments agreed needed addressing in the mid-1990s: that is, whether there is concrete, independent evidence of halting the ongoing decline in the environmental health of one of the world's great river basins, and whether the Basin has been put on a path where its health is improving materially.

Sustainable diversion limits (SDLs)

The Basin Plan introduces sustainable diversion limits (SDLs) for surface water and groundwater from July 2019, to replace the current "cap" mechanism that only applies to surface water. *The first watch point for the Basin Plan is how the new SDLs are administered when they are eventually applied, how aggregate water use within the Basin will respond, how "interception" (water extraction or use outside of the entitlement framework) is managed and whether the resultant water use satisfies a "sustainable water use" benchmark.*

SDLs for surface water

The Basin Plan proposes that the SDLs for surface water, operational from 2019, will reduce the quantity of surface water available for consumptive use by 2750 GL per year across the basin, to 10,873 GL per year, or a reduction of around 20% from the 2009 benchmark.[3] The proposed reduction in surface water SDLs is by any measure large and a major step forward from "Cap" arrangements. However, the final aggregate surface water SDL is clearly a compromise that left many interests dissatisfied with the size of the proposed reduction (some regarding it as too large, and others as too small).

The proposed reduction is at the bottom end of scenarios modelled by the MDBA over the 2009–2011 period that it argued would achieve sustainable outcomes into the future. The MDBA suggests that "positive environmental outcomes would be achieved with water recovery of 2800 GL/y" (MDBA, 2012c, p. 3). This writer's judgment is that, with both environmental and socio-economic considerations in mind, the proposed reduction could have a positive material impact on the environment, while still keeping socio-economic adjustment issues within basin communities at manageable levels. The technical evidence presented by the MDBA also seems to suggest that with current river operational constraints in place, the benefit from additional environmental water flows would be small (see for example MDBA, 2012c, 2012i). The Basin Plan requires that the MDBA put in place a constraints management strategy by the end of 2013 (MDBA, 2012a, p. 40). What remains to be seen is the nature of the trade-offs if these constraints are addressed.

It is worth remembering that the proposed reduction in surface water availability is much larger than any scientist or environmental group called for before the Australian government announcement in 2007, even though it is very much at the lower end of current scientific estimates. It is likely that this observation just says something about the state of political discourse and a lack of scientific data, at that point in time, on how much water was actually required to make a difference. Moreover, it does not mean that the proposed 2750 GL/y reduction in take for consumptive purposes is the last word to achieve the objectives of the Basin Plan in the longer term, but it is certainly large enough to make a very significant start, and one that will require removal of man-made constraints to water flows to optimize outcomes. The uncertainty surrounds not only the 2750 GL reduction but also how the state and Australian governments manage water interception activities over the coming decade.

The Australian government has set aside AUD1.5 billion of new funding (over and above what remains from Water for the Future funding) to finance on-and off-farm efficiency projects to achieve an additional 450 GL per year of water for the environment, beyond the mentioned 2750 GL per year. It has also set aside AUD 200 million for projects to remove constraints in the river system that may impede delivery of environmental water.[4] While there are major questions around the efficacy of using public money to finance further "efficiency" projects (the task could be undertaken much more cost-effectively, and directed much more precisely, by buying water entitlements directly in the market), this additional funding is ongoing evidence of the centrality of politics in crafting a sustainable "solution" in the MDB. It appears that the Regional Australia Committee's inquiry into the Murray-Darling (led by one of the independents holding the balance of power in the House of Representatives, MP Tony Windsor) continues to have a significant impact on the government's preparedness to pursue a balance between water purchases in the market and efficiency measures through enhanced infrastructure (for the case for purchasing water directly, see for example Productivity Commission, 2010; Grafton and Jiang, 2009; Wentworth Group of Concerned Scientists, 2010). The twin interests of farmers wishing to sell their entitlements and minimizing the cost to the public purse have, it seems, been set aside.

There are some significant risks to reaching the target for reduction in water use. The first is that the compromise 2750 GL/y reduction in surface water SDLs is buttressed by an SDL "adjustment mechanism", whereby some of this quantity can potentially be met through "mak[ing] more water available for environmental management without reducing consumptive take, or allow[ing] environmental managers to achieve equivalent environmental outcomes more efficiently" (MDBA, 2012f, p. 12). The SDL adjustment mechanism comprises "supply" and "efficiency" measures.

A supply measure

> increases the quantity of water available before consumptive take. The measure may do this either by making water available for environmental use without reducing the volume of water available for consumptive take (e.g. through reducing evaporation losses at suitable storages) or by allowing environmental managers to achieve the same environmental outcomes more efficiently, thus reducing the volume of water needing to be recovered for the environment. Supply measures allow equivalent environmental outcomes to be achieved without needing to reduce consumptive take as much as originally anticipated in the Basin Plan. (Minister for Sustainability, Environment, Water, Population & Communities, 2012, paragraph 157)

A supply measure increases the water available for consumptive use because it replaces water that was to have been recovered from consumptive use and made available for the environment. The government argues that a supply measure therefore potentially increases the SDL. Calculation of a supply contribution is based on Schedule 6 of the Basin Plan (MDBA, 2012a). How this will work in practice has not yet been determined.

An efficiency measure, by contrast,

> is one that makes savings in the amount of water required for consumptive purposes. Examples include investment in more efficient irrigation infrastructure. (Minister for Sustainability, Environment, Water, Population & Communities, 2012, paragraph 158)

Water saved by an efficiency measure will be counted towards environmental use because, it is argued, the water saved is no longer required to maintain output, so socio-economic outcomes are unaffected. It would result in a potential reduction in the SDL. Unfortunately, it is not clear whether this approach applies to efficiency measures already undertaken, or, if it does not, what the starting-point for consideration is.

The Basin Plan allows for supply and efficiency measures up to a net amount of 5% of the total surface water SDL. If achievable and agreed, these types of measures would allow improvements in environmental outcomes without any adverse socio-economic impact. However, one must ask, if they were straightforward, surely they would have been raised seriously at some point over the past decade? Supply measures (such as the efficacy of river system flows or rules) have been mooted for many years, but few have been realized. In many cases, they have the quality of a "magic pudding" in that their ability to actually deliver an effective equivalent to the purchase of water entitlements has yet to be proven.[5] It could be argued that another reason is that no funds have been previously set aside for this purpose, but that is not the case. For example, money was set aside to reconfigure Menindee Lakes arrangements (or any cost-effective alternative) but failed to secure the support of the government of New South Wales (NSW). (Department of Sustainability, Environment, Water Population & Communities, 2011). Of course, none of the above suggests that potential measures should not be properly explored; but any measure put forward will need to be evaluated in an independent and rigorous manner.

A second watch point is that any proposals to acquire water through supply and efficiency measures accepted by the MDBA should be independently and rigorously verified against clear criteria, not simply approved by the MDBA.

SDL for groundwater

The Basin Plan introduces for the first time aquifer by-aquifer limits on groundwater extraction, aggregating to basin-wide limits on groundwater extraction. Clearly, this is important, not least because of the connectivity between groundwater and surface water resources. This has been a controversial part of the preparation of the Basin Plan over the past two years, as shown in Table 1. MDBA estimates of "sustainable" extraction have jumped around massively.

In the draft Basin Plan that was released in November 2011, proposed groundwater SDLs for NSW grew dramatically, without sensible explanation, relative to the figures contained in the Guide to the Proposed Basin Plan. The proposal to increase access to deep groundwater was in itself not objectionable; what was and remains at issue is the approach taken to arrive at the draft groundwater SDLs.

Indeed, without acknowledgment at the time (despite the information being public), known connectivity between surface water and groundwater would have resulted in increased pressure on surface systems as more water from them flowed into aquifers in response to increased extraction from the aquifers. For most of the previous decade there had been wide acceptance of the fact that growth in groundwater use needed to be arrested, and extraction from many aquifers reduced (see for example NWC, 2009). Small reductions were proposed for only two groundwater water resource plan areas in the November 2011 draft, a far cry from proposals for reductions relative to current diversion limits and use and from the proposals for diversion limits outlined in the Guide to the Proposed Basin Plan a year earlier (MDBA, 2010, Table 9.1, 2011, Table S4.1). After the commonwealth environment minster expressed deep concern at this development (Burke, 2012a), the proposed SDLs were trimmed by over one-quarter, although in total they were still massively above current use.

Table 1. The process of developing MDBA estimates of sustainable groundwater extraction.

• October 2010 Guide to the Basin Plan – groundwater diversion baseline of 1786 GL
o Groundwater was being overused
o Recommended reductions in 11 areas
• November 2011 Draft Basin Plan – groundwater SDL of 4340 GL
o Only two reductions below the baseline diversion limit (BDL); large increases in unassigned areas[a]
o Adoption of NSW methodology on limits in place, resulting in higher SDLs
o Claimed "improved" estimates of BDLs leading to increased SDLs
o Large increases for "new" deep water resources
• May 2012 Revised Basin Plan – groundwater SDL of 3184 GL, a reduction of 26% from November 2011 but still nearly double the 2010 groundwater diversion baseline
• November 2012 Basin Plan – groundwater SDL not directly specified
o 3335 GL minus an unspecified amount (possibly unchanged from May 2012)

Note: [a] A baseline diversion limit for groundwater determines the baseline from which to determine reductions in diversions (see Minister for Sustainability, Environment, Water, Population & Communities, 2012).
Sources: MDBA, 2010, 2011, 2012a, 2012g.

The November 2011 draft proposal had all the hallmarks of a political deal with the NSW government. There was no clear and transparent enumeration of why the draft proposed that the diversion limits of the 2010 Guide to the Basin Plan be increased. All the key reasons subsequently provided by the MDBA were challenged (see MDBA, 2012h). Hearsay has it that the proposed draft plan was agreed as part of the political price for NSW acquiescence to support for the Basin Plan, supposedly to ensure future coal-seam gas producers' and other miners' access to adequate water supplies via access to new deep aquifer reserves. Whatever the case, the process left much to be desired.

It is very clear that the groundwater SDLs are subject to much greater uncertainty than surface water estimates. Notwithstanding this, groundwater use has grown steadily during the decade and a half that the cap on surface water has been in operation, even as state governments sought to restrict issuance of new entitlements in many groundwater districts. If the consumptive use of groundwater grows from its current volume of 1760 GL per year to the SDL estimated at between 3073–3334 GL per year[6], it can be argued that the Basin Plan for groundwater and surface water as a whole is actually proposing only a very small reduction in total potential water diversions. *The third watch point is that the MDBA needs to be very transparent in the way it assesses compliance with groundwater SDLs and the impact higher use is having on both aquifers and surface water systems.* Sharply increased use of the groundwater SDLs could undermine one of the key objectives of the Basin Plan, that of ensuring sustainability of water extraction, and a sustainable environment.

While a precautionary approach has apparently been adopted, this is one area that will need revisiting once further scientific work, currently underway, is complete (see Independent Expert Scientific Committee on Coal Seam Gas and Large Coal Mining Development, 2013).

Implementation delays and the cost of future adjustment

A feature of the Basin Plan is that some key elements will not be activated for many years, for example the introduction of the SDLs is delayed until 2019. Originally, the bulk of the Basin plan was to be fully operational in 2014. While it is disappointing that the introduction of some key elements of the plan has been delayed well into the future, the 2007/2009 reforms are already setting the stage for an improvement in the sustainability of the MDB (Horne, 2012a). For example, governments already hold a significant volume of the entitlements for environmental use, and have already released large quantities of water for use at environmental sites. Indeed, the Australian Department of Sustainability, Environment, Water, Population and Communities (SEWPAC) estimates that as of the end of December 2012, 1630 GL of surface entitlements (on a long-term average annual yield basis) had already been recovered for the environment, or around 60% of the target reduction (SEWPAC, 2013b). SEWPAC figures are presented in Table 2 below.

As indicated in Table 2, around two-thirds of this water recovery has come from water purchases in the market by SEWPAC, which if a survey of purchases is any indication, was very positively regarded by those selling water into the market (Cheesman and Wheeler, 2012). The claims of some that there would be insufficient sellers, that market sales would harm communities or that market purchases were tantamount to "buying air" have proved unfounded. Water purchased in the market has been very cost-effective, has provided environmental water where it has been required, has enabled transactions to be completed in a very timely fashion (where states have allowed it), has allowed irrigators to better

Table 2. Water title acquisitions to cover the reduction in SDLs.

SEWPAC list the following as "recovered" as of 31 December 2012
• 1117 GL of secured water purchases in the water market
• 346 GL received, estimated or agreed under signed infrastructure works contracts
• 154 GL recovered through state government actions (as of 30 September 2012)
• 11 GL gifted by the Queensland Government and 2 GL of other recovery
• Total 1630 GL

Note: All figures are estimated long-term average annual yields. Under the Basin Plan, water recovered from 2009 contributes to the water recovery target of 2750 GL/y. It is not clear whether any actual water contributions outside of water purchases have been finalized – the document refers to "received, estimated or agreed".
Source: SEWPAC, Environmental Water Recovery Strategy for the Murray-Darling Basin, November 2012. retrieved from http://www.environment.gov.au/water/policy-programs/water-recovery-strategy/pubs/draft-recovery-strategy.pdf), updated where possible using SEWPAC, 2013, Progress towards meeting environmental needs under the Basin Plan (retrieved from http://www.environment.gov.au/water/basin-plan/progress.html

manage their balance sheets and outstanding debt, and has resulted in injections of funds back into communities in contrast to the risks, cost overruns and uncertain estimation of water savings from many infrastructure projects (Horne, 2012a). So, notwithstanding implementation delays on the Basin Plan, the actual task of making the environment, agriculture and communities of the MDB more sustainable than they would otherwise have been has already commenced.

According to the Australian government, as of the of end December 2012, some 1845 GL of commonwealth water had been delivered to environmental sites (bolstered by a further 943 GL from "The Living Murray" [TLM] and state-government sources and private donations) since 2009 (Commonwealth Environmental Water Office, 2013b). In 2012–2013, 612 GL had already been delivered, and a further 775 GL is available for delivery (Commonwealth Environmental Water Office, 2013a). The amount of water being carried over year by year has also been gradually increasing (over the short period that the environmental water manager has been operational). All this suggests that the era of large-scale environmental water planning and delivery has arrived, and all participants need to gear up to fully participate.

The fourth watch point is policy makers need to ensure that the initial momentum from implementing Water for the Future is not lost, now that the first stage of the political task of agreeing the Basin Plan is finished. In particular, an effective basin-wide use strategy for environmental water is needed, building on the work of the Commonwealth Environmental Water Holder.

Environmental water managers and their scientific advisors will have their work cut out in coming years to use the water accruing to the environmental water portfolios in a way that demonstrably produces improved environmental outcomes. By the time the SDLs are operative in 2019, there will be nearly a decade of experience delivering large volumes of water to environmental sites, and a decade of evidence of its impact. If early experiences are anything to go by, this will require substantial change in the behaviour of many state and MDBA water managers, where it is not yet clear that all parties are working with Basin Plan objectives, and the basin-wide scale of the initiative, in mind.

Plan fails to account for climate change

The Basin Plan as introduced does not factor in an SDL adjustment for the reduction in water availability consequent on the expected impact of climate change. The revised approach to this issue occurred in the movement from the Guide to the Basin Plan to the

Draft Plan, indicating a clear intent in the latter towards reducing the size of the adjustment contained in first Basin Plan. *The fifth watch point is that if action is needed to address the impact of climate change it is taken and not deferred, because it is likely to be the environment that will play catch-up.*

But it is not a crippling flaw. There is a very considerable task before all governments in properly implementing the Basin Plan that is now in place. That is, correcting the balance between consumptive use and the environment on the basis of the current climate is in itself a first-order task that needs the full attention of governments. Past experience in water policy suggests that both state and national governments will struggle with even this implementation task. The adjustment for climate change can be undertaken when the plan is revisited in the early 2020s. The task for now is to thoroughly and completely implement the Basin Plan that has been accepted by the Australian parliament.

Water recovery strategy

The water recovery task over coming years is dependent, inter alia, on the success of water accumulation methods used. Without speculating on its reasons, the Australian government has already indicated it is planning to place less weight on buying water entitlements in the market, favouring so-called "efficiency" measures (see SEWPAC, November 2012), with greater emphasis on much more expensive, less reliable approaches, and "supply" measures. The Federal opposition's stated approach is to limit market purchases of entitlements to 1500 GL.

While there may be a case for some on-and-off farm infrastructure subsidies to assist the adjustment of irrigation to a lower level of consumptive water use, focus on efficiency is clearly "inefficient" from a perspective of minimizing the cost and maximizing the location effectiveness of increasing the share of water available for the environment. On-and off-farm infrastructure measures have a history of being very expensive, taking longer to implement than initially proposed, suffering from cost overruns, and under-delivering in terms of water saved (for example ANAO, 2012, Productivity Commission, 2009). They also tend to stifle socio-economic adjustment and the process of water being used in areas of highest value.

The sixth watch point is that, over coming years, it will be important to ensure that the public is getting value for money in implementing the water-acquisition programme, particularly if it relies on on-farm and off-farm infrastructure works, and to ensure that it does not become another in the long list of poorly targeted regional support programmes. If the government is intent on establishing regional support programmes, it should do so transparently, specifying clear objectives for each programme.

The government has pencilled in 650 GL of the remaining 1120 GL as coming from "possible contribution from supply measures". These have been touted for many years, but few concrete, costed proposals have been made public. The feasibility of one project relating to the Lindsay River in Victoria, is currently being examined (Burke & Walsh, 2013). The national environment minister has indicated that he would revert to buy-backs if the states do not bring forward appropriate projects. There are significant questions with respect to how long the minister will wait, and what quality of project will be accepted (see Burke, 2012b).

Efforts to remove constraints on moving actual environmental water are also critical to achieving environmental objectives and "positive environmental outcomes", and it is sensible to devote substantial resources to removing major constraints. As noted above, the Australian government has set aside AUD200 million for this purpose. It should be engaging in this task immediately, based on the environmental water flows needed to deliver environmental watering plans established or to be established under the Basin Plan.

In January 2013 the NSW government announced the introduction of a new restrictive regulation regarding water purchases in the market for environmental purposes that is sharply at odds with the spirit and the letter of the trading rules in Section 12 of the Basin Plan (NSW Government, 2013; MDBA, 2012a). At first blush, this appears much more restrictive than the infamous "four per cent rule". This NSW regulation promises to be an early test for the MDBA, as will be putting in place adequate Basin Plan implementation plans with the states.

MDB joint programmes

One of the great surprises over the latter part of 2012 was a major financial threat to the joint natural resource management programmes run by the MDBA. In financial terms, the key programmes are River Murray operations and asset maintenance, and management of TLM assets (water entitlements held by the MDBA). Other programmes include a number of cooperative environmental management programmes such as the Sustainable Rivers Audit, the Native Fish Strategy, the River Murray Water Quality Monitoring Program and contributions to the South Eastern Australian Climate Initiative (MDBA, 2012e, p. 49). In 2011–2012, these programmes received funding of approximately AUD 110 million. Details of expenditure on each programme, and forecast of expenditure in the forward estimate years, are surprisingly not publicly available.

In June 2012, NSW announced that it would reduce its resourcing of joint programmes from around AUD32 million in 2011–2012 to AUD12.4 million in 2012–2013 and to under AUD9 million in 2013–2014 and 2014–2015. In December 2012, South Australia announced a cut of over 50% in its contribution to joint programmes from 2014–2015: from AUD26.4 million to AUD12.1 million (MDBA, 2012d). As over AUD60 million is currently spent annually managing River Murray assets of some AUD2.5 billion, maintenance and services are likely to suffer, although the proposed cutbacks provide a good reason to examine all cost structures closely.

The MDBA also currently manages TLM assets valued at around AUD0.5 billion. This asset portfolio has no strategic coherence, and alternative options for its future management should be explored. For example, the assets could be dispersed to individual states for individual management, or passed to the Commonwealth Environmental Water Holder (and be managed along with the Australian government's water portfolio). Adopting the first approach would seem very odd, as the purpose of TLM assets was to undertake management of key assets cooperatively in a basin-wide framework. From an efficiency perspective, the second approach seems to make sense. In examining approaches, governments should take a hard look at the portfolio composition of TLM.

Even if there are no further financial cuts by other jurisdictions, and even after a radical programme of cost savings, the forecast funding will require significant programme cutbacks. Some minor programmes could be eliminated with little impact, but the axing by the Ministerial Council of the Sustainable Rivers Audit – which provides an independent health check of the river system – seems inexplicable, except as a blatant attempt to shift costs to the Australian government (MDBA, 2012d). Some may argue that the function is likely to be undertaken under the Basin Plan, and thus paid for by the Australian government. That may well be the case, but until new monitoring and evaluation approaches are in place it seems premature and irresponsible to eliminate the key independent programme assessing the health of the basin.[7]

While overarching state fiscal issues are very important, the resourcing cuts announced by NSW and South Australia undermine any position the two states might hold that MDB issues are critical or a priority. They appear to be further evidence that state governments give very little weight indeed to holistic management of the Murray-Darling Basin or the preparedness to contribute persistently to achieving better outcomes, and provide a timely reminder of why the Australian government sought to become more involved in water matters in the MDB. *This underscores the seventh and final watch point: that implementation issues outside the Basin Plan – such as the existing joint programmes that fall outside the coverage of the Basin Plan but contribute to outcomes within the MDB – should be treated sensibly and not axed by state actions without careful examination of the implications.*

Conclusion

The water policy framework in Australia's MDB is now more secure than it was half a decade ago, and the political agreement to the Basin Plan is a further important step forward, putting in place a framework to address some long-standing shortcomings in water policy and cementing in place a regulatory and planning framework to drive more sustainable outcomes.

However, no one should be under the misapprehension that the job of water reform in the MDB is complete. Recent announcements by several states underscore the fragility of cooperation in implementing policy. This paper provides a number of watch points and examples that underscore the importance of concerted effort on implementation over the coming years and of political commitments being converted into actions supporting the key objectives of the Basin Plan. Currently, there is only a very fragile consensus for moving forward.

One thing that is very clear is that the development and implementation of water policy over the past half-decade has not been built around a steady, strong consensus, nor has it reduced the level of politics in decision making. Indeed, with the ebbing impact of the crisis of the Millennium Drought, there is a sense that politics rather than scientific evidence is again playing a determining role. This is a step back from what appeared to be loose consensus in the time of crisis. Clearly, politics will always play a central role in the management of the MDB, because there are important social, economic and environmental trade-offs to be managed. It is hoped that the Basin Plan will provide a clearer framework in which trade-offs can be managed more transparently.

Acknowledgements

The author would like to thank several colleagues for poignant and useful comments on an earlier draft of this paper.

Notes

1. Some commentators would argue with this premise; see for example Byron (2010).
2. See Independent Audit Group (1997) for a description of the earlier arrangements capping surface water extractions.
3. Of this, around 2700 GL is estimated to be interception activities.
4. For transparency, the government should reveal the total financial savings that have been extracted from Water for the Future water programmes since 2008, and the total savings built into the remaining forward estimates years. This would allow us to estimate the *actual* total new money involved in the Basin Plan.

5. Some water entitlements, which depend on discretionary behaviour of governments, are also subject to some uncertainty. For example, Victorian Goulburn and Murray low-reliability entitlements purchased under the Living Murray programme have not yet delivered any water.
6. The overall groundwater SDL is not transparently presented. Several groundwater area SDLs in Schedule 4 are not precise figures but ranges. The two imprecise areas have a total SDL of 261 GL per year. See Schedule 4 of the Basin Plan.
7. For a recent reaction by the chair of the MDBA, see Knowles (2013).

References

ANAO (2012). *Administration of the Private Irrigation Infrastructure Operators Program in New South Wales*. June 2012. Retrieved from http://www.anao.gov.au/Publications/Audit-Reports?year=2011-2012&portfolio=29&topic=1

Byron, N. (2010). What Can the Murray-Darling Basin Plan Achieve? Will it be Enough? In Daniel Connell & R. Quentin Grafton (Eds.), *Basin Futures: Water Reform in the Murray-Darling Basin*. Canberra: ANU E Press. Retrieved from http://epress.anu.edu.au/apps/bookworm/view/Basin+Futures+Water+reform+in+the+Murray-Darling+Basin/5971/ch24.xhtml

Burke, T. (2012a). Press Conference – Revised draft Murray-Darling Basin Plan. *E&OE only*. Retrieved May 28, 2012, from http://www.environment.gov.au/minister/burke/2012/tr20120528.html

Burke, T. (2012b). Address to the National Press Club. *E&OE only*. Retrieved November 22, 2012, from http://www.environment.gov.au/minister/burke/2012/tr20121122a.html

Burke, T., & Walsh, P. (2013). Lindsay Island Environmental Works Project. *Joint media release*. Retrieved January 9, 2013, from http://www.environment.gov.au/minister/burke/2013/mr20130109b.html

Cheesman, J., & Wheeler, S. (June 2012). *Survey of water entitlement sellers under the Restoring the Balance in the Murray-Darling Basin Program*. Report by Marsden Jacob Associates for Department of Sustainability, Environment, Water, Population and Communities.

Commonwealth Environmental Water Office. (2013a). *About Commonwealth Environmental Water*. Retrieved January 2013, from http://www.environment.gov.au/ewater/about/index.html

Commonwealth Environmental Water Office. (2013b). *How much Commonwealth environmental water has been delivered?*. Retrieved January 2013, from http://www.environment.gov.au/ewater/about/water-delivered.html

Commonwealth of Australia. (2009). *Water Act 2007*. reprint 1. Canberra.

Department of Sustainability, Environment, Water Population and Communities. (2011). *Menindee Lakes Project*. Retrieved from http://www.environment.gov.au/water/policy-programs/srwui/menindee-lakes/index.html

Grafton, RQ, & Jiang, Qiang (2009). Economics of Water Recovery in the Murray-Darling Basin. Submitted to PC, Retrieved September 17, 2009, from http://www.pc.gov.au/__data/assets/pdf_file/0009/91467/sub018.pdf

Horne, J. (2012a). Economic approaches to water management in Australia. *International Journal of Water Resources Development*, 1–18. doi: 10.1080/07900627.2012.712336.

Horne, J. (2012b). Australian water policy in a climate change context: some reflections. *International Journal of Water Resources Development*. doi:10.1080/07900627.2013.725537.

Howard, J. (2007). Address to the National Press Club, Great Hall, Parliament House, 25 January 2007. Retrieved from Prime Minister of Australia Media Centre: http://pandora.nla.gov.au/pan/10052/20070321-0000/www.pm.gov.au/media/Speech/2007/speech2341.html

Independent Audit Group. (1997). *Review of Cap Implementation 1996/97*. Murray-Darling Basin Ministerial Council, Canberra.

Independent Expert Scientific Committee on Coal Seam Gas and Large Coal Mining Development. (2013). *Research and Knowledge Projects*. Retrieved from http://www.environment.gov.au/coal-seam-gas-mining/research-projects/index.html

Knowles, C. (2013). *Speech to the 8th Annual Water Symposium 2013*. Retrieved February 22, 2013, from http://www.mdba.gov.au/media_centre/media_releases/chair-speech-8th-annual-water-symposium

MDBA. (2010). *Guide to the proposed Basin Plan: overview*. Canberra: Murray–Darling Basin Authority. Retrieved from http://download.mdba.gov.au/Guide_to_the_Basin_Plan_Volume_1_web.pdf

MDBA. (2011). *Plain English summary of the proposed Basin Plan – including explanatory notes.* Canberra: Murray-Darling Basin Authority.

MDBA. (2012a). *Basin Plan.* Retrieved from http://www.mdba.gov.au/basin-plan

MDBA. (2012b). *Addendum to the proposed Groundwater Baseline and Sustainable Diversion Limits: Methods Report.* Canberra, p. 41.

MDBA. (2012c). *ATTACHMENT G – Synthesis of analysis associated with the determination of an environmentally sustainable level of take (ESLT) for surface water and groundwater in the Basin Plan.* Retrieved from http://www.mdba.gov.au/basin-plan

MDBA. (2012d). *Statement from the MDBA chair Craig Knowles.* Retrieved December 20, 2012, from http://www.mdba.gov.au/files/Statement-from-Chair-SAbudget.pdf

MDBA. (2012e). *Murray–Darling Basin Authority annual report 2011–12.* Retrieved from http://www.mdba.gov.au/about/corporate_documents/annual-reports

MDBA. (2012f). *Basin Plan – Authority's views on the Minister's suggestions on the altered proposed Basin Plan.* MDBA publication no: 83/12. November 2012.

MDBA. (2012g). *Proposed Basin Plan – A revised draft.* May 2012.

MDBA. (2012h). *Addendum to the proposed Groundwater Baseline and Sustainable Diversion Limits: Methods Report.* Canberra. MDBA publication number: 62/12. Retrieved http://download.mdba.gov.au/revised-BP/Addendum-to-Groundwater-Methods.pdf

MDBA. (2012i). *Hydrologic modelling of the relaxation of operational constraints in the southern connected system: Methods and results.* Retrieved October 2012, from http://www.mdba.gov.au/draft-basin-plan/science-draft-basin-plan/hydrologic-modelling-of-relaxed-constraints

Minister for Sustainability, Environment, Water, Population and Communities. (2012). *EXPLANATORY STATEMENT Basin Plan 2012. Canberra.* Retrieved from http://download.mdba.gov.au/Basin-Plan/Explanatory-Statement-Nov2012.pdf

NSW Government. (2013). *Access Licence Dealing Principles Order (No 1) 2013 – Murray Darling Basin.* Retrieved from http://www.legislation.nsw.gov.au/sessionalview/sessional/sr/2012-687.pdf

National Water Commission. (2009). *Australian Water Reform 2009: Second biennial assessment of progress in implementation of the National Water Initiative.* Canberra: NWC.

Productivity Commission. (2010). *Market mechanisms for recovering water in the Murray-Darling Basin: Final report.* Retrieved from http://www.pc.gov.au/projects/study/water-recovery/report

SEWPAC. (November 2012). *Environmental Water Recovery Strategy for the Murray Darling Basin, Draft for Consultation.* Retrieved from http://environment.gov.au/water/policy-programs/water-recovery-strategy/index.html

Sinclair Knight Merz. (2012). *Impacts of groundwater extraction on streamflow in selected catchments throughout Australia, Waterlines report.* Canberra: National Water Commission.

Wentworth Group of Concerned Scientists. (2010). *Sustainable diversions in the Murray-Darling Basin: An analysis of the options for achieving a sustainable diversion limit in the Murray-Darling Basin.* Retrieved from http://www.wentworthgroup.org/uploads/Sustainable Diversions in the Murray-Darling Basin.pdf

Environmental water management in Australia: experience from the Murray-Darling Basin

Benjamin Docker[a] and Ian Robinson[b]

[a]Commonwealth Environmental Water Office, Canberra, ACT, Australia; [b]Commonwealth Environmental Water Holder 2008–2012, Canberra, ACT, Australia

Recent water reform in Australia has focused on seeking to balance the needs of the environment and consumptive users through improved flow regimes. This is in response to declining ecological conditions, exacerbated by drought and the threat of climate change particularly in the Murray-Darling Basin. A programme of environmental flows integrated through multiple governance layers and managed by an independent federal-government entity operating in the water market on behalf of the environment has been established to help rectify the decline. While a challenge for this new entity involves determining when to release, trade or carry over water in storage so as to maximize environmental outcomes, early results point to real environmental gains within a highly regulated and diverse river system.

Introduction

Since 2007, the Australian federal government has been implementing a programme of water reform that includes a focus on rectifying environmental degradation and the over-allocation of water resources in the Murray-Darling Basin. The introduction of the programme reflected growing public concern over the environmental condition of the basin and the difficult situation faced by irrigators in the grip of a lengthy and worsening drought. The reforms are being implemented with significant federal government funding and increased federal government involvement in the management of the basin's water resources.

The legislative and institutional changes which have been central to the reforms, including the Commonwealth Water Act (2007) and its establishment of two new federal government entities, the Murray-Darling Basin Authority (MDBA) and the Commonwealth Environmental Water Holder, have accelerated a shift that was already occurring in the way that water is recognized and managed. Concepts such as those of sustainability and resilience, of the interconnected nature of the whole river basin and of the environment being a legitimate user of the available resource have come to the fore.

This paper provides a perspective on the Australian experience in environmental water management. It focuses on the Murray-Darling Basin, where policy intervention has been most significant due to the ecological stress caused by the previous over-allocation of water to consumptive use. It is also the area where the federal government has been the most active, due to the need for more coordinated management of the resources of a single basin that is subject to the competing claims of four states and one territory.

The Murray-Darling Basin covers an area of one million square kilometres, or one-seventh of the Australian continent (Figure 1). It contains Australia's three longest rivers, the Murray, the Murrumbidgee and the Darling, and amongst its 30,000 wetlands sixteen are listed as internationally important under the Ramsar Convention. Home to two million people, it is a region of vital economic interest and one of the most productive areas for irrigated agriculture, producing one-third of the nation's food supply. The basin's agricultural produce is valued at an average of AUD15 billion per year in the national economy (MDBA, 2011a).

The water resources of the Murray-Darling Basin are highly variable (Figure 2) both spatially and temporally, and are characterized by frequent droughts and floods. As a result, water resource management, including the construction of large public storages and other control structures to reduce flow variability, has been integral to the agricultural development that has occurred. This highly variable natural flow regime has also seen a

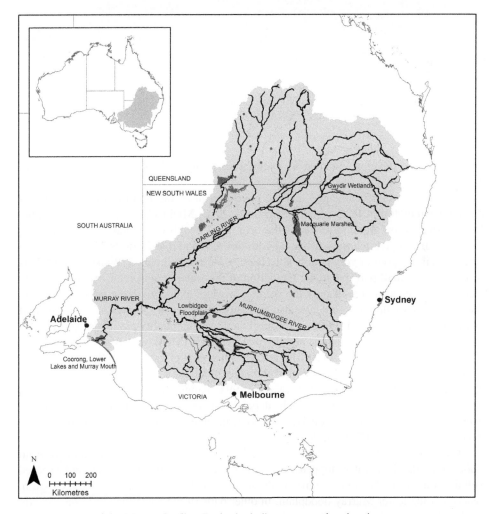

Figure 1.   Map of the Murray-Darling Basin, including states and major rivers.

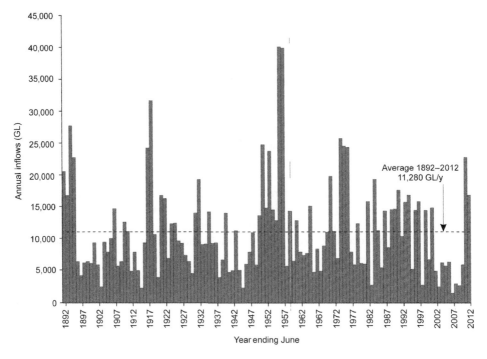

Figure 2. Murray River inflows over 120 years including Menindee Lakes inflows but excluding Snowy River system releases. Source MDBA (2012b).

unique ecology develop, adapted to cycles of wetting and drying (Kingsford, 2006; Young, 2001).

It has been well documented that the environment of the basin has been in serious decline (Arthington & Pusey, 2003; Kingsford, 2000; MDFRC, 2011). The Sustainable Rivers Audit, a programme to assess the ecological health of the basin based on three themes – macro invertebrates, fish and hydrology – found that 20 of its 23 valleys where rated as being in poor or very poor health (Davies, Harris, Hillman, & Walker, 2008). This result is in no small part due to the regulation of the water resource for irrigation, which has not only reduced significantly the volume of water available to the environment and the frequency of flooding, but has also in many cases led to a reversal of the natural seasonal flow (Thoms et al., 2000) and contributed to water quality problems ranging from salinization to toxic algal blooms and thermal pollution (MDBA, 2010).

As reported by the MDBA (2011b), at least 90 per cent of the Gwydir Wetlands, 75 per cent of the wetlands of the Lower Murrumbidgee floodplain, and 40–50 per cent of the Macquarie Marshes have been lost (Keyte, 1994; Kingsford & Thomas, 1995, 2004). These floodplain ecosystems, which depend on intermittent flooding to function effectively, have seen inundation, particularly from small and medium-sized flow events, become less frequent (CSIRO, 2008).

The state of the basin's ecology received increased attention during the drought from 2000 to 2010, when water stopped flowing from the mouth of the Murray and exposed sulfidic soils which began to acidify on the bed of South Australia's Lower Lakes and in reaches of the lower Murray floodplain. In other parts of the basin the stress was equally visible. For example, in the Macquarie Marshes over half the river red gum forest and woodland had more than 40 per cent dead canopy, and over 40 per cent had more than 80 per cent dead canopy (Bowen & Simpson, 2009).

The growth in water resource development between 1950 and 1995 occurred during a period of generally wetter climatic conditions during which public water storage increased six-fold (CSIRO, 2008). Irrigators who had rarely had reason to question the security of their water entitlements had to make do during the drought with a fraction of the expected annual allocations of water against their permanent entitlement rights. Forecasts of climate change increased the recognition that the volume of entitlements issued by state governments for consumption was unsustainable. Apart from the direct environmental issues, this threatened the long-term prosperity of the agricultural industries and communities that rely on basin resources.

Evolution of environmental water policy and governance

For some time now, governments of the Murray-Darling Basin have been seeking to address the ecological decline with more sustainable management practices, most notably through a 1995 intergovernmental agreement to cap extractions for consumptive use and through agreement by federal and state governments to the National Water Initiative (NWI) in 2004. The NWI aims *inter alia* to phase out the overuse of water, reform the water entitlement system and develop an active water market (National Water Commission (NWC), 2004). In doing so it seeks to recognize the environment as a legitimate user of water resources with statutory rights.

As highlighted by the NWI, central to achieving more sustainable water resource management is the concept of environmental water or environmental flows. The World Bank (2009, p. xiii) defines environmental flows as the "quality, quantity, and timing of water flows required to maintain the components, functions, processes, and resilience of aquatic ecosystems that provide goods and services to people". Environmental water is water that is made available either directly for the purpose of achieving environmental flows or indirectly through protection from use for any other purpose. While this is a relatively straightforward concept, defining and accounting for environmental water use in practice is a complex and highly sensitive process with much uncertainty.

The traditional approach to managing environmental flows in Australia is based on establishing minimum passing flow requirements or end-of-system flows as rules within water-sharing plans (NWC, 2010). As a result, the environmental water, including the total volume and the flow pattern of that water, is heavily influenced by the limits and demands of consumptive water use. This approach is often at odds with ecosystem requirements for the full range of flows to function effectively (Bunn & Arthington, 2002; DNRE, 2002; Poff et al., 1997). Meeting such requirements efficiently within a highly regulated system requires more active management which has led to the establishment of environmental water reserves or contingency allowances which allow river operators more discretion over the timing and volume of releases (Schofield, Burt, & Connell, 2003). One example of such a water reserve is the Barmah-Millewa environmental water allowance, which was established in 1993 by the Murray-Darling Basin Ministerial Council. This agreement is based on a system of banking, borrowing and payback of water by irrigators in order to meet periodic ecological objectives in the Barmah-Millewa Forest, a Ramsar site on the mid-Murray floodplain.

While for the most part these reserves are still provided for as rules in water-sharing plans, in recent years market-based mechanisms for acquiring environmental water have grown in significance. The shift towards market-based acquisitions is a response to the growing body of evidence of the benefits of such an approach (Kirby, Qureshi, Mainuddin, & Dyack, 2006; Murphy et al., 2009; Qureshi, Connor, Kirby, & Mainuddin, 2007; Wheeler, Garrick, Loch, & Bjornlund, 2013). While the use of market mechanisms to acquire water is relatively new in Australia, there is considerable experience with such approaches in the western United States in both private and state organizations (Burke, Adams, & Wallender, 2004; Landry, 1998; Simon, 1997), using a range of contract types including leases and options (Wheeler et al., 2013). Siebert, Young, and Young (2000) and Garrick, Siebentritt, Aylward, Bauer, and Purkey (2009) explore the policy and regulatory requirements to enable market transactions for the environment. The latter highlight two of the key conditions as a cap on water rights so that scarcity exists and recognition of the environment as a legitimate user, so that the transfer of property rights to in-stream use does not lose the underlying priority of the right. Both conditions are central to recent water reforms in the Murray-Darling Basin.

In 2007, the Commonwealth Water Act established the independent MDBA and charged it with developing a plan for the management of the water resources of the whole of the basin (Commonwealth of Australia, 2007). The 'Basin Plan', which was passed by the Australian Parliament in November 2012, prescribes sustainable diversion limits (SDLs) or limits on extraction which reflect an environmentally sustainable level of 'take' (consumptive use) (MDBA, 2012a). To ensure that there is sufficient water to meet the basin's environmental water requirements, the federal government is acquiring water both through direct market purchases and through investment in irrigation efficiency. In accordance with the NWI, it is the legally enforceable SDLs which reduce consumptive use (and therefore increase scarcity), and the government's acquisition programmes which ensure that the environment is a legitimate user with transferable property rights.

An important difference between the acquisition of environmental water in Australia and in the United States has been the greater acceptance of the role of government in the management and provision of water resources in Australia, as outlined by Connell (2007) and Crase (2008). This means that the institutional arrangements established here have evolved to include a government entity acting on behalf of the environment, rather than public trusts or non-government organizations, as advocated by a number of commentators (Bennett, 2010; Young, 2010). The latter approach is more the norm in the western United States with its greater emphasis on riparian rights and use of the courts (or the threat thereof) to provide for environmental flows (Connell, 2007).

Commonwealth Environmental Water is the federal government function established through legislation to manage the water entitlements being acquired. The Commonwealth Environmental Water role is constituted as a holder of tradeable water entitlements, rather than as a manager of a water reserve or of environmental flow rules. The aim of this approach is to add a significant amount of water to the environment over and above what is currently available, while ensuring the same degree of security to the environment as provided to consumptive users (Docker & Robinson, 2009).

The Basin Plan requires a decrease in consumptive use of 2750 GL on average each year (although this can vary between 2100 GL and 3200 GL subject to opportunities to achieve the same environmental outcomes with less water or recover more environmental water with no socio-economic impact [MDBA, 2012a]), and much of this is proposed to be acquired as entitlements for environmental use. The additional environmental water is significant but needs to be managed in the context of much larger environmental flows. Even with the amount of water to be reallocated from consumptive to environmental uses as required by the Basin Plan, and with a government policy commitment to acquire this full amount, the vast majority of environmental water in the basin will still consist of water provided by rules in state water-sharing plans (MDBA, 2012a). An integrated approach to environmental watering across the basin is therefore necessary, and this is to be coordinated through an environmental watering plan, which is part of the Basin Plan. Whilst part of a wider picture, Commonwealth Environmental Water has quickly become the largest holder of entitlement-based environmental water that can be actively managed within the basin, with an average of 1113 GL of water available per year as of February 2013.

Commonwealth environmental water: experience to date

The first water entitlements were acquired for the Commonwealth's environmental water holdings in 2008, and the first yield of annual allocation against them was received shortly after. Because the first two years of operation were dominated by drought, the water available to those entitlements was limited in these years. However, during 2010–11 there was a significant shift in water availability, including one of the wettest summers on record. In that year the Commonwealth's holdings yielded 744 GL of water, of which 387 GL was used for environmental purposes. Consistent with provisions of catchment water-sharing plans, 331 GL was carried over in storages for use in subsequent years, thereby improving the capacity to meet future needs.

Early in the establishment of the Commonwealth Environmental Water role it was considered important to have in place an assessment framework that was adaptable to changed water availability circumstances but that also could be used to consistently assess the options for environmental water use across the basin. A framework (CEW, 2011a) was prepared and is regularly updated as further experience is gained. It builds on work undertaken in state jurisdictions and under the joint-government Living Murray programme and outlines ecological and management objectives for different water availability circumstances (Figure 3).

Individual water-use proposals are assessed against criteria that include the ecological significance of the river or wetland asset; the expected ecological outcomes; the potential risks of the watering action; the long-term sustainability of the asset; and the cost-effectiveness and operational feasibility of undertaking the action. The approach is informed by the advice of an independent science advisory panel with respect to strategies for environmental water use, monitoring and evaluation, and the knowledge and research requirements to improve the decision-making process. Such advice is essential because most aquatic science has, to date, not been of the scale required to fully inform a whole-of-basin approach to environmental water management, generally being focused on individual wetlands or species requirements without the framework to apply these findings more broadly.

Extreme dry	Dry	Median	Wet	Very wet
Avoid damage to key environmental assets	Ensure ecological capacity for recovery	Maintain ecological health and resilience	Improve the health and resilience of aquatic ecosystems	Build future capacity to support ecological health resilience

Damage avoidance	Capacity for recovery	Maintained health and resilience	Improved health and resilience

Figure 3. Ecological objectives under water availability scenarios. Source CEW (2011a).

Management arrangements for delivery of water vary across the basin, with a number of different river operators, catchment-based natural resource management agencies, irrigation infrastructure providers, government agencies (for example national park agencies) and private landowners. In most cases the delivery of the environmental water is managed through established state-government arrangements. This has the benefit of enabling the engagement with local knowledge and expertise that is essential to ensuring efficient management. As further volumes of environmental water become available in different parts of the basin it can be expected that these arrangements will be strengthened. The role of regional organizations in managing environmental water is a developing area that has been discussed by Roberts, Seymour, and Pannell (2011) and others. Garrick, Bark, Connor, and Banerjee (2012), through an exploration of the subsidiarity principle in environmental water management, identify many of the opportunities and limitations to local management, particularly in relation to upstream−downstream trade-offs, economies of scale and cost sharing, capacity building, and accountability mechanisms in support of the national interest.

As water availability has improved, the options for delivery have expanded from small volumes delivered to individual sites to include multi-site actions and options that connect the rivers and floodplains and provide flows through the system. An example of this type of use was the provision in June 2011 of 161 GL of water to the Murrumbidgee River system with the objective of connecting the river channel to wetlands along the mid-section of the catchment while also providing additional flows to the Murray River and the Ramsar-listed Lower Lakes at the end of the system (CEW, 2012).

Coordination of the various sources of environmental water has occurred through direct liaison between both state and federal entities; to the end of February 2013, approximately 2000 GL of Commonwealth environmental water had been delivered in conjunction with 950 GL of water supplied by state governments and others.

Assessing outcomes

The outcomes from the use of Commonwealth environmental water are reported to the federal Parliament each year in an annual report and in a separate annual outcomes report (CEW, 2012). Although the new environmental watering programme is at an early stage, and yields against the entitlements were relatively low during the drought, monitoring of environmental responses to date has detected encouraging changes, such as better health in river red gum trees and improved habitat for birds, fish and frogs (CEW, 2011b, 2012).

The most significant benefits will take time to materialize, however, and benefits to the health of the entire system will only be identified through the implementation of the monitoring and evaluation programme being established as part of the Basin Plan. This programme seeks to coordinate the monitoring arrangements of state and Commonwealth agencies so that a coherent basin-wide picture of environmental improvement can be obtained. It establishes the outcomes that progress will be measured against, principles to be applied in monitoring and evaluation, and the reporting requirements imposed on basin states and Commonwealth entities, including for the use of Commonwealth environmental water (MDBA, 2012a).

Determining the effectiveness of the basin's environmental watering plan will require several levels of environmental-flow monitoring over an extended period. This includes operational monitoring, which establishes volumes delivered and immediate hydrological outcomes from environmental flow releases; intervention monitoring, which seeks to establish the ecological outcomes from a particular environmental-flow event or events;

and programme level monitoring, which seeks to identify the overall trends in ecosystem health in response to the basin-wide programme of action.

Operational monitoring of environmental flows is largely implemented through existing arrangements applied by state water resource agencies. As for irrigation purposes, all flows are gauged at an identified reference point so that the volumes and flow rates delivered can be recorded. Intervention monitoring is more challenging because there is less consistency in monitoring protocols and standards. However, there are a number of well-documented examples of ecological response to flow, particularly for bird-breeding events but also for fish spawning and recruitment (see King, Tonkin, & Mahoney, 2007).

Programme-level monitoring to detect changes in response to a programme of environmental flows at the basin scale requires further development. The expected ecological outcomes that the programme will contribute to are described by the MDBA (2011b) and include: improvements in the extent and diversity of healthy wetland habitat and in hydrologic connectivity; flow regimes that support recruitment of native water-dependent species and critical environments in times of drought; and flows that enable salts and nutrients to be flushed from the Murray River to the ocean.

The interaction of different jurisdictions with responsibility at different scales poses a number of challenges in ensuring consistency in results that can be integrated at a basin scale. An intensive programme of work will be required over the coming years to develop and agree on protocols, methods and standards, to ensure this integration can occur in a cost-effective manner, building on existing investment.

Challenges and opportunities

Any initiative the size of the Murray-Darling Basin reforms will inevitably raise implementation challenges and opportunities. Given the complexity of the institutional arrangements and the range of actors involved, these will need to be managed over some years to come, including by adaptively changing the approach as opportunities arise and as there is greater collective experience in managing the increased volume of environmental water.

A key challenge for the management of the Commonwealth's environmental water holdings will be one of portfolio management: how to manage the total portfolio of entitlements and allocations in each valley throughout the basin to achieve the maximum environmental outcome over time. This is an emerging area of inquiry with little precedent elsewhere in the world, particularly at this scale. The environment will be a market participant with approximately AUD 5 billion of water entitlements in its portfolio, based on prices paid to date (DSEWPaC, 2013). Just as irrigators do to maximize irrigation outcomes this must be done by active management of the water entitlements and the annual allocations that are made available for use as announced by state-government agencies. Doing so should enable more efficient use, meaning desired environmental outcomes can be achieved with less acquired water. Just as consumptive users have benefited from the expansion in the water market in recent years, it is expected that so too will the environment.

Active management of water entitlements for the environment provides substantial benefits beyond that available through planned or "rules based" environmental water. The security of the water is the same as of that provided to irrigators, and management options include calling it for use, carrying it over for use in future years or trading it to consumptive users (Figure 4). All of these options involve risks and implementation costs, and it may be at times that none of the options are appropriate or available, in which case

Option	Issues to consider
Use of water within current year	- What water is available? - What water use options are in scope under various scenarios? - What are the ecological priorities for the year? (relative to future years) Assess: - expected environmental outcome - risks of water use (and non-use) - costs of use - management arrangements - operational constraints
Carryover of water in storage for use in subsequent years	- What carryover arrangements apply to the relevant entitlements? - What are the ecological priorities for future years(relative to the current year)? - What water is likely to be available in future? - What are the costs or risks of carryover (e.g. dam spills; forgoing future allocations)? - Can carryover be enhanced by transfer of water between accounts?
Trade of water for use in a different valley and/or in subsequent years	- What are the costs and benefits of using water in a particular valley in the current year relative to using that water in a different valley or at a future time? - What trading rules/restrictions apply to the relevant licences? - What are current and probable future market prices and how are these likely to be impacted by decisions to enter the market? - What is the likelihood of having sufficient buyers/sellers at an appropriate time? - How can transaction costs be minimized?

Note: Assessment of the above issues will occur in an environment where there is a high degree of uncertainty about future conditions. The assessments include judgements about the balance of probabilities under a range of future scenarios.

Figure 4. Portfolio management options – issues to consider.

the water allocations may be re-distributed according to the rules of the relevant water resource plan. These are the same arrangements as exist for other water users.

Calling water from storage in regulated parts of the basin involves the release of water to a particular point in the system at a time and flow rate that will help to achieve environmental outcomes. The water may be diverted to particular wetlands, for example, using infrastructure or pumps, or retained in channel to restore a part of the natural flow regime.

Carrying over water in dams for use in subsequent years can provide greater certainty about environmental flows in drier periods or the option to supplement future natural events. The objective is not to entirely "drought-proof" the system, because droughts are a natural part of the Australian environment; but carrying over water allows increased volumes to be built up over time for use in larger, less frequent flow events, thereby reintroducing some of the natural flow variability that river regulation has reduced.

In addition to use and carryover, there are options to use market mechanisms such as trade of water to improve environmental outcomes both across the basin and across time. Trading water should provide benefits in terms of establishing capacity to meet future environmental needs; responding to varied conditions across the basin; adapting to changing circumstances and new information; dealing with delivery constraints or opportunities; and realizing value when immediate environmental requirements have been met and carryover of water between years is not available.

There are legislated conditions on trading, but where better environmental outcomes can be enhanced by doing so, this is an important flexibility mechanism. For example, if flow conditions dictate that a particular entitlement is no longer needed for the environmental objectives for which it was intended, the trading of that water to consumptive users will enable water to be acquired for greater benefit elsewhere. Such an approach should also support improved asset risk management and cost-effective use (Burke et al., 2004) by ensuring that water is held where it can best serve desired environmental objectives.

The capacity of the holdings to achieve environmental outcomes might also be enhanced by realizing value from the sale of temporary water allocations in relatively dry years and using the proceeds to acquire water to supplement flows in moderately wet years. This approach is sometimes referred to as "counter cyclical" trade; benefits would arise both for the environment and for agricultural users due to the different timing of demand for water between the two uses (English, Brearley, & Coggan, 2004; Kirby et al., 2006). Other inter-sectoral trading arrangements could include entitlement leasing and options contracts (Wheeler et al., 2013).

Whilst management of the portfolio has the potential to provide significant advantages over "rules-based" approaches, operating within a water management system established principally to provide security of use for irrigation offers a number of significant challenges, particularly given that arrangements often vary considerably from one valley to the next.

Water entitlements are typically established to provide the rights to extract a share of the water from the channel at a particular point, traditionally for agricultural use. Environmental water use confined to a particular wetland is to some degree concordant with this. For example, environmental water has been used at the Ramsar-listed Hattah Lakes in Victoria over recent years by calling it from storage and pumping it into the wetland. As the volume of available water increases, however, there will be a broader range of environmental uses, including using large volumes delivered as flow events to restore some of the natural connectivity throughout the system. These flows transfer carbon and nutrients along the system and export salinity to improve water quality. These events are also typically a more efficient use of water, because it is possible to target multiple sites with the same event thereby using less water compared to a "site-by-site" approach.

Because the system was not designed for this type of use and the rules that govern how the rivers are operated generally do not allow it, there is a need to review some of these arrangements. For example, current approaches to management of the system make it difficult for environmental water holders to supplement natural flows. User requirements, including demands placed by environmental water holders, are generally met from the existing flow where possible rather than from an additional dam release, and so a desire on the part of an environmental water manager to supplement the natural flow with additional water cannot always be achieved. Other challenges involve protecting water left in-stream from subsequent extraction and accounting for use when a substantial amount of environmental water provided to the floodplain returns to the river and would otherwise provide further environmental benefit downstream.

Environmental water managers also need to operate within the physical capacity constraints of the system – constraints that quite correctly are designed to protect the communities and industries which have developed since the river was regulated. The MDBA and jurisdictions have previously acquired easements to increase the capacity and flexibility of river management, and there are likely to be further options for this in the future. There will also be options for removing constraints through infrastructure works and other measures to ensure access when higher flows occur (MDBA, 2012a). Not all constraints are resolvable, though, and the SDLs prescribed in the Basin Plan take into account that the system has developed as a working river and cannot be returned to natural conditions.

The portfolio management challenge, particularly at the basin scale, is further complicated by the variety of entitlement types and rules that exist in different parts of the basin. Murray-Darling Basin water entitlements have been put in place in a manner that reflects historical water availability and the development of agricultural industries and infrastructure in particular catchments. The resulting differences, and the fact that a number of state jurisdictions are involved, mean that the characteristics of the entitlements in the Commonwealth's holdings vary substantially. As of December 2011 there were 38 different types of entitlement in the holdings, across 20 individual catchments. The estimated long-term average annual yield for individual types of entitlement ranged from 14% to 100%.

Of the 38 different entitlement types, 17 do not provide for carryover of water between years, including those that exist within unregulated parts of the basin. Of the 21 types that do provide for carryover, the amount of water that can be carried over varies between 30% and 200% each year. Six entitlement types in the state of Victoria have provision for "spillable" water accounts that provide for water carried over beyond the total entitlement volume to be credited to a separate account; but the volume is reduced if the dam spills.

Given this complexity, an additional portfolio management option includes the transfer of water allocations between different entitlement accounts held within hydrologically connected systems, for instance between accounts in the southern connected system, which includes the Murrumbidgee and Lower Darling Rivers in NSW, the Murray River, and a number of its Victorian tributaries. There are constraints on these transfers, primarily for hydrological and water-security reasons, but within this system the available options can facilitate the delivery of environmental water for different outcomes and improve the scope to carry over water to subsequent years. These management options exist for all water users, and like other users an environmental water manager must make the best decisions possible given available knowledge. Information about environmental requirements and water availability are continually improving, but inevitably decisions will be made that are subsequently impacted by changes in circumstances – particularly changes in inflows and water availability.

The adaptive management approach provided for in the Basin Plan offers significant opportunities to learn about river-basin-scale responses to management intervention in the form of environmental flows, allowing an improved understanding of the sustainability and resilience of aquatic ecosystems in a semi-arid environment subject to intensive water resource development.

Conclusion

Increasing the share of environmental water and improving environmental water management are central elements of current water reform in the Murray-Darling Basin. The reform is significant both in terms of the new institutional arrangements and in the scale of the effort being brought to bear. The development of a basin-wide environmental watering plan and a federal government entity acting on behalf of the environment, both as market participant and manager of environmental flows, aims to enact one of the central concepts of integrated water resources management, that of the interconnected nature and dependencies of the whole drainage basin. By considering the environmental water requirements of the entire system, irrespective of state boundaries, both the MDBA and Commonwealth Environmental Water are seeking to build the resilience of a living basin ecosystem subject to regular droughts and floods, which are forecast to become more frequent and intense due to climate change.

The reform is being supported by substantial federal-government funding with the aim of restoring a more sustainable balance between consumptive and environmental use. The water being acquired is that of entitlements previously held for irrigation and therefore can be actively managed as irrigation water is. This is changing the landscape of environmental water management in the Murray-Darling Basin because the environmental manager must assess the expected environmental outcomes from options that can be implemented across valleys and through time.

Early results from the approach point to real environmental gains within the framework of a highly regulated and diverse river system. Good progress has been made on establishing the structures and implementation arrangements to manage such a significant portfolio of public assets, but there is a long way to go before all the potential gains can be achieved. A system of water management that evolved over more than a century, primarily for one particular use, will need to adapt further to accommodate an alternative use with equivalent rights. Achieving optimal social, economic and environmental outcomes is going to require continued intergovernmental cooperation and effort for many years to come.

Acknowledgements

We would like to thank Dr James Horne and an anonymous reviewer for useful comments that helped improve the manuscript. Alana Wilkes prepared the map in Figure 1.

References

Arthington, A. H., & Pusey, B. J. (2003). Flow restoration and protection in Australian rivers. *River Research and Applications, 19*(5–6), 377–395.

Bennett, J. (2010, November 5). Murray money a monopoly game. *The Australian*. Retrieved from: http://www.theaustralian.com.au/opinion/murray-money-a-monopoly-game/story-e6frg6zo-1225948007692

Bowen, S., & Simpson, S. (2009). *Changes in extent and condition of the vegetation communities of the Macquarie Marshes floodplain 1991–2008*. Unpublished report for the NSW Department of Environment, Climate Change and Water, Sydney.

Bunn, S. E., & Arthington, A. H. (2002). Basic principles and ecological consequences of altered flow regimes for aquatic biodiversity. *Environmental Management, 30*(4), 492–507.

Burke, S. M., Adams, R. M., & Wallender, W. W. (2004). Water banks and environmental water demands: Case of the Klamath project. *Water Resources Research, 40*(9), 1029–1038.

CEW. (2011a). *A framework for determining Commonwealth environmental water use.* Canberra: Commonwealth Environmental Water.

CEW. (2011b). *Commonwealth environmental water 2009–10 outcomes report.* Canberra: Commonwealth Environmental Water.

CEW. (2012). *Commonwealth environmental water 2010–11 outcomes report.* Canberra: Commonwealth Environmental Water.

CSIRO. (2008). *Water availability in the Murray-Darling Basin. A report to the Australian Government from the CSIRO Murray-Darling Basin sustainable yields project.* Canberra: CSIRO.

Commonwealth of Australia. (2007). Commonwealth Water Act. Retrieved from http://www.comlaw.gov.au/Details/C2007A0013

Crase, L. (2008). *Water policy in Australia: The impact of change and uncertainty.* Washington DC: Resources for the Future.

DNRE. (2002). *FLOWS – A method for determining environmental water requirements in Victoria.* Department of Natural Resources and Environment. Melbourne: Victorian Government.

DSEWPaC. (2013). *Progress of water recovery under the restoring the balance in the Murray-Darling Basin program.* Canberra: Department of Sustainability, Environment, Water Population and Communities. Retrieved from http://www.environment.gov.au/water/policy-programs/entitlement-purchasing/progress.html

Davies, P. E., Harris, J. H., Hillman, T. J., & Walker, K. F. (2008). *SRA Report 1: A Report on the Ecological Health of Rivers in the Murray–Darling Basin, 2004–2007.* Prepared by the Independent Sustainable Rivers Audit Group for the Murray–Darling Basin Ministerial Council.

Docker, B., & Robinson, I. (2009). The Commonwealth as water holder: A basin-wide approach to environmental watering. *Australian Water Association Conference Paper.* 16–18 March, Melbourne.

English, B., Brearley, T., & Coggan, A. (2004). Environmental flow allocations and counter-cyclical trading in the River Murray system. *Australian Agricultural and Resource Economics Society Conference.* 11–13 February, Melbourne.

Garrick, D., Siebentritt, M., Aylward, B., Bauer, C. J., & Purkey, A. (2009). Water markets and freshwater ecosystem services: Policy reform and implementation in the Columbia and Murray-Darling Basins. *Ecological Economics, 69*(2), 366–379.

Garrick, D., Bark, R., Connor, J., & Banerjee, O. (2012). Environmental water governance in federal rivers: Opportunities and limits for subsidiarity in Australia's Murray-Darling River. *Water Policy, 14*(6), 915–936.

Keyte, P. (1994). *Lower Gwydir Wetland – plan of management 1994–1997.* Report by NSW Department of Water Resources for the Lower Gwydir Steering Committee, Sydney.

Kingsford, R. T. (2000). Ecological impacts of dams, water diversions and river management on floodplain wetlands in Australia. *Austral Ecology, 25*(2), 109–127.

Kingsford, R. T. (2006). *Ecology of desert rivers.* Cambridge: Cambridge University Press.

Kingsford, R. T., & Thomas, R. F. (1995). The Macquarie Marshes in arid Australia and their waterbirds: A 50-year history of decline. *Environmental Management, 19*(6), 867–878.

Kingsford, R. T., & Thomas, R. F. (2004). Destruction of wetlands and waterbird populations by dams and irrigation on the Murrumbidgee River in arid Australia. *Environmental Management, 34*(3), 383–396.

King, A. J., Tonkin, Z., & Mahoney, J. (2007). *Assessing the effectiveness of environmental flows on fish recruitment in Barmah–Millewa Forest.* Heidelberg, Victoria: Arthur Rylah Institute for Environmental Research, Department of Sustainability and Environment.

Kirby, M., Qureshi, M. E., Mainuddin, M., & Dyack, B. (2006). Catchment behavior and counter-cyclical water trade: An integrated model. *Natural Resource Modeling, 19*(4), 483–510.

Landry, C. (1998). Market transfers of water for environmental protection in the western United States. *Water Policy, 1*(5), 457–469.

MDBA. (2010). *Guide to the proposed Basin plan.* Canberra: Murray-Darling Basin Authority.

MDBA. (2011a). *Delivering a Healthy Working Basin: About the draft Basin plan.* Canberra: Murray-Darling Basin Authority.

MDBA. (2011b). *The proposed environmentally sustainable level of take for surface water of the Murray-Darling Basin: Method and outcomes.* Canberra: Murray-Darling Basin Authority.

MDBA. (2012a). *Basin plan*. Canberra: Murray-Darling Basin Authority. Retrieved from http://download.mdba.gov.au/Basin-Plan/Basin-Plan-Nov2012.pdf

MDBA. (2012b). *Murray-darling Basin authority annual report 2011–12*. Canberra: Murray-Darling Basin Authority. Retrieved from http://www.mdba.gov.au/annualreports/2011-12/MDBA-annual-report-2011-12-web.pdf

MDFRC. (2011). A Review of River Ecosystem Condition in the Murray-Darling Basin. Murray-Darling Freshwater Research Centre, Publication 01/2011.

Murphy, J. J., Dinar, A., Howitt, R. E., Rassenti, S. J., Smith, V. L., & Weinberg, M. (2009). The design of water markets when instream flows have value. *Journal of Environmental Management, 90*(2), 1089–1096.

National Water Commission (NWC). (2004). *Intergovernmental agreement on a national water initiative*. Canberra: National Water Commission. Retrieved from http://nwc.gov.au/__data/assets/pdf_file/0008/24749/Intergovernmental-Agreement-on-a-national-water-initiative.pdf

NWC. (2010). *Australian environmental water management report*. Canberra: National Water Commission.

Poff, N. L., Allen, J. D., Bain, M. B., Karr, J. R., Prestegaard, K. L., Richter, B. D., . . . , Stromberg, J. C. (1997). The natural flow regime: A paradigm for river conservation and restoration. *Bioscience, 47*(11), 769–784.

Qureshi, M. E., Connor, M., Kirby, M., & Mainuddin, J. (2007). Economic assessment of acquiring water for environmental flows in the Murray Basin. *The Australian Journal of Agricultural and Resource Economics, 51*(3), 283–303.

Roberts, A. M., Seymour, E. J., & Pannell, D. J. (2011). The role of regional organisations in managing environmental water in the Murray-Darling Basin, Australia. *Economic Papers: A journal of Applied Economics Policy, 30*(2), 147–156.

Schofield, N., Burt, A., & Connell, D. (2003). *Environmental water allocation: Principles, policies and practices*. Canberra: Land and Water Australia.

Siebert, E., Young, D., & Young, M. (2000). *Market-based opportunities to improve environmental flows*. Scoping Report to Environment Australia. Adelaide: CSIRO Land and Water.

Simon, B. M. (1997). Federal acquisition of water through voluntary transactions for environmental purposes. *Contemporary Economic Policy, 16*(4), 422–432.

Thoms, M., Suter, P., Roberts, J., Koehn, K., Jones, G., Hillman, T., & Close, A. (2000). *Report of the River Murray Scientific Panel on Environmental Flows: River Murray – Dartmouth to Wellington and the Lower Darling River*. Canberra: Murray Darling Basin Commission.

Wheeler, S., Garrick, D., Loch, A., & Bjornlund, H. (2013). Evaluating water market products to acquire water for the environment in Australia. *Land use Policy, 30*(1), 427–436.

World Bank. (2009). *Environmental flows in water resources policies, plans and projects: Case studies*. Washington: WorldBank.

Young, W. J. (2001). *Rivers as ecological systems: The Murray–Darling Basin*. Canberra: Murray–Darling Basin Commission.

Young, M. (2010). Managing environmental water. *Making decisions about environmental water allocations* (pp. 51–60). Sydney: Australian Farm Institute. June 2010.

Connell, D. (2007). *Water politics in the Murray-Darling Basin*. Sydney: The Federation Press.

Index

For Product Safety Concerns and Information please contact our EU
representative GPSR@taylorandfrancis.com Taylor & Francis Verlag GmbH,
Kaufingerstraße 24, 80331 München, Germany

Printed and bound by CPI Group (UK) Ltd, Croydon, CR0 4YY
08/05/2025
01864326-0001